"Linda Goldman offers wise intentio empower children, parents, and teac world's consciousness, to ring the fire Linda Goldman's work becomes wide., ..uu anu implemented, a future generation will demand of me and millions of my contemporaries: 'And what did you do to alleviate climate change?' Goldman offers a blueprint for our imaginations and her ideas will inspire the imaginations and creativities of many."

—**Harold Ivan Smith, DMin, FT,** *author of* ABCs of Healthy Grieving

"The mess we've made of the earth is causing existential anxiety for today's youth, ignited by record-breaking fires, floods, and the covid-19 pandemic, and other disturbing environmental realities. This book could not be timelier. Jump in and join the youth and organizations working hard to make a difference."

—**Donna Schuurman, EdD, FT,** *senior director of advocacy and training at the Dougy Center: The National Grief Center for Children and Families*

"In this newest book, Linda Goldman applies her years of expertise in the field of grief and loss to the struggles faced by today's youth about climate change. Goldman uses case studies and practical techniques to help us help today's young people process grief and loss and begin to cope with the anxiety and depression. I am confident that this will be a great resource to help all of us move to action and hope."

—**Emilio Parga, MeD,** *founder of the Solace Tree Center for Grieving Children*

"This book shows that climate change awareness is not just about sharing concerns about the future—it is about taking action, particularly by living more sustainably, eating less meat, the four R's, and, most importantly, demanding better climate laws from our local politicians."

—**Barton Rubenstein,** *cofounder of the Mother Earth Project and Parachutes for the Planet*

"Goldman expertly interweaves her erudite knowledge of the impact of grief and loss in children with the modern world's current global warming crisis. In this volume, the existential dread that we see in our youth from the impending environmental disasters going on all around us is balanced with expressive, familial, and community-based projects toward inner healing for both individuals and Mother Nature herself. A groundbreaking, timely, much-needed book to help us help our youth become actionable, mindful, and respectful of the planet we must protect in a symbiosis to ultimately protect humanity."

—**Eric J. Green, PhD,** *author of* The Handbook of Jungian Play Therapy

Climate Change and Youth

Climate Change and Youth is a pioneering book that opens the door to understanding the profound impact climate change has on the mental health of today's young people.

Chapters provide age-appropriate language for a meaningful dialogue and resources for acknowledging children's voices, separating fact from fiction about environmental issues, encouraging participation in activism, creating tools to reduce stress, and highlighting inspirational role models and organizations for action. The book includes firsthand examples, research, children's work, interviews, and terminology. It also shares age-appropriate resources and websites relating to climate change and challenges.

Filling a large void in the literature on this topic, this essential resource offers techniques and tools that professionals and caring adults can use to address the stresses associated with climate change and offer strategies for hope, resilience, and action.

Linda Goldman has been a teacher and guidance counselor in the public schools and grief therapist for over 30 years and is the author of several books, including *Life and Loss: A Guide to Help Grieving Children Classic Edition* and *Raising Our Children to Be Resilient: A Guide to Helping Children Cope with Trauma in Today's World.*

Climate Change and Youth

Turning Grief and Anxiety into Activism

Linda Goldman

Routledge
Taylor & Francis Group

NEW YORK AND LONDON

Cover image: Photo by Max Goncharov on Unsplash

First published 2022
by Routledge
605 Third Avenue, New York, NY 10158

and by Routledge
4 Park Square, Milton Park, Abingdon, Oxon, OX14 4RN

Routledge is an imprint of the Taylor & Francis Group, an informa business

Library of Congress Cataloguing-in-Publication Data
Names: Goldman, Linda, 1946- author.
Title: Climate change and youth: turning grief and anxiety into activism / Linda Goldman.
Description: New York, NY: Routledge, 2022. | Includes bibliographical references and index.
Identifiers: LCCN 2021050759 (print) | LCCN 2021050760 (ebook) | ISBN 9780367494544 (hbk) | ISBN 9780367494537 (pbk) | ISBN 9781003051770 (ebk)
Subjects: LCSH: Anxiety in children. | Grief in children. | Youth. | Resilience (Personality trait) | Climatic changes.
Classification: LCC RJ506.A58 G65 2022 (print) | LCC RJ506.A58 (ebook) | DDC 618.9285/227--dc23/eng/20211130
LC record available at https://lccn.loc.gov/2021050759
LC ebook record available at https://lccn.loc.gov/2021050760

ISBN: 978-0-367-49454-4 (hbk)
ISBN: 978-0-367-49453-7 (pbk)
ISBN: 978-1-003-05177-0 (ebk)

DOI: 10.4324/9781003051770

Typeset in Times New Roman
by MPS Limited, Dehradun

"We humans are the only species with the power to destroy the Earth... and so, too, do we have the capacity to protect it."

Dalai Lama, 2021

Contents

8 Youth Activists for the Environment   195

9 Families Activities to Support a Healthy Planet   219

PART IV
Change: *Environmental Justice, Nature Deprivation, Climate Action, Resources*   245

10 Environmental Justice and Young People   247

Preface

The concepts within this book seek to embolden children, teens, parents, and caring professionals to join in taking action for the health and well-being of everyone on planet Earth. Climate change, global warming, fossil fuels, carbon imprints, toxic environments, deforestation, pollution, and recycling are a few of the many terms needed to increase understandings and clarifications for today's young people. This topic of youth and climate change has a vocabulary that is being introduced at lightning speed, with changes in words, definitions, and meanings moving so swiftly, that what may have been valid at the time of writing might be outdated by the time the book prints. The essence is true and constant … too many of our young people have become fearful, and even grief stricken, after a lifetime of bombardment by media information and visualizations illustrating their planet could become so injured it might die during their natural lifetime.

Eco-anxiety is a new term recognizing the widespread worries young people and adults experience associated with climate change, discussed in Chapter 1 of this resource. "Eco-anxiety is anxiety about ecological disasters and threats to the natural environment such as pollution and climate change" (Wikipedia, 2019).

Girls and boys absorb the constant information pool and ongoing media impute that the world is getting hotter, weather is more extreme, and natural disasters are increasing. These phenomena are all related to climate change issues that deeply impact everyday life. Adults must recognize and work with children's anxieties and fears, give children accurate age-appropriate language for discussion, and create an atmosphere of hope, resilience, and action that brings confidence for their future.

As this resource illustrates in Chapter 4, discussion can be ongoing and developmentally appropriate as kids mature. Young girls and boys can be part of a dialogue about the environment and join with adults in promoting activities that encourage a love of nature and creation. These conversations can progressively continue through high school, eventually becoming part of the curriculum as discussions on fossil fuels, bio-extinction, and so on, become more in-depth. A lifelong snapshot of the ever-changing challenges and successes surrounding climate change evolves. This book lays a foundation for terminology, accurate understandings, activities for action on the planet, state of the art projects within the schools, global environmental youth communities, and older generation environmental involvement as well.

Climate Change and Youth is a needed tool for enabling professionals and all caring adults to recognize the stresses associated with environmental challenges and help young people externalize the impact of these challenges. By providing clear language for a meaningful dialogue, acknowledging children's voices, separating fact from fiction about climate issues, encouraging participation in activities for the planet, creating tools to reduce stress, highlighting inspirational role models and organizations, we can ultimately transform anxiety and depression into hope, resilience, and a shared involvement with our children. We can travel with young people toward a path whereby everyone, young and old, resets their moral compass to a commitment, a resolve, and a willingness to act in a way that ensures unity for ourselves and the world around us.

Mr. Fred Rogers stated, *"Anything that's human is mentionable, and anything that is mentionable can be more manageable"* (2019, p. 15).

Let us help our young people feel safe in their environment. This needed, cutting edge resource, *Climate Change and Youth,* openly speaks of the hazards and hopes of climate change, man-made or natural.

It shares guidelines that allow girls and boys to express feelings, reduce fears, and transform **grief** and anxiety into **activism** and action in their homes, communities, nation, and world. Only then can they be inspired to join a global community for the welfare of the planet.

Figure 0.1 Hope Photo by Ben White on Unsplash

"I have learned you are never too small to make a difference."

Greta Thunberg, UN COP24 Climate Talks, 2018,
(Firth-Bernard, 4/8/2020)

Part I

The Challenge

Mental Health Perspectives,
Climate Change, Grief, and Loss

1 Climate Change and Mental Health: Laying a Foundation of Understanding

You have stolen my dreams and my childhood with your empty words.
–Greta Thunberg UN Climate Summit, NY,
September 2019 (Davis, 2019)

Figure 1.1 The Future.
Source: Photo by Gift Habeshaw on Unsplash.

DOI: 10.4324/9781003051770-2

*"Climate change poses a threat to "children's mental and physical health…
And that "failure to take prompt, substantive action would be an act of
injustice to all children."*

–The American Academy of Pediatrics Policy Statement 2015

Introduction

The writing of this book was actually initiated by my son-in-law John. "If
you really want to write about an overriding grief and loss topic concerning
this younger generation," he explained, "write about climate change and
the anxiety and depression it is creating with young people." As I begin to
research the topic and talk to children, teens, and young adults, I realized
how right he was! A true millennial sparked the birth of this resource.

Youth and climate change are a topic that has risen from obscurity to
accountability in a very short time. Increasingly youth are harboring feelings
of grief, depression, and anxiety, as they are constantly flooded with negative
outcomes for themselves, and the world they live in. Continuous exposure to
this negativity for their future has left many girls and boys terrified of
growing up, or even more petrified they will not have a planet to grow up on.

Whether one is a non-believer of climate change or extreme activist, all
caring adults can agree upon the reality of the tremendous toll taken on
the mental health of many of our children. This toll in terms of worry,
fear, and inability to see an optimistic future must be addressed with the
same vigor as helping the planet.

Understanding Generation Z

*The influence of Gen Z – the first generation of true digital natives – is
expanding.*

–Francis and Hoefel, 2018

Young people belonging to the Gen-Z were born between 1995 and 2010.
Francis and Hoefel (2018) refer to this generation as

Our true digital natives: from earliest youth, they have been exposed
to the internet, to social networks, and to mobile systems. That
context has produced a hypercognitive generation very comfortable
with collecting and cross-referencing many sources of information
and with integrating virtual and offline experiences.

One may ask what this has to do with climate change. The answer lies in
the astute technological abilities of this generation that have resulted in a
savvy group of youngsters who display an intense focus on what is
happening to planet Earth. With all of these resources and adaptive
qualities in their possession, they have become a potent force of influence
for others in their generation and of all ages. This influence of this generation concerning change in the environment is far reaching.

The following four core Gen Z behaviors were found in the study by Francis and Hoefel (2018). Gen Zers might be called "identity nomads" because they do not define themselves through only one stereotype but rather for individuals to experiment with different ways of being themselves and to shape their individual identities over time (Francis & Hoefel, 2018, p. 4). They live pragmatically and approach life realistically. Throughout this resource you will see these attributes of truth, activism, and fierce determination to dialogue and pursue change for themselves and the planet. Their search for truth is at the root of these behaviors:

1. Gen "Z"ers value individual expression and avoid labels.
2. They mobilize themselves for a variety of causes.
3. They believe profoundly in the efficacy of dialogue to resolve conflicts and improve the world.
4. Finally, they make decisions and relate to institutions in a highly analytical and pragmatic way.

This rising Gen Z generation has made their life purpose to reverse the damage done by humans on Earth, and Ho (2019) explains they are "bracing for the most devastating impacts of our environmental damage." Gen Z's have exemplified climate activism through demonstrating, striking, and consciously educating and carrying through ideas and processes to implement a healthier planet. Out of this Gen Z movement come many youth activists, including Greta Thunberg *Time Magazine Person of the Year 2019*, highlighted in Chapter 8.

Millennials Understood

In contrast to Gen Z, the previous generation – the millennials or Gen Y, sometimes called the "me generation" – got its start in an era of economic prosperity and focuses on the self. Its members are more idealistic, more confrontational, and more willing to question diverse points of view. Millennials are the first generation to be born into the advent of technology such as the Internet, virtual reality, and artificial intelligence. Because this generation has witnessed the growth and advancement of technology, millennials may identify with more progressive, creative thinking than past eras. Gen Y's share common traits with Gen Z's. These mutual characteristics from *The Career Guide* are the following (2020):

*   Value meaningful motivation.
*   Challenge the hierarchy status quo.
*   Place importance on relationships with superiors.
*   Intuitive knowledge of technology.
*   Open and adaptive to change.
*   Openly receptive to feedback and recognition.
*   Freethinking and creative.
*   Value social interactions in the workplace.

Media Influence Growing Up

My son, Jonathan, a millennial, reminded me that millennials and Gen Z's were greatly influenced by the media they grew up with. Three TV shows specifically impacted young people of both generations on environmental issues and care of the planet: *Captain Planet*, *The Magic School Bus*, and *Dora the Explorer*. All three boldly carried the message to our now climate-focused younger generations that they should care about the environment, act, and create change.

Captain Planet and the Planeteers

Captain Planet and the Planeteers was an animated environmentalist superhero television series in 1990. The show developed into the *New Adventures of Captain Planet* from 1993 to 1996, the years our young millennials were developing and learning. One episode dealt with a polluting counterpart, Captain Pollution, who is capable of duplicating himself to his allies, the eco-villains. These antiheroes are only weakened with pure elements such as water and sunlight.

Captain Planet left each episode with the inspirational message to young viewers, "The power is yours!," planting the seeds of action for these young minds, and that they can and should make a difference. That wave of speaking out and sharing information has helped to form the essence of the millennial outcry to help Mother Earth heal.

The Magic School Bus

The Magic School Bus was an animated children's TV show initially running from 1994 to 1997. Its airing and playing coincides with the formative years of millennials and Gen Z's. Based on the book series of the *Magic School Bus* published originally by Scholastic Publishers, these TV shows were aired for 18 years, until 2017, when the shows were canceled. It now has been envisioned as a sequel on Netflix called the *Magic School Bus Rides Again.*

The impact of *The Magic School Bus* on many generations developing from preschoolers to teens and young adults has remained steadfast. Initially, the first books were meant to help kids learn about science in interesting ways. Conceived by authors Joanna Cole and Bruce Degen, it was as an idea to create relatable school children who partake in scientific field trips with their teacher, Ms. Frizzle.

Ninety-three million copies of the book series have been printed for over 100 countries. Many of today's youth globally were greatly influenced in book and video form about science, climate, and nature through fieldtrips with Ms. Frizzle. One of the newest of the books is for Generation Alpha, *The Magic School Bus Gets Cleaned Up,* was written in collaboration with the EPA and Scholastic Publishers in 2021 (see Chapter 11). It explores pollution from diesel engine school busses.

Dora the Explorer

Dora the Explorer was a TV show that began in 2000 and was presented on Nickelodeon for almost 20 years. Dora traveled the world with her popular backpack and map, entertaining preschoolers and influencing the perceptions of the world, nature, and climate. Groundbreaking as a Latinx character on TV, Dora shares with young minds throughout the years, information about caring for the planet and each other in ways very few shows presented to children. Dora has now come of age in a new film, *Dora and the Lost City of Gold*, taking place in the Amazon rainforest (NPR, 2019).

Many shows for kids illustrate the beauty of nature, its trees, and animals, but few deal directly with climate change. In 2008, an episode of Dora, *Dora Saves the Snow Princess*, made a giant effort in a gentle way to bring up the topic of climate change for preschoolers. Cathy Galeota, Nickelodeon SVP of preschool production, explains, "that storyline dealt with climate change, but in a very child-friendly way of a snow princess. I think these are complex issues that have to be explained in simple ways." Galeota adds,

> We have more *Dora* episodes about keeping our oceans clean from excessive garbage, and about cleaning up the beaches. A *PAW Patrol* episode (was) about rescuing a baby whale from an oil spill, which won an Environmental Media Association Award. We have a wide library of other series with episodes centered about topics like deforestation, drying rivers, endangered animals, alternative energy and community gardens. (Whyte, 2017)

Youth Inspired Progress

Both millennials and Gen Z's are also expected to be the majority of voters in the next generation. Many of these global youngsters are likely to strive to make progress on climate change (see Chapter 8). Organizations are initiating ways to engage these generations. Some initiatives, such as *The Green New Deal* in Congress, are sparking keen interest. *Our Children's Trust* (see Chapter 10) and *Zero Hour* (see Chapter 7) are initiatives inspired by youth, emphasizing their voices be heard in legal systems and climate policy. Our youth are becoming involved, and inspiring peers and older generations to join them. The power they are creating is exciting and documented throughout this resource.

As we journey together to experience what information and fears youth are inundated with from early childhood to early adulthood, we will see this generation of kids and young adults, Gen Z (born 1995–2010) and millennials (born 1980–1994), as citizens of the planet who often fluctuate between fear and sadness, and activism and resilience.

Figure 1.2 Despair.

Source: Photo by Arno Senoner on Unsplash.

Before leaving the subject of creating an understanding of today's youth, their characteristics, and media exposure, we must address the newest generation. This growing generation, Generation Alpha, is of kids born from 2011 to the present.

Generation Alpha

Sixty seven percent of six to nine-year old's want to make saving the planet their career mission.

–Sally Ho, 2019

Generation Alpha children are under the age of 12. They are the first generation to be born entirely within the twenty-first century. We might come to define these very young people by "their commitment to saving our planet" (Ho, 2019). They are born to millennials and many times siblings to Gen Z. When they have all been born by 2025, they "will number two billion, the largest generation in the history of the world" (McCrindle, 2021). As McCrindle points out, they were born with the same year birth as the iPad and Instagram, and their digital literacy transforms their formative years into a new label, screenagers.

Ho maintains,

> Born in the midst of a biodiversity crisis, deteriorating natural ecosystems, food insecurity, and escalating climate emergency, this generation, made up of children eleven years old and younger, is already committing to undo what previous generations have done,

and to reshape the future by putting climate change on the agenda. (Ho, 2019)

Most of these kids will have millennial parents that are well educated, technologically confident, and world travelers. They were born and grew up in an environment of great climate change, and politics and government often unwilling or unable to turn the tide to a healthy Mother Earth.

Although it may be difficult to define behavior before these children reach their teens, Pinsker (2020) maintains,

> They are or will grow up to be the best-educated generation ever, the most technologically immersed, the wealthiest and the generation more likely than any in the past century to spend some or all of their childhood in living arrangements without both of their biological parents. These are notable features, but some of them are broad and fairly low-stakes observations, given that the global population has been getting richer, better educated, and more exposed to digital technology for a while now.

JW Thompson Intelligence reported research that brands were realigning to meet the mindset of Gen A's, finding that even toy companies are making new products to "better align with this socially liberal, inclusive, eco-consious and health-aware market demographic" (Ho, 2019).

Sesame Street is rich in providing these Generation Alpha young children words to use, dialogues, and activities to promote health and well-being for themselves and the planet (see Chapters 3 and 5). This includes videos on hygiene, nature, and even a televised town hall (CNN) meeting for preschoolers to discuss racism (June 6, 2020).

Figure 1.3 Generation A.
Source: Photo by Anthony Tran on Unsplash.

Media Effects on Mental Health

Yet, many of these young people have entered the world of adults and they are deadly serious about it. Instead of partying and maintaining an active social life on weekends, some are protesting the abuse of the planet, terrified there will not be a future. They are inundated and consistently confronted with the adult message – it is up to them to fix the world. Too many feel a sense of despair and hopelessness, confiding it is useless to study or have children when they perceive peril in their future. Many carry signs with the same poignant message, "Earth will survive climate change, we won't!"

Plautz (2020) relays his interview with two school children, sixth-grader Arianna, and second-grader Colin, who both took part in a protest at the Capitol in Washington, DC. Colin carried a sign he made with a picture of coal on one half of the page, and next to it the word "Why?" On the other side of the picture, Colin drew a sun with the words "Why not?" Colin explained he is very scared about the planet's survival but feels comforted that so many people at the protest feel the same way. Ariana explained, she cried over the destruction of the coral reefs and looks to activist Greta Thunberg as an ally. Ariana's parents felt proud of their children's caring for the planet and their incredible activism, yet they confided they often fear their children are becoming overwhelmed "by predictions about the environment that seem to be growing ever more dire" (Plautz, 2020).

Media Bombardment

> There is a growing concern about the mental health impacts of climate change, even for those who are simply observing events unfold (McDonald, 2019).
>
> –The American Psychological Association, 2017

The following illustrates some of the threatening information inundating young people about climate change and disturbing their vision of a peaceful future and a healthy life. The United Nation Intergovernmental Panel on Climate Change cautioned policymakers that there is only a-12-year window to avert the worst consequences of global warming (Plautz, 2020).

The images bombarding their auditory and visual perceptions hold realistic accounts of devastating natural catastrophes with foreboding warnings about an unstoppable devastation of the planet. The following news items exemplify the media coverage about climate change throughout the spring and summer of 2021. Thousands of young people were directly impacted by these climate disasters, and countless more were terrified by what they saw and heard in the media.

Smoke exposure: Smoke from a fire can have a dangerous impact on your physical and mental health, even from thousands of miles away.

–Julia Ries, 08/09/2021 Huffpost

Figure 1.4 Smoke Exposure.

Source: Photo by Ryan Arnst on Unsplash.

Wildfires: The Dixie Fire in Norther California destroyed seventy five percent of the town. It is the largest wildfire in the U.S., expanding over 361,812 acres in three weeks.

–Xiange August 7, 2021, Yahoo News

Drought: Climate change is starting to shape where Americans relocate. For many, turning on the faucet is becoming a source of stress, because the drought in Southern California is causing a water shortage. Many Americans have moved due to climate-related trends such as wildfires, heat waves, drought, and hurricanes.

–Ramaswamy, August 2, 2021, *USA Today*

Hurricanes: Ida Flooding: After dozen die in the East, NYC mayor urges cities prepare differently and states, "This is a new world."

–Holcombe & Hanna, September 3, 2021, CNN

Emissions: West Coast facing uptick in wildfire thanks to climate change. Danielle Butcher, executive vice president of the American Conservation Coalition explains, "A changing climate can lead to warmer, drier conditions, which allows for more frequent and intense fires. As the fires increase, so do their emissions, which worsen the condition of our climate."

–Garin Flowers July 8, 2021. National Reporter

Heat wave: The Pacific North West endured the most extraordinary heat wave of our time. Portland, Oregon rose to a record breaking 116 degrees. The world Weather attribution team found that climate change made this heat wave at least 150 times more likely and almost four degrees hotter than it would have been before.

–Jeff Berardelli. July 8, 2021. CBS News

Extreme heat: Climate change is clearly increasing the severity and frequency of unprecedented extreme heat events globally.

–Daniel Swain, climate scientist at University of California.
David Knowles, June 28, 2021c.
Yahoo News

Abnormal weather: Climate change is increasing the frequency, intensity and duration of heat waves... When you look at this heat wave, it is so far outside the range of normal.

–Professor Kristie Ebi, Center for Health and the Global
Environment at the University of Washington. Vjosa et al., June 30,
2021, *New York Times*

Heat-related deaths: "The big lesson coming out of the past number of days is that the climate crisis is not a fiction." John Horgan, premier of British Columbia. Thirty seven percent of heat-related deaths could be linked to climate change, with significant increase in deaths linked to extreme weather.

–Vjosa Isai et al., June 30, 2021, *New York Times*

Weather-related disasters: "A hurricane blasts Florida. A California dam bursts because floods have piled water high up behind it. A sudden, record-setting cold snap cuts power to the entire state of Texas... These are also emergencies that require immediate action. Multiply these situations worldwide, and you have the biggest environmental emergency to beset the Earth in millennia: climate change," explains Scientific American senior editor Mark Fischetti.

–David Knowles April 12, 2021a.
Yahoo News

Climate emergency: Scientific American magazine is replacing *climate change with climate emergency* in articles about man-made global warming.
–David Knowles, April 12, 2021a. Yahoo News

Impending doom: A draft report by the United Nations Intergovernmental Panel on Climate Change warns that unless drastic and immediate action is taken to limit greenhouse gas emissions and keep global temperatures from rising further, life on Earth is poised for a catastrophic reckoning.
–David Knowles, June 23, 2021b.
Yahoo News

Irreversible damage: The UN report on Climate Change (2021) is "a code red for humanity... Global heating is affecting every region on Earth, with many of the changes becoming irreversible."
–UN Secretary General Antonio Guterres Brandon Miller,
August 9, 2021, CNN

A dire prediction: Without rapid, strong, and sustained cuts in carbon dioxide and other greenhouse gases, we're heading into a world where it will be not pleasant for many, particularly the vulnerable, to live.... So, in that sense it is a stark warning; it is a dire prediction.
–Professor Richard Allan, Intergovernmental Panel on Climate
Change Report 2021 (Hartley, 2021)

Youth Carry the Climate Change Burden

Young people have become the poster children for climate change awareness, forcefully carrying on their shoulders the burden of educating the planet and miraculously curing the problems. Not only is this unrealistic but also it is unfair. The over responsibility placed on this generation of youth has led to anger, frustration, sadness, and nervousness. Panic attacks about wildfires, incredulity of artic storm devastation, and disillusion about plant and wildlife injury have increased depression in our youth that needs to be explored by parents, teachers, and counselors.

A *Washington Post-Kaiser Family Foundation Poll* (September 2019) indicated that teenagers feel scared about climate change, and 52 percent said it made them feel angry. Only 29 percent of young people felt optimistic about the future. The consensus with most caring adults is that open and honest discussion is the most helpful, whereby girls and boys can share feelings in a safe environment and feel understood.

Concern of alarmism with no possible alternatives is becoming more pronounced, and the mindsets of many scientists and mental health professionals seem to weigh in on pulling back from the message of terror and allowing for forward vision. Kate Marvel, a climate scientist voiced her feelings in the following way. The message that

> We're all going to die – that's just not supported by science. I'm not saying we can all rest, and I'm not saying we live in the best of all possible worlds. But one can have a sense of optimism by working towards a solution. (Plautz, 2020)

Plautz also interviewed Michael Shellenberger, founder of the nonprofit Environmental Progress, who shared the following: "These scenarios of apocalypse of cataclysmic climate change that people are scaring children around, are in the realm of an extreme unpredictable event" (2020). Shellenberger shared his 14-year-old daughter grows more worried about the planet and reflected on the eco-anxiety this concern creates. He stresses information should be presented seriously but not with threat of mass extinction. This fear that manipulates the psychology of young people needs to be addressed and dissolved for their well-being. "What people need to understand is that there are extreme scenarios ... and they are not the same thing as predictive science" (Shellenberger in Plautz, 2020). The following questions ring true for all of us to ask ourselves when working with young people, climate change, and mental health.

> *How do you raise a generation to look toward the future with hope when all around them swirls a message of apparent hopelessness?*
>
> *How do you prepare today's children for a world defined by environmental trauma without inflicting more trauma yourself?*
>
> *And where do you find the line between responsible education and undue alarmism?*
>
> –Plautz, 2020

Climate Grief and Loss

Although research on climate grief is just beginning to appear, researchers have begun to substantiate the impact of climate change on young people and their mental health. The US government's National Climate Assessment cited mental health concerns as a side effect of climate change, and the American Academy of Pediatrics issued a policy statement warning that climate change poses threats to "children's mental and physical health" (Plautz 2020).

Environmental Grief

Thanatologist Kriss Kevorkian has defined environmental grief as "the grief reaction stemming from the environmental loss of ecosystems by natural and man-made events" (Rosenfield, 2016). Cunsolo and Ellis (2018) define environmental grief as "the grief felt in relation to experienced environmental change (or anticipated ecological losses, including the loss of species, ecosystems, and meaningful landscapes due to acute or chronic)."

Anticipatory Grief

This anticipatory grief young people carry is their fear of impending loss. Usually this could be the upcoming loss of a dying loved one, but in the case of climate change, it may very well be the fear of a dying Earth. Too many of our youths see the future in a terminally ill planet, with dying wildlife, ocean life, and plant life. One teenager explained to his mom why he did not want to do his homework. "Why should I do anything? The planet will probably be uninhabitable by the time I grow up, if I live to grow up." This attitude, shared by many adolescent peers, leads to apathy, resignation, and an inability to move forward.

Many professionals in the field of grief and loss have recognized the anxiety young people feel about climate change, and their fears about future safety because of anticipatory grief. It is characterized by fear of the future, apprehension about an unsafe future, and despair many feel because of inability to make real change.

Anticipating negative outcomes may serve as an explanation for the sorrow and gloom we find so prevalent in our children. David Kessler, author, and specialist for traumatic events, shares his lifelong observations on the importance of acknowledging the grief and expressing these feelings in order to move forward and find meaning in the present (Berinato, 2020).

Disenfranchised Grief

Often the grief felt with climate change is disenfranchised, cut off from the natural channels of empathy and compassion. Disenfranchised grief is frequently ignored or invalidated, creating a secondary loss of isolation and helplessness that kids may experience. Many youngsters feel their cries for help to older generations are discounted. This lack of acknowledgment of what they perceive as a life-threatening situation produces a feeling of hopelessness.

Collective Grief

Kessler maintains there exists a "collective grief in the air" which might stem from 9 to 11, COVID-19, and climate change, and "a feeling we get about what the future holds when we are uncertain" (Berinato, 2020). This can lead to a disturbing image of what will come that shakes our sense of safety.

The constant daily deluge on the psyches of young people, the smartest social media users, has sparked the rise of a new phenomenon labeled climate depression. Instantaneously, they are seeing and hearing through technology about devastation wreaked on people, animals, plants, and Mother Earth herself through floods, wildfires, melting ice caps, fuel emissions, and rising sea levels. Undoubtedly this creates depression, anxiety, and over-responsibility for the planet collectively held by our younger generations.

Prolonged Grief

Prolonged grief does not disappear over a long period of time and inhibits healing with persistent thoughts and feelings. Findings underscore the emerging paradigm that more and more young people are experiencing grief, loss, anxiety, and depression over longer periods of time because of changes in the environment. This is impacting their mental health. Whether one agrees climate change is natural or human induced, whether one agrees there is climate change or not, there is an agreement young people are experiencing *sustained* depression, hopelessness, anxiety, and fear about their future.

Re-traumatized Grief

Re-traumatization of grief is becoming more common with the increasing weather disasters directly impacting children and families. As climate change becomes more real, families have begun to face the truth of its destruction personally. They relive the unbearable emotional roller coaster of yet another storm. Almost to the day, Hurricane Ida 2021 wreaked similar havoc to Hurricane Katrina 16 years before. Now residents of the same area are re-traumatized as they experience a second devastating assault. "Experts say that as the planet continues to warm, and climate change's effects become more apparent and severe across the globe, more people than ever could experience serious challenges to their mental health as a result" (Baker, 2021).

Relentless Grief

Relentless grief is a term explaining the constancy of accumulated loss and grief due to climate change. Not only are these extreme situations repeated once or twice but also many are ongoing, persistent, and continuous. Therapists are beginning to see more requests for therapy concerning climate change, as well as a strong interest in discussion groups about climate. "We've been for so long in social denial. Now, with the smoke drifting all the way back East and the phenomenal fluctuation in temperature, people can't deny it anymore" (Masters in Baker, 2021).

Psychiatrist Gary Belkin explains,

> We are psychologically unprepared to face the accelerating existential crisis of climate and ecological change... The mental health system works on the idea of discrete illnesses that are treated and have a distinct beginning and end, whereas mass population effects like climate change... are relentless. (Baker, 2021)

Persistent flooding, forest fires, and drought emerge as never-ending life-threatening forces.

Climate Despair

Young people are perhaps the most vulnerable. They ponder a deadly future, asking if it is worth it go to college, get married, or have a career or family. One young person striking on September 20, 2019, illustrated her disturbing feelings by lying on the ground and pretending to be dead. She held a poster saying, "You will die of old age. We will die of climate change."

Figure 1.5 Climate Change Death.
Source: Photo by Markus Spiske on Unsplash.

This "die-in" was an event of over 200 young people staging death in front of the Ministry of Natural Resources and Environment in Thailand. It is symbolic of the impact climate change is having on youth. Another young person held up the poster "There is no Planet B." This phrase had become a mantra for youth activists, and steadfast reminder we all live on the only planet we have, Earth. Humanity needs to take care of everyone and everything.

Figure 1.6 There is NO Planet B.

Source: Photo by Markus Spiske on. Unsplash.

What Is Eco-anxiety?

The following are examples of definitions for eco-anxiety:

1. Eco-anxiety is anxiety about ecological disasters and threats to the natural environment such as pollution and climate change. Variations to the definition exist such as the broader description explaining it as the "worry or agitation caused by concerns about the present and future state of the environment" (Wikipedia, 2020).
2. *Medical News Today* defines eco-anxiety as "a fear of environmental damage or ecological disaster. This sense of anxiety is largely based on the current and predicted future state of the environment and human-induced climate change" (Huizen, 2019).

3. Eco-anxiety or climate anxiety is defined by the American Psychological Association's guide, *Mental Health and Our Changing Climate*, as "a chronic fear of environmental doom" (Clayton et al., 2017, p. 68).

Eco-anxiety often manifests in children as constant worry about their environment, their future, and their inability to control what is happening. They may feel panic, helplessness, and experience persistent, repetitive thoughts about what will happen to their world. Anxiety surrounding extreme environmental issues can manifest with actual experiencing of near experienced climate-related extreme weather such as wildfires, floods, droughts, and hurricanes. Debilitating anxiety can increase as young people fear they have no control as to what is happening around them yet feel responsible for saving the planet at the same time.

> Depression, anxiety, grief, despair, stress—even suicide: The damage of unfolding climate change isn't only counted in water shortages and wildfires, it's likely eroding mental health on a mass scale, too, reports the American Psychological Association, the preeminent organization of American mental health professionals. (Schlanger, 2017, Quartz)

The American Psychological Association (APA) joined by Climate for Health and Eco America, reports the increase in chronic psychological consequences resulting from daily despair caused by the environmental impact of climate change. The constant bombardment of facts and fiction experienced by preschoolers to college students leaves them with fearful, even terrified emotions, about their future and the future of the planet.

These evolving thought forms have led to a new term, eco-anxiety. The APA explains that climate change is causing Post-traumatic Stress Disorder, anxiety, and depression on a massive scale. Many young people feel they are unable to make a difference in changing the course of the planet and feel helpless to improve the overwhelming present conditions and prophecies. The APA has recognized the "profound connection between climate change and mental health, that the changing environment is a legitimate source of distress already affecting many young people, and it has the potential to be psychologically destabilizing" (Schlanger, 2017).

Climate Adjustment

Reser and Swim (2011) define climate change as "the threat and unfolding environmental impact" of current climate issues. In their research on adaptation to and coping with the impact of climate change they have begun a conversation on adaption. The Intergovernmental Panel on Climate Change (2007) defines climate adaptation as "adjustment in natural or human systems in response to actual or expected climatic stimuli or their effect, which moderates harm or exploits beneficial opportunities" (Parry et al., 2007, p. 869). This threat of the consequences of climate change exposed by the media has become a forefront issue and recurring nightmare for many informed youngsters capable of accessing instantaneous updates on dire facts and predictions. Adapting to climate change for kids includes understanding the natural shifts too.

Climate change produces multiple stressors in children and teens that present processes for adaptation and coping as seen in Figure 1.1. Reser and Swim (2011) maintains the idea of discrete and continuous stressors and natural and technological disasters. Discrete events can be sudden and catastrophic, such as wildfires, floods, and earthquakes. Severe changes of weather can be disturbing to kids, due to their unpredictable and damaging nature. Prolonged or continuous stressors can be drought or excessive rainfall, producing for young people on both ends of the spectrum a realistic uncertainty about the future.

Natural and technological disasters can be equally cataclysmic, as they too are unpredictable and can be life threatening. Government policies that impact energy protocols and environmental well-being are a piece of the threat, as well as the recognition that "global climate change is unique in that it presents multifaceted global impacts that will be chronic over a dramatic time frame and constitutes a phenomenon not amenable to conventional, national, or jurisdiction agencies or disaster policies and procedures" (Marshall et al., 2007).

Reser and Swim conclude in the context of human response and adaptation to climate change there are the following essential and important avenues of consideration (2011, p. 286).

1. More research and documentation are needed to assess psychological and social response to environmental threat due to climate change.
2. The subject of local versus global environment should be researched, and that psychological adaptation to local and global environmental challenges can be joined.
3. Research on the direct exposure to and experience with environmental changes.
4. Research on how media depiction and images and popular science influence public understanding. Develop interventions with existing knowledge on copying and adaptation to help psychological and physical adaptation to climate change.

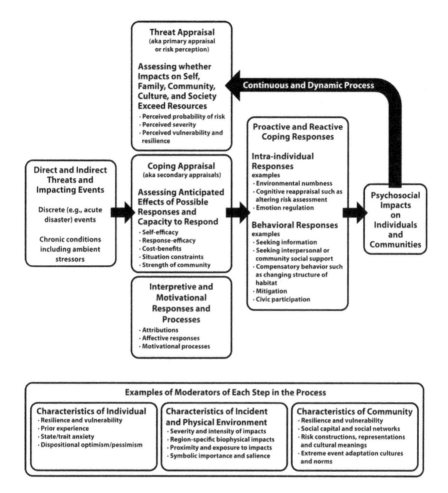

Figure 1.7 Psychological Processes That Influence Adaptation to and Coping with Climate Change.

Source: Adapted from *Psychology and Global Climate Change: Addressing a Multifaceted Phenomenon and Set of Challenges* (Figure 1.8, p. 54) by the American Psychological Association Task Force on the Interface between Psychology and Global Climate Change, 2009, Washington, DC: American Psychological Association. Copyright 2010 by the American Psychological Association. Reproduced with permission. American Psychologist May-June 2011 e-figure 1 page 279.

Climate Grief Defined

Ecological grief, also known as climate grief, can be a psychological response to loss caused by environmental destruction or climate change. Cunsolo and Ellis (2018) explain that "grief is a natural and legitimate response to ecological loss, and one that may become more common as climate impacts worsen."

Journalist Mike Pearl in (2019) asserted "people are suffering from what could be called 'climate despair', a sense that climate change is an unstoppable force that will render humanity extinct and renders life in the meantime futile." The emerging model of climate grief suggests that young people may process climate despair or climate anxiety as a true grief and loss issue, and their need for social support is a part of that grief process.

Child psychologist Dr. Jillian Roberts explains her experience with young people and climate change. Dr. Roberts states, "eco-anxiety can invoke the fight, flight, or freeze response in children in the following three ways" (Egan-Elliott, 2019).

1. Fleeing by avoiding the subject altogether or trying to escape
2. Freezing as in a "complete paralysis," that can move toward depression and result in feelings of helplessness
3. Fighting or acting

One example of fighting and acting were young activists in front of the Ministry of Housing and Urban Affairs in New Delhi, India. They were part of a worldwide protest of young people for action to guard against climate change. Many youths around the globe joined together that day, with slogans and statements that demanded action by government and the adult world. One poster read, "The climate is changing, so should we! #Act now."

Figure 1.8 Change Now.
Source: Photo by Markus Spiske on Unsplash.

Still another poster challenges those of all generations that too easily ignore climate change challenges with a simple statement: "No intelligent species would destroy their only home and planet."

Figure 1.9 Be Intelligent.

Source: Photo by Markus Spiske on Unsplash.

Generation Z and millennials have become the activists of the planet, moving forward with a strong voice for the urgency of care for themselves and the planet. They come together to protest and explain to older generations the urgency of their mission and their disappointment and anger that they must be the ones to enlighten adults and spur them to action. Young Generation Alpha has begun to join them. Gen A has produced child advocates to educate older youth and adults about climate change challenges (see Chapter 8).

Conclusion

Climate instability is one of the most urgent public health threats of the twenty-first century. Mental health is profoundly impacted by the disruptions associated with climate change.

–Climate Psychiatry Alliance, 2020

The media has become a surrogate parent and extended family to us and our children. Adults must regain their birthright to keep young people safe by dissolving their apprehensions and apathy, and joining young people as co-creators of healthy minds, healthy bodies, and a healthy world. The following questions needs to be addressed by all concerned grownups:

- How can we ease the burden these youngsters carry as the future protectors of the planet?
- How can we instill positive news and information that will uplift their spirits?
- How can we support activities and imagery that create a beautiful, harmonious environment?
- How can we support resilience by underscoring change is ongoing and calls for flexibility and endurance?
- How can we promote activism and resources for themselves and mother earth with a vision of working together to co-exist on the planet?

To move young people forward by dissolving uncertainty about their future and engaging in successful actions – we need a framework to alleviate stress and enhance optimism toward positive outcomes. Mental health professionals, educators, and parents must look at climate change with a new lens. This lens focuses on our youth and what they say and feel with a fresh perspective ... one that solidifies hope, participation, and harmony within our homes, schools, communities, and government for achieving well-being for young people and planet Earth.

This perspective allows children and adults to *acknowledge* what is happening to themselves and the world they live in, to *accept* what cannot be changed, and to *act* on what can be changed in a productive and unified fashion. The three A's – *acknowledge, accept, and act* – transform challenges into opportunities for growth.

We need to help our youth balance the anxiety of the destructive images of what their future could bring with equally empowering images of a future that contains a thriving planet as well. Often this balance can be achieved through action and hope.

Figure 1.10 A Healthy Planet.
Source: Photo by Joshua Clay on Unsplash.

2 Childhood Losses in the Twenty-First Century

In this most materially blessed nation on Earth, no one should want for food, clothing, shelter, or other basic necessities of life.
–Dr. Carol Weyland Conner, Founder of White Pony Express and Following Francis Website. www.Followingfrancis.org

Figure 2.1 The Future.

Source: Photo by Katie Moum on Unsplash.

DOI: 10.4324/9781003051770-3

Introduction

In my work as a teacher and therapist with kids and grief and loss for the past 30 years, I have often heard the prevailing myth that children are too young to grieve. And yet, if a child is capable of loving, she or he is certainly capable of grieving.

One five-year-old took part in a climate change protest with her family. She carried a poster she made that read, *Mother Earth is crying*. Tears rolled down her eyes.

Figure 2.2 Grief.

Source: Photo by Omar Elsharawa on Unspash.

Grief and loss in childhood, adolescence, and early adulthood is an ongoing process. Throughout time children and teens have experienced childhood losses ranging from the loss of a toy, the wilting of a flower, the death of an oyster, or the destruction of a home. The fast-pace digital world of today's youth has left them swirling with information and visual imagery that inundates their minds and hearts and impacts them deeply. These are very perceptive young minds and hearts. These are the first generations born into social media, and their inherent aptitude to become tech smart can at the very least be overwhelming. This barrage of wanted and unwanted data serves as an unstoppable and ever-present overlay to all existing personal, social, and societal grief and loss issues living in their home, school, community, country, and planet (see Chapter 1).

Climate Change Losses

The new age losses associated with climate change range from the perceived loss of health, nature, government, and the future, culminating in an evolving new category of childhood loss, the loss of the planet and the loss of the world itself. These timely losses are included in the following childhood loss categories that young people experience (Goldman, 2017, p. 18).

- The loss of relationship
- The loss of environment
- The loss of skills and abilities
- The loss of routines and habits
- The loss of privacy
- The loss of self/self-esteem
- The loss of external objects
- The loss of the safety and protection of the adult world
- The loss of a future

  - ° The loss of health
  - ° The loss of trust
  - ° The loss of nature
  - ° The loss of the planet and the world itself

Today's children carry the burden of losses not recognized in the past in working with young people. These losses have become profound considering the climate change issues, including a health pandemic, demonstrations on racism, and social and economic inequity. These immediate losses act as an overlay for all losses existing before these events. Social distancing and isolation have created multiple losses for kids as well that include:

- The loss of income
- The loss of physical contact with friends and family
- The loss of being in school and socialization
- The loss of the daily routine and outdoor play
- The loss of the environment and nature
- The loss of childhood
- The loss of faith in government
- The loss of hope

Underlying emerging losses for young people in relationship to climate change include loss of hope, health, income, nature, friends, privacy, school, and a future. Greta Thunberg has often stated her generation has lost their childhood due to the realities of climate challenges. *Global*

Citizen maintains the following information on its website regarding poverty, pollution, and climate change.

> Climate change threatens people and the planet. From rising carbon emissions to plastic in our oceans, the degradation of our environment could reverse progress made in tackling poverty. It's already having a shocking impact – reports show people in the world's poorest countries would be thirty percent richer if not for climate change. And this is only the beginning. In order to halt this crisis, world leaders must immediately focus on reducing carbon emissions, helping communities adapt to the effects of climate change, and ensuring there's a price on pollution. (Global Citizen, 2020)

Other losses emerge due to climate change. Elliot Haspel (2021), reported in *The Washington Post* explained that climate change is forcing kids to indoors – and warns childhood will never be the same. "Go out and play" was a phrase used very often by parents to their children. With the extreme weather conditions throughout the globe, this phrase is no longer the norm. Now climate change threatens childhood experiences. Wildfires, smoke, extreme heat, flooding, hurricanes, and chaotic climate patterns drive children indoors, forcing them to be less active and more device oriented.

Richard Louv coined the term *nature-deficit disorder* and explains that increased screen time and decreased outdoor time are causing "a narrowing of the senses, greater rates of depression, and myopia among children" (Haspel, 2021). Louv describes *nature-deficit disorder* as "not being a medical diagnosis, but a useful term—a metaphor—to describe what many of us believe are the human costs of alienation from nature: diminished use of the senses, attention difficulties, higher rates of physical and emotional illnesses, a rising rate of myopia, child and adult obesity, Vitamin D deficiency, and other maladies" (Suttie, 2016). The report on health and climate by the *Lancet Medical Journal* 2019 stated that, "Children are among the worst affected by climate change." They are very vulnerable to extreme heat and air pollution (see Chapter 10).

A groundbreaking study by Hickman (2021) presents an enormous broad scale investigation into climate anxiety for young people throughout the planet and their reactions to government response. About 10,000 young people indicated having eco-anxiety (see Chapter 1) that produced a negative impact on their lives, and expressed frustration that governments are not doing enough to avoid climate disaster. Sixty percent said they felt very worried or extremely worried about climate change and felt the future was threatening. Eighty one percent stated they felt ignored or dismissed (Thompson, 2021).

W. Thiery et al. (2021) maintain under present conditions that younger generations are expected to face more climate extremes across their lifetimes compared to older generations. Their recent study on intergenerational inequities in exposure to climate extremes explains:

> If the planet continues to warm on its current trajectory, the average 6-year-old will live through roughly three times as many climate disasters as their grandparents, the study finds. They will see twice as many wildfires, 1.7 times as many tropical cyclones, 3.4 times more river floods, 2.5 times more crop failures, and 2.3 times as many droughts as someone born in 1960. (Kaplan, 2021b)

Thiery et al. (2021) highlight findings that indicate climate change poses "a severe threat to the safety of young generation and calls for drastic emission reductions to safeguard their future."

Children's Understandings at Developmental Stages

Young people's understanding and integration of the losses that impact their life directly or vicariously are influenced by their cognitive understanding at different stages of their growing up. The Swiss educator Piaget (Wadsworth, 2003) explained children's cognitive understanding through the following developmental stages:

- *Sensorimotor stage: Approximately 0–2.* A child's concept of death is characterized by "out of sight, out of mind."
- *Preoperational stage: Approximately 2–7.* A child's concept of death includes magical thinking, egocentricity, reversibility, and causality.
- *Concrete operations: Approximately 7–12.* A child's concept of death is curious and realistic.
- *Formal operations: Approximately 13 and up.* An adolescent's concept of death is self-absorbed, and they see death as remote and rely on their peers for support (Goldman, 2014, pp. 39–40).

Children in the pre-operational stage often display magical thinking. They can feel a traumatic event is their fault – when a plant dies; an animal gets sick, or even causing Mother Earth to cry. Little Maggie was five years old. She continually heard her older brother Sean talking about the planet dying and Mother Earth crying. One night, mom was reading her a story about trees and animals, and suddenly she burst into tears. "It is my fault Mother Earth is so sad. I forgot to water my plant and it died." Only when Maggie could share her feelings with mom could she begin a dialogue that helped her understand climate change was not her fault. Natural and man-made events may cause despair in the environment, but there is certain activities Maggie can do to help. She can plant another flower, recycle waste, and not use plastic straws.

In the concrete operations, stage kids want to know the facts. What is a carbon imprint, how much plastic is destroying the oceans, and why are ice caps melting? Teens look to their peers during the formal operations stage, seeking support and support peer groups. Joining a compost project, writing to a senator, planting trees in the park, and striking together for the good of the planet help create connection, peer support, activism, and resilience in their lives.

Adolescents usually feel death is far away, but the Gen z's have embraced the notion that it is their job to rescue the planet. The global youth activation (see Chapters 7 and 8) to rescue the planet had indeed created a worldwide network and support group for young people wanting to feel united and strengthened. Looking to peers for support is a characteristic of this developmental stage.

Common Signs and Symptoms of Climate Grief

It is essential that parents and professionals educate themselves on the following common feelings, behaviors, and thoughts of grieving young people, and the physical symptoms that can be a by-product of grief. These common patterns can be seen in our youth in relation to climate grief explained in Chapter 1.

Common Behaviors Associated with Grief

Sleeplessness	Crying	Social withdrawal
Loss of appetite	Sighing	Dreams of deceased
Listlessness	Clinging	Nightmares
Overactiveness	Verbal attacks	Fighting
Excessive touching	Bed-wetting	
Poor grades	Excessive hugging	
Absentmindedness	Extreme quiet	

Common Physical Signs of Grief

Headaches	Stomachaches
Fatigue	Heaviness of body
Dry mouth	Tightness in chest
Dizziness	Tightness in throat
Headaches	Sensitive skin
Hot or cold flashes	Empty feeling in body
Increased illness	Muscle weakness

Common Thought Patterns Associated with Grief

Inability to concentrate	Poor self-image
Self-destructive thoughts	Preoccupation
Difficulty deciding	

Common Feelings Associated with Grief

Anger	Intense feelings
Guilt	Loneliness
Confusion	Depression
Sadness	Anxiety
Disbelief	Relief
Mood swings	Hysteria
Rage	Feeling unreal
Helplessness	Pounding heart
Shortness of breath	Fear

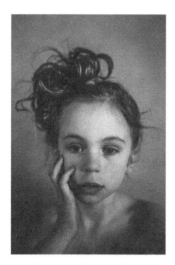

Figure 2.3 Common Feelings.

Source: Photo by Sarah Driscoll on Unsplash.

Common Signs of Grieving Young People

- Child retells events or perceived future events over and over.
- Child dreams about climate loss.

- Child has nightmares about the future.
- Child rejects old friends and seeks new friends with a similar loss.
- Child wants to call home during the school day.
- Child cannot concentrate on homework or classwork.
- Child bursts into tears in the middle of class.
- Child seeks scientific information on the environment.
- Child worries excessively about his own health and health of the planet.
- Child sometimes appears to be unfeeling about loss.
- Child becomes the "class clown" to get attention.
- Child is overly concerned with caretaking of the environment.
- Child feels overly responsible for the planet's survival.

Pain-Based Behavior: Coping by "Acting Out"

A crucial paradigm is the concept of pain-based behavior as an adaptive mechanism to an overwhelming life event, such as climate change. When we can place the children's fear of the loss of their environment, and the overwhelming anxiety they feel about their health and their future, the tendency for some to act out can indeed fit into the landscape of pain-based behavior. "Young people who have experienced trauma are literally living in a world of pain which shows in their challenging behavior" (Anglin, 2014, p. 4). Anglin defines the term *pain-based behavior* as "behavior, either of an 'acting out' or withdrawn nature ... triggered by the re-experiencing of psycho-emotional pain. Pain based behavior is a common human experience" that can be triggered by students' unresolved problems, often producing volatility and chaos in the classroom (Goldman, 2017, p. 45).

Tamara was listening to her third-grade teacher, Mrs. Samson, read a story about penguins and their inability to cope with their changing environment. "The penguins can't find food, and it's getting too hard for them to keep going." When Tamara heard this, she burst into tears and shouted, "I can't stand to hear this. It's not fair. I hate everyone. Why can't we save the penguins!!" Then she ran out of the room. As Mrs. Samson went to calm her down, Tamara fell into her arms sobbing: "I don't want the animals to die. I had a nightmare last night that my doggy was dying. What can we do?"

Mrs. Samson decided to help her answer that question. The class began a project of finding good things people were doing to save the animals. Tamara joined the school club that worked to help the environment. She initiated a project to create a school fundraiser to help penguins. A few weeks later Tamara told Mrs. Samson, "I feel better because I am doing something to help with other kids. I don't feel so alone."

Figure 2.4 What Can We Do?
Source: Photo by Julia Scagliol on Unsplash.

"Unfortunately, professionals, and caregivers often react in ways that perpetuate conflict and pain" (Anglin, 2014, p. 53). Tamara is an example of approaching a troubled child with a calm, heartfelt listening approach, and a dedication to help an overwhelmed student find avenues of action to feel empowered. Tamara's seemingly defiant attitude displayed as troubling behaviors with outbursts, emotional explosions, and an over-reaction to authority could have escalated into teacher/student conflict. She may have been labeled "a troublemaker" rather than seeing her behavior as a cry for help that may have escalated continuous time-outs, punishments, and even exclusion and school expulsion. However, Mrs. Samson maintained a mindset that incorporates love, understanding, and respect for her students, resulting in the ability to transform problems into opportunities for learning and growth.

An Example of Pain-Based Behavior

A comprehensive example of a pain-based behavior was cited in a CNN article (Ebrahimji, 2021) explaining how a principal, Mr. Smith, took an act of defiance and turned it into an act of compassion. A middle school boy Anthony refused to take off his hat in class, a behavior that was against school policy. He was sent to the principal's office for a reprimand. When the principal asked Anthony why he refused, he explained he hated his new haircut and wanted to hide it so no one would laugh.

The principal, who was adept at cutting his own hair for years, drove back to his home in the snow to retrieve his clippers. With the permission of the boy and his mother, he shaped Anthony's hair to his liking, and off to class Anthony went. This principal, with great empathy, understood the embarrassment of a perceived haircut for this age boy and how traumatic it feels. Instead of punishment, he enabled this student to feel better and go back to learning. It was indeed a pain-based behavior driven out of fear of being ridiculed by peers for a bad haircut.

Mr. Smith checked on the boy throughout the day and found he was participating quite well without his hat on in class. This principal's gesture of kindness was far more meaningful than a reprimand for disobedience. Normally, an in-school suspension would be the consequence for not complying with the dress code. Then the student's parent picks him up which Mr. Smith explains, "would have prevented him from being in front of a classroom teacher and giving him the education, he deserves, so it really worked out well" (Ebrahimji, 2021).

Principal Smith explained his following educational perspective that resonates with and validates the understanding that underlying causes of misconduct can be pain based.

> All behavior is communication and when a student is struggling, we need to ask ourselves what happened to this child instead of what's wrong with the child – What need is the child trying to get met and really, the future of urban education rests on that question. (Ebrahimji, 2021)

A Trauma Sensitive Approach

Certainly, many of our present school population have been traumatized by direct effects of climate change, and vicariously through media bombardment of devastating climate events. Jim Sporleder, a former high school principal, transformed an at-risk student population into a trauma sensitive safe environment by eliminating the pitfalls of a school system that only uses punishment to shape behavior. He implores educators to see the benefits of establishing heartfelt connections with students that help modify destructive or unproductive ways of acting, even caused by traumatic or perceived traumatic events.

Sporleder explains,

> Once I became trauma-informed and grew a deeper understanding of what our kids were going through, I walked away from my strong traditional disciplinary practices. I learned quickly that the Zero Tolerance policies had no positive effect, and we were missing

the root of the problem. Once I left my traditional past, what my students taught me about resilience transformed me. I learned the power of a caring adult relationship, and how we can influence a life path. When you look at Lincoln High School's statistical data and transformation, you will see the power of our paradigm shift and how it has impacted our students. (Goldman, 2017, pp. 295–296)

This shift went from punishment to heartfelt connections.

Katie's Case Study: Aftermath of a Natural Disaster

Disaster struck Paradise, California, 2019, with wildfires that destroyed over 1,000 homes and businesses, communities, and life. Not only was this traumatic natural disaster devastating at the time but myriads of loss issues that remained present for months afterward only served to keep seven-year-old Katie, a little girl impacted by the Camp Fire, in a state of heightened traumatic grief. She became withdrawn, hypervigilant, and easily aroused. Katie's dad, Adam, had recently died in a tragic car accident. Adam had abandoned her at age two. Her father's visits were infrequent and explosive, with Adam often going into an alcoholic rage of physical and emotional abuse that terrified Katie and her mother.

These outbursts of violence remained silently buried in Katie after her dad's sudden death. Katie began to have repeated emotional outbursts in school. She was unable to stay in the classroom and performed poorly in school. After the fire, she had frequent nightmares, crying out in her sleep, "Help me, the fire is coming." Her house had been destroyed and the family lived in tents for quite some time. She anticipated future disaster, obsessively listening to the news to see if the fire was coming back.

Sometimes Katie was unable or unwilling to talk about her father's death or the experience of the fire. Projective techniques were helpful in unlocking hidden feelings. In one grief therapy session, she drew a scribble picture. I asked her if she could see something inside the scribble and give it a name.

Katie called the scribble picture *Fire*. "If the fire could talk, what would the fire say?" I asked. She replied, "Help me!"

Her sadness and feelings of being overwhelmed by the Camp Fire were represented in her scribble picture, with a plea for help over an experience she had no control over. She explained that "the fire was so scary. I kept looking for help. I didn't know how to stop the fire. What could I do?"

Figure 2.5 A Fire (Goldman, 2002, p. 124).

Source: Insert Permission Taylor and Francis.

She became very anxious over her pet dog Gracie, who was missing in the fire. She wondered. "Is she Ok? Is she hungry? 'Is she alive?' It's my fault she's gone. Why didn't I stay and wait for her?" Then she began to sob.

Figure 2.6 Gracie.

Source: Linda Goldman Photo.

Figure 2.7 Life Before and After (Goldman, *Life and Loss*, Classic Edition, 2022, p. 75).

Source: Image Permission Taylor and Francis.

Katie shares her frustration through the above drawings of life with her family before the fire and after the fire. Before the fire she drew a lot of idealized love and happiness. After the fire she drew a lot of frustration and anger.

A youth survivor of the snow and ice Texas catastrophe February 2021, David, explained his feelings before and after the winter storm in this way. "Before the freezing temperatures and ice, mommy, daddy, and me were always happy. Now we always feel worried and sad. We lost heat, water, and we were freezing. And we have a lot of busted pipes. Now we are scared the cold, cold, weather will come back." David, mom, and dad constantly checked television and cell phones for the return of the bad weather.

What Will Life Be Like in the Future?

Katie liked to create stories, reproduce them with toy figures, and take photographs to share with others. By projecting her feelings onto drawings and written work, Katie was beginning to safely place them outside of herself. The following image is Katie's magical place – the imagery of her peaceful nature environment and meaningful visualization.

Katie was asked what life would look like for her in the future. She drew this picture and relayed the following story. Through her drawing, Katie creates a tangible image of a happy future that she could view when more difficult images of the fire arose. She explained it was a place with rainbows and flowers, and everyone got to meet God. Katie kept the drawing in her bedroom. She liked to look at it because she said it helped her feel better.

My Magical Place by Katie

Once there was a girl named Katie. She dreamed of a magical place where plants were everywhere and every color – green, red, orange, yellow and pink.

Figure 2.8 My Magical Place (Goldman, 2002, p. 118).
Source: Image permission Taylor and Francis.

Animals were everywhere too. It was beautiful. There was a magic rainbow and a house with the sun over it. I would live with the animals and plants. I wish I could always be there!

Yet sometimes Katie would say she did not want to live. One day she told her teacher life was too hard, and she could not take it anymore. Her teacher took her words seriously and joined the guidance counselor and me to create a contract with Katie about her feelings of hopelessness. Here is what this team decided on. Katie read it aloud, and Katie, the teacher, the guidance counselor, and Linda signed it.

The Katie Contract

Specific single goal behavioral contracts were made with Katie. The following was one of our first contracts:

> *I agree to raise my hand in math class when I want to say something for one week. If I get frustrated, I can tell or call...*
>
> *   *My math teacher*
> *   *Linda*
> *   *The guidance counselor*
> *   *My journal*
>
> *I will get my favorite treat at the snack bar from Linda at the end of the week.*
> Katie, Linda, The Guidance Counselor, The Teacher

Children may need to repeat back in their own words the terms of the contract to be sure they understand the agreement. Katie's math teacher reported that there was a significant improvement in her ability to participate in class, and she was rewarded for this behavior by receiving her favorite snack.

Look for the Helpers

Katie's family lived in a tent after the fire. They had no money, no food, no clothing except for what they were wearing. In the beginning help came, but they wondered how long it would last. They did not even have money for gas, and they had no way to cook. Katie became despondent. How will we ever make it? How will I live through this?

Katie's mom remembered she read an article that talked about disaster and recalled Mr. Rogers's words:

> For me, as for all children, the world could have come to seem a scary place to live. But I felt secure with my parents, and they let me know that we were safely together whenever I showed concern about accounts of alarming events in the world. There was something else my mother did that I've always remembered.

Mr. Rogers shared his mother's advice: "Always look for the helpers," she would tell me. "There is always someone who is trying to help." Mr. Rogers did follow his mother's advice and came to see that "the world is full of doctors and nurses, police and firemen, volunteers, neighbors and friends who are ready to jump in to help when things go wrong" (Craig, 2020).

Service Recognition for Paradise: White Pony Express

> *An act of helpfulness, a word of comfort, the spontaneous warmth of selfless love, gives to others what they really need.*
> –Dr. Carol Weyland Conner, www.whiteponyexpress.org, 2021

Dr. Carol Weyland Conner, founder of the White Pony Express, and her White Pony Express volunteers exemplified Mr. Rogers's concept of helpers. Dr. Conner was awarded one of the highest public service awards in California from the American Association of Retired Persons (AARP) for the help given during the deadly Camp Fire. The Camp Fire started at Camp Creek Road in Paradise, California, and was one of the most destructive wildfires in the history of California. Dr. Conner accepted the AARP award on behalf of the entire staff who worked tirelessly for ten months. The White Pony Express is organized to serve one Bay Area County, which was a three-to-four-hour drive from the fire region. The group had never attempted anything of this kind before.

The fire was contained after 17 days, with nearly 20,000 structures destroyed and 50,000 people displaced. The towns of Paradise, Concow, Magalia, and Butte Creek Canyon were largely destroyed. By January 2019, the total damage was estimated at $16.5 billion; one-quarter of the damage, four billion dollars, was not insured. The Camp Fire also cost over $150 million in fire suppression costs, bringing the total cost of the fire to $16.65 billion (Wikipedia, 2018).

Families displaced by the 2018 wildfire were brought food, clothing, and money to help them get on their feet again. While the Camp Fire was still raging, Dr. Conner gathered 182 volunteers to respond, not only during the fire but also every day for the next ten months. The White Pony Express completed ninety-one 300-mile trips to Butte County communities that were now burned areas, and brought relief supplies of food, clothing, and cash needed for gas, bills, and other essentials.

White Pony Chief Operations Officer Isa Campbell explained, "We [gathered and] gave away almost 58,000 pounds of food and 1,800 articles of clothing. We gave away thousands of dollars in cash for necessities and put gas in vehicles" (Vacar, 2020). The White Pony Express volunteers gave more than food. They gave understanding and love. All of us caring for each other as one unified family is the White Pony Express perspective put into practice.

Following Francis: Francis on the Hill

Francis on the Hill, Washington DC is a program under Following Francis, born in 2018 to beautify and clean the Meridian Hill Park area by picking up trash and planting colorful flowers in concrete planters. In March 2020, the program grew out of the need to feed families during the COVID-19 epidemic. Francis on the Hill is comprised of a small but mighty volunteer team that includes many senior citizens determined that no one should go hungry, especially not during the pandemic.

Its mission is to gather food surplus donations and distribute or deliver the groceries to underserved families. When families are sick and cannot pick up the groceries themselves, the food is delivered to them. Through the generosity of community and national donors, Francis on the Hill was able to grow from feeding 30 families weekly to over 400 families a week.

> Francis on the Hill is dedicated to supporting children and families in Washington DC – helping to alleviate economic insecurity by providing fresh, wholesome groceries and new clothing for neighborhood residents.
>
> –Following Francis, 2021

Figure 2.9 Grocery Donation.
Source: Photo permission Following Francis.

During the winters of 2020 and 2021 a special coat and toy drive was initiated for families who were very much in need. Every child and adult identified by a local school in Washington DC as homeless (in transition) received a holiday gift bag of a new coat and toys and toiletries.

Figure 2.10 Holiday Gift Bag.

Source: Photo permission Following Francis.

One teenager had explained to her teacher that she could not participate in after-school activities because she needed to go home right away so that her mom could go to work. They only had one coat, and they had to share it each day. After the coat drive, they had two.

Figure 2.11 New Coats.

Source: Photo permission Following Francis.

The mission of Francis on the Hill and Following Francis is clear. "Our mission is to help eliminate hunger and poverty by delivering the abundance all around us to those in need – with love."

Following Francis, www.followingfrancis.org, 2021

Kindness Day at Healdsburg School

Children and schools also played a part in the helpers Mr. Rogers spoke of that exist all around us. The students and teachers at The Healdsburg School decided to create a kindness day project. Their compassion for other children who lost so much in the Camp Fire was palpable.

The school community was stunned by the devastation that families had experienced after the Camp Fire, which caused unconscionable destruction of home, property, and life to the inhabitants of the town of Paradise. The students created a recorded video of the song, "Better Place" that they sang and sent to schools impacted by the fire.

Along with the recording were handwritten notes of caring and encouragement for other kids. The children at Healdsburg had become fearful the fire was too close, and the opportunity arose to take the moment to reach out to others.

One student wrote, "I know what you have been through. I was you a year ago" (Minkiewicz, 2018). Others simply wrote "We care" and "I'm sorry." "I'm so sorry your house burnt down. I hope it gets rebuilt." This morphed into the Kindness Club at school where students began a fire relief program, collecting donations for Paradise school children. The club began meeting regularly to initiate projects that give back to the community.

Trauma-Informed Care for Kids and Climate Change

Young people like Katie experiencing trauma can exhibit many pain-based behaviors that manifest as hyperarousal, hyperactivity, inability to concentrate, fear, and anxiety. These are common prevailing signs of stress, resulting from direct or vicarious exposure to climate change challenges and natural disasters such as wildfires, earthquakes, and even viral pandemics. Greenwald (2005) explains, "Parents, counselors, teachers, coaches ... and others are all in a position to help a child heal" (p. 37).

Establishing a safe environment at home, in schools, and with mental health professionals that includes an understanding that many of the behaviors and difficulties in learning and relating to others are pain-based rather than merely "oppositional" or an indicator of attention deficit disorder can quicken the healing process for our students. Bath (2008a) maintains that

One does not need to be a therapist to help address these three crucial elements of healing: the development of safety, the promotion of healing relationships, and the teaching of self-management and coping skills ... the three critical pillars for intervention outlined here are fundamental and universal. (p. 18)

The Three Pillars of Trauma-Informed Care

These three pillars of trauma-informed care for students are safety, connections, and managing emotions. Bath (2008a) explains, "Unfortunately, the defining experience of any child who has experienced complex trauma is that of feeling unsafe. *The first imperative is creating a safe place for them*" (p. 19). Including children in decision-making, giving them choices, maintaining consistency, and being honest, and reliable are factors that can help educators to create and sustain that "oasis of safety" for kids. *Connections, the second pillar, are essential in developing trust that leads to safety.* Educators (mental health professionals) who are available, honest, and able to become mentors and cheerleaders for students provide an integral step for their healing, their growth, and their learning. Bath (2008a, p. 20) suggests the following:

> From a neurodevelopmental perspective, it appears that the brains of traumatized children have learned to associate adults with negative emotions by suspicion, avoidance, and/or outright hostility. The task for care providers and other mentors is to help restructure these associations so that the children can develop positive emotional responses (e.g., happiness, joy, feelings of security) with some adults and can learn to accurately distinguish between those who threaten harm and those that do not. If the establishment of safety is the first consideration with traumatized children and yet it is the responses of adults that often bring further pain to the children, Anglin's (2002) central challenge might be re-formulated as follows: How to prevent the corrections adults use from sabotaging connections they need! Too often educators unknowingly create a punitive environment that adds to their perception that school is not safe for them. (Goldman, 2017, p. 20)

The third pillar highlighted is emotion and impulse management. Reactivity is a common reaction of students exposed to trauma and complex grief issues that can lead to challenging behaviors. Bath maintains, "A primary focus of work with traumatized children needs to be on teaching and supporting them to learn new ways of effectively managing their emotions and impulses" (2008a, p. 20).

As discussed in Chapter 1, many of the seemingly acting-out incidents of our students who have experienced grief and trauma stems from pain that needs to be recognized and acknowledged. Trauma-informed methods of educating student self-regulation include adults modeling calming practices, identifying children's feelings, responding in a heartfelt way, and actively listening to foster self-awareness.

Play Therapy as an Avenue of Expression

Play is considered a fundamental aspect of early life, and it has been shown to improve the social, emotional, cognitive, and physical domains of children.

–Eric Green, 2014

Child-Centered Play Therapy (CCPT) is a very relevant theoretical model in working with children and grief and loss. This model allows children to explore their experiences in a secure space psychologically and physically. In this environment, a therapist, teacher, or counselor unconditionally accepts without judgment the thoughts and feelings expressed in a child's play. Child-centered play therapy involves children leading and directing their own play, while an adult observes and participates. Responses such as following play behavior, reflecting kids' feelings, promoting self-esteem, setting therapeutic boundaries, helping to promote understanding, and broadening a child's meaning are beneficial in creating avenues for expression and empathy during a child's grief journey.

Landreth (2012) suggested that children should have access to a fully equipped playroom that contains real-life toys, aggressive toys, and toys that facilitate expression, such as a counselor's office or early childhood classroom. The use of sand trays is recommended from this theoretical perspective because of the unstructured properties of sand and water. Children have access to scooping, shifting, piling, and burying in the sand with various types of items and toys. The teacher, counselor, or therapist does not need to direct the student in any way, and the experience during play can be relaxing and soothing for the child.

To begin the session, the child-centered play educator or mental health professional may simply say, "Welcome to the playroom. In here, you can play with all of the toys in most of the ways you'd like." This open invitation sets the stage for the child to be in control of the healing process. Afterward, children typically play out different themes (e.g., power, seeking safety, good versus bad, nurturing, etc.) occurring in their lives and work out solutions to old problems through the symbols afforded by the various toys and the beneficial relationship within the playroom (Goldman, 2017, p. 247).

Projective Techniques

Projective techniques such as storytelling, drawing, clay, anger props, and toys offer ways to safely project difficult feelings. They also help release frozen feelings. Children of all ages can use props to recreate projective play about a climate disaster. They can re-create the setting of the catastrophe with doctors, nurses, firefighters, and police.

After the wildfires subside, youngsters could use projective play in many ways. Isabella chose a nurse toy and pretended to help people that were hurt. Tommy and Seth dressed up as action figures, firefighter and soldiers, and imagined they were saving people using fire hats, army hats, and gloves as props. Max explained he was National Guard and shouted, "Don't worry, I'll save you."

Through projection that involves action, young people "felt empowered through play to take action and control over the difficult experience they had witnessed" (Goldman, 2022, p. 66).

Figure 2.12 Play Props.
Source: Photo permission Taylor and Francis.

Sophie survived Hurricane Katrina. She too used projective play at the sand table in counseling and toy figures of people. "This is my mom and dad and my dog Lucy." She explained. "I couldn't find my dog, my house was gone, and all of my stuff was missing. Me and my mom and dad were scared. We didn't know if help would ever come." Shen (2002) conducted a statistical study effectiveness of CCPT (child-centered play therapy) after the Taiwanese earthquake. These findings suggested a significant reduction in anxiety and suicidal ideation in children who received this play therapy after a Taiwanese earthquake that supports play therapy's usefulness.

Emma had just heard a story in kindergarten about the polar caps melting, making life more difficult for the polar bears to survive. That night when mom was reading a story, she began to cry. "I can't tell you mom, but I'll show you." Emma went to her shelf and got her angel doll and her polar bear stuffed animal. "Dear Angel. I'm so worried about the polar bears. Will you help them?" And she began to sob again. Only when she could share her feelings out loud could Emma's mother begin to have a conversation with her about it!

Figure 2.13 Emma's Angel.
Source: Linda Goldman Photograph.

Artwork

Artwork becomes a safe vehicle of expression in many ways for young people. Too often young people are unable or unwilling to articulate deep feelings surround grief and trauma. Artwork is a safe avenue of expression that allows kids to increase memory retrieval, share narratives, and reduce anxiety. A simple drawing can speak volumes.

A Keepsake Book

Dr. Laila Gupta has done much work with children living with war, disaster, and trauma. During a keynote speech at the Montreal Association for Death Education and Counseling Conference (2008), she shared the experience of a boy from Rwanda that had witnessed his being murdered before his eyes.

Dr. Gupta invited the boy to create the following four drawings: (1) life before the tragic event, (2) the boy's experience of the event, (3) how life is now, and (4) what would he like life to be in the future. Dr. Gupta incorporated the concept of creating a keepsake book, ending with a future hopeful outlook. Through art expression, the boy was encouraged to share his experience, ending with a hopeful future outlook. The boy drew himself in the future as an automobile mechanic.

Positive Outcomes for Climate Grief

Two sixth grade girls, Shantal and Da'Iman, created a poster in response to the question, "What we can do to make this world a better place?" They were very concerned about Mother Earth. When their school held a contest for the best poster representing the world as a better place, these students moved their sadness, worry, and fear about the health of the planet into an action plan. Depressed by all the trash they saw, and the inability of many to recycle or plant, they chose to draw action activities such as planting trees, cleaning up trash, watering flowers, and recycling paper, glass, and plastic.

Their goal of caring for nature, animal life, and the planet in a proactive way is reflected within their drawing. The artists included diverse groups of children circling the planet – visually illustrating we all need to work together to make a better world. The following pictures are examples of parts of the poster. The first shows the importance of recycling and the second represents the goal of cleaning the environment by picking up trash. The welcoming nature of adults and the happiness of a child singing while caring for plants was expressed in their work.

Shantal and Da'Imah won the prize for the best poster!

Figure 2.14 A Better Place/Planting (Goldman, 2006, p. 201).

Source: Image permission Taylor & Francis.

Figure 2.15 A Better Place/Trash.

Katie's scribble drawing (Figure 2.5) shared her fear and anxiety after the Camp Fire destruction in Paradise. Overwhelmed with feelings too difficult to verbalize, Katie projected her anxiety and fear onto her artwork – a safe avenue for expression.

Props and Projective Toys

Toy telephones can create an intimate role-play dialogue with a loved one, allowing children to say safely what they are feeling. Katie worried a lot about her missing dog Gracie. She was never found after the fire. Was Gracie living? Did she die? Is she hungry? And "Why didn't I stay and save her!" She began an imaginary phone conversation. "I really miss you, Gracie. I am so sorry I didn't stay and save you. I love you so much, I hope you are OK." This ongoing, ever-present dialogue with Gracie helped her to add something very important, "Gracie, I got you a new ball in case you come home." Through using the telephone as a projective prop, Katie could safely verbalize challenging feelings. This imaginary dialogue creates a secure pathway for thoughts and feelings children experience during life challenges.

After the hurricane in Puerto Rico, Tony used props of fire trucks, boats, and toy figures to re-create the traumatic event. He pretended to be a rescue worker and throw a life raft to save people.

Billy, aged six, watched Hurricane Ida destroying his house. He re-enacted the scene with toy figures and a house he made with clay. He repeatedly knocked down the clay house and said, "Hurricanes make houses fall down." Jared, a classmate of Billy's, drew a similar picture and wrote at the bottom: "Run for your life!!!" Both students had outbursts in class, inattention, and an over-reactivity to stimulus.

> Play allows children to use symbolic expression, so that they often feel safer to reveal difficult feelings… Children who are considered to have avoidance symptoms may be more able to articulate their traumatic experiences in a play therapy setting. (Ogawa, 2004, p. 25)

During the COVID-19 pandemic, Cory decided to take toy figures and show on the sand table what his mom does at work. Cory's mom was a nurse and went on the front lines every day to help other people. He took a nurse doll and made a mask for mom and explained. "I worry about my mom. She wears a mask, but I don't know if she can still get the virus. I hope she is safe. I wanted her to stay home, but she said her job is to help people."

Monica prepared her teddy bear to go to the doctor. "We have to wear our mask and take our temperature," she explained.

Figure 2.16 Wearing Masks.

Source: Photo by Kristine Wook on Unsplash.

Recommendations for Parents and Professionals

Educators, parents, and health professionals need to responsibly help children cope with trauma, loss, and grief within their homes, schools, communities, and nations. Providing information, understanding, and skills on these essential issues may well aid them in becoming more compassionate, caring human beings and thereby increase their chances of living in a future world of inner and outer peace (Goldman, 2012, p. 14).

Look for Common Signs of Complications of Loss and Grief

These signs may become red flags, indicating a child needs help, and Katie demonstrated quite a few. They are characterized by their increase in frequency, intensity, and duration.

- Outbursts of aggressiveness and rage
- Extreme feelings of unworthiness and despair
- Nightmares and bedwetting
- Hypervigilance
- Conflicted relationship with a parent
- Poor grades, impulsivity, and inability to concentrate
- Poor eating
- Lethargy
- Excessive drug and alcohol use
- History of multiple losses
- Expressing not wanting to live
- Giving possessions away

Memory work is a useful tool for grieving kids suffering with complex grief issues. It provides a creative outlet to help remember a person, a place, or pet to help release feelings and discharge pain. In Katie's case, all pictures and memorabilia were destroyed in the fire. We helped Katie by asking friends and relatives to send pictures of the family and the house and help Katie make a new picture album called *My Life*. Katie chose the pictures for the book and wrote a sentence about it. In it, new pictures would be taken of the family and friends. Katie carried this album as an important linking object to the losses she had, and the hope for the future.

Memory books can be interactive story and workbooks that allow children to express feelings and thoughts. *Children Also Grieve 2020* is a free downloadable storybook and memory book on the website www.grievingchildren.net. Examples of questions or ideas Katie can use to reflect on or discuss thoughts and feelings include the following:

Figure 2.17 Children Also Grieve.
Source: Linda Goldman Cover Permission.

- If you could see your pet or person, what would you say?
- If you could change one thing or do one thing over, what would it be?
- Draw what your family was like before traumatic event, and after.
- Write a letter to your loved one. Tell him or her how you feel.
- List or draw your top five worries (Goldman, 2014, p. 74).

Memory boxes provide a place to store treasured items of a loved one. They can be made from a painted shoebox decorated to house the precious belongings. Katie decorated her memory box with stickers and pictures of the new house she hoped to live in one day. She put in a picture her Aunt Susie had of her dog, Gracie. She collected different ideas from magazines and put them in her memory box. It gave Katie something to look forward to in the future.

A memorial service: Katie and her family decided to create a memorial service in memory of the house and community that was demolished. The family went to the site of the wreckage and took rubble from the house and placed it in a bag each person had chosen. Katie put the ruble from her home in her *memory box*. Together they light a candle and said a prayer of thanks that they survived. Then each person told a memory about the house.

Lucy Lets Go (Goldman, 2014) is a resource for children, which includes ideas for a child-oriented memorial service and other memory projects. It is an interactive storybook and memory book at www.grievingchildren.net.

Figure 2.18 Lucy Lets Go.
Source: Cover permission *Linda Goldman.*

Suggestions for Trauma

Seek professional help if needed when signs of complex issues become a red flag. Evaluations, therapy, school team conference, and possible referrals or placement can facilitate a child's grief process. The following national resources may be helpful: American Academy of Experts in Traumatic Stress (www.schoolcrisisresponse.com), National Association of School Psychologists (www.nasponline.org), and National Child Traumatic Stress Network (www.nctsnet.org).

Maintain a resource library of grief, loss, trauma, climate change resources, and ways to express feeling (see Chapter 12).

Become aware of characteristics of students with chronic psychoemotional pain. The following combinations of feelings and thoughts were found in young people who had experienced abuse, neglect, or other overwhelming life events that carried deep-seated and prolonged pain (Anglin, 2014, p. 54):

- Grief at abandonment and loss, often the death of someone close to them.
- Persistent anxiety about themselves and their situation.
- Fear, or even terror, of a disintegrating present and a hopeless future.
- Depression and dispiritedness as a lack of meaning or purpose in their lives.
- Psycho-emotional paralysis in a state of numbness and withdrawal.

The manner in which adults respond to pain is a key indicator of the quality of care experienced by the youth. Lingering effects of abuse, rejection, or neglect (of professionals) can be re-awakened in the intense interaction with youth in pain. This highlights the critical importance of self-awareness training and personal development, and entails ongoing supervision of practice, especially in relation to worker "anxiety" which is pain-based fear. Effective intervention requires a deeper understanding of the origins and management of this pain-based behavior so that responsive human relationships can help these young people heal (Anglin, 2014, p. 55).

Recognize the loss of the trust of the emotional environment because of climate crisis. Too many adults have turned a deaf ear to youth cries for climate reform. This is exasperated by government apathy and denial of a climate problem. Ruth Berlin, executive director of Maryland Pesticide Education Network, begs the questions we must ask our children to enhance their ability to trust what they see and hear. In an interview on August 9, 2021, Ruth offers the following guided questions to initiate regaining trust in the adult world and increase ability to discern information. (1) Who do you trust? (2) How do you distinguish truth from misinformation? (3) Who is providing those truths? (Lawmakers, scientists, parents, teachers, or young people) (4) Who do you listen to? (Is the motivation self-interest or altruism?)

Her advice for young people is hopeful. Remain active, volunteer, donate, research, follow scientific data, listen, stay open, and move toward a paradigm shift in daily discussions about climate and planetary health and well-being. Only then when an authentic problem is recognized can we begin to examine all sides and find a solution that offers hope for our youngsters.

Provide training for parents, educators, and mental health professionals on pain-based behavior. These trainings can open doors to communication and healing and serve as is a useful paradigm for adults to incorporate when formulating a safe environment for the grieving, traumatized child. "If professionals (and parents) can acknowledge and express thoughts and feelings involving grief and loss, they can serve as role models for the ever-increasing population of students experiencing traumatic loss" (Goldman, 2017, p. 171).

An exercise that allows students to express grief and release trauma was created by a third-grade teacher, Kyle Schwartz. Kyle used the lesson *I wish my teacher knew,* which allowed students to write a note with a simple message inviting them to share life issues. The actual lesson began as a community building experience of collecting notes and then reading them aloud to classmates. The children sat in a circle, and happily took turns reading. Empathy grew with each note read. One classmate read, "I wish my teacher knew my dad left me and my mom." None of the students laughed or made fun of him. One boy put his arm around his friend and patted his shoulder. "A chorus of voices echoed around the room saying a frequently used phrase in our classroom: 'We got your back'" (Goldman, 2017, p. 60).

On one level, the *I wish my teacher knew* is a process that informs adults of a child's reality. It can help a parent or teacher understand what is happening in a young person's life and how best to support their grief experience. Some comments from various classrooms were related to climate change and the pandemic. "I wish my teacher knew we slept in our car last night." "I wish my teacher knew my aunt died of COVID-19. I didn't get to say goodbye." "I wish my teacher knew my dad lost his job during the pandemic." "I wish my teacher knew I'm scared the planet will burn up."

When there is a foundation of trust, students can feel safe enough to share challenges involving death, illness, poverty, climate change, loneliness, climate injustice, and so on. They can feel their "vulnerability of sharing their life experiences as well as the strength that comes from advocating for their own needs" (Schwartz in Goldman, 2017).

Conclusion

In an era of unprecedented weather events, challenging health issues, racial unrest, quarantines, and contemptuous politics, our children have become the savviest and most articulate generation ever to grow up on the planet. With lightning speed, issues and problems are posted without regard for the younger population that is all too present in the relentless turbulence in their life.

–Linda Goldman Life and Loss Classic Edition Preface, 2022

Within a few days a new normal swept through the Northeast United States with the unexpected devastation thrust upon children and adults by Hurricane Ida in August 2021. Joey, a kindergarten student living in Montgomery County, Maryland, suddenly experienced his daily routine vanishing when the entire student body was evacuated and sent home for fear of immense flooding expected very soon. Joey and his mom were glued to the TV set that afternoon and evening. This kindergartener continually saw images of people trapped in floating cars, subways bursting with water and people desperately trying to escape, cities without electricity and food, people dying, and a tornado 40 minutes away that swept through a busy area destroying all the property in its way.

Besides the barrage of devastating visual images, Joey heard frightening scenarios from news commentators and public officials. "Mother Earth is very angry today," said one governor. Joey wondered and worried, as a young child would, "What did I do to make Mother Earth this angry?" Governor Hochul of New York explained, "No longer will we say, that won't happen again in our lifetime, this could literally happen again next week" (Caspani & Harte, 2021). Joey went to bed sobbing that night. "Mommy," he explained. "I am so sad all those people aren't safe, and people died. I am scared the planet will die too. Can I stay home from school tomorrow?" As much as we remind adults to monitor television and social media, it is almost impossible with technically knowledgeable youngsters to hide events happening in their world. Knowing this, it is essential adults create meaningful teachable moments when good things happen. Mr. Rogers suggested to look for helpers. Dr. Carol Weyland Conner, the White Pony Express, and Francis on the Hill exemplify those people willing to help when there is a need.

During the pandemic, many students lost their homes and possessions. Francis on the Hill heard from school officials that certain youngsters needed backpacks and supplies to begin school. Miraculously, they produced a backpack event September 2021. Almost 100 brand new backpacks and supplies were given to students that otherwise would not have had them to begin the school year. Rosie was a high school student that had called her teacher to say she might not return to school because she could not afford the necessary supplies. After hearing about the backpack and supply donations, Rosie told her mom, "Now I can go to school!"

Losses such as life, health, income, school time, school supplies, food, home, routine, environment, and safety created by climate change events have become more commonplace for kids. We must help our children remember there are adults working very hard to keep them safe and secure.

Figure 2.19 Backpack Drive.

Source: Photo permission Following Francis.

3 The Coronavirus and Climate Change

To me the quilt means people care that people died. It means I care. It means there is still good in the world (Callahan, 2020).
—Madeleine Fugate, age 13, Creater of the Covid Memorial Quilt

Figure 3.1 Wear a Mask.
Source: Photo by Atoms on Unsplash.

DOI: 10.4324/9781003051770-4

And the people stayed home. And read books, and listened, and rested, and exercised, and made art, and played games, and learned new ways of being, and were still. And listened more deeply. Some meditated, some prayed, some danced. Some met their shadows. And the people began to think differently.

And the people healed. And, in the absence of people living in ignorant, dangerous, mindless, and heartless ways, the earth began to heal.

And when the danger passed, and the people joined together again, they grieved their losses, and made new choices, and dreamed new images, and created new ways to live and heal the earth fully, as they had been healed.

–And the People Stayed Home by Kitty O'Meara,
Published by Tra Publishing, Nov. 2020

Introduction – A New Beginning

While writing this book, the epic of epics, the most surreal global experience, and perhaps the most terrifying, began. I, like many inhabitants of our planet, was thinking the same unifying thoughts – stay healthy, wash hands, maintain social distancing, and pray.

I found myself calling loved ones I had not spoken with, letting go of past grievances, and appreciating heartfelt kindness in this shared terrifying experience. Gradually a new paradigm crept into my overburdened mind and heart – perhaps this is the *very moment* in time all human beings on planet Earth can be unified in one common goal – to stay healthy and take good care of ourselves, each other, and our world. As the pandemic spread throughout the planet, there was no more obvious lesson learned than this one truth, "We are all in it together." I realized there were no differences, no judgments, no grudges, only the pure hope that everyone will rise up to renew life on a new level of understanding, empathy, and cooperation, remembering to honor each other and Mother Earth.

Three Lessons

As the days merged, and the quarantine felt endless, I wondered if this book was relevant to the new epoch we are stepping into. Then the realization grew that this coronavirus and climate change were intrinsically connected. The lessons for our children are paramount. The first lesson is to stay steadfast in our personal hygiene as an ongoing health protection, and steadfast in our planetary hygiene to protect the planet. Mother Earth and nature are powerful and must be respected.

Another critical lesson for young people is the realization of the connection between self-interest and collaboration. We are not separate from each other. If children and adults can consider the self-interest part of ourselves as the thread that binds us to each other, a light will emerge that leads to the realization that when we join together as a global team, we are truly caring for the collective self.

The third lesson for our children is that every action we do impacts other people and nature. Good can spread as well as global challenges when we join forces for the welfare of all. Through the emergence of a global cohesiveness never before imagined, we can help our youth step forward into a world they still feel protected in, and model how they can carry the new emerging paradigms onward in their lifetime. This change is inevitable, the challenges are palpable, and the rewards are mighty.

The mobilization to combat the virus was one that no one thought possible, no precedent before in creation, yet each country rallied inwardly and outwardly to save lives and help all human beings. This swift action, inspired by fear and bravery, is the same fear and bravery our young people feel necessitates climate change action. Now the world has seen a model of what can be done in the immediacy of an unprecedented emergency, and children, young people, and adults can view climate change through the same lens.

As Mother Earth rests during this epidemic, we too can breathe in the dawning of a new age. An age where politics and divisiveness give way to collective reason and care. The children are leading the way through their pressing urgency to make changes in the environment that promote the health and well-being of our planet Earth.

Flexibility, Climate Change, and the Virus

> *We are not watching a movie; we are creating it*, together, until the end.
> –Peter Baker, March 31, 2020 The Guardian

The reality that climate change and the coronavirus are deeply intertwined becomes apparent as the days turn into weeks and months. The urgency that humanity feels about protecting, saving, and caring for every human being on the planet parallels the urgency so many have felt before the epidemic about climate change. We have seen governments, nations, enemies, and loved ones join together to aid and assist all people during the coronavirus crisis. We have ripped open the band aid of normalcy and gone deeper into ideas that could not be considered before this unprecedented event. In the ever-present moment, we are creating the new normal, and its seeds are being planted and beginning to manifest.

The silver lining is the knowledge that everyone can come together for the good of all to save lives and health during the COVID-19 pandemic. Now we know we can use the same magnitude of energy, surplus, and future thinking ideas to help planet Earth and its children transition to a new world – achieved through addressing and acting upon what is needed for climate change. We can begin to see we are one organism vibrating together on planet Earth. When we join as a collective body – this miracle of unity can create a new Earth and a loving way to live together on it. We are creating the future in the present.

Climate change, COVID-19, and our young people are fused together in an awakening of a fresh mindset that highlights cleanliness and health for ourselves, others, and the environment. As the pandemic spreads, skies become bluer, birds chirp more cheerfully, and distant mountains become visible in the absence of pollution. Nature is unmistakably singing a song of thank you for the rest created for planet Earth by the virus. Children are learning to wash their hands carefully, sanitize their home and belongings, cover their sneeze into an elbow, and pick up liter wherever they may see it. The seemingly unrelated events of climate change and the pandemic have now merged into a new way of being ... in a cleaner, more caring world. These unprecedented occurrences are now interwoven with the psyches of young people to emerge as "teachable moments in time" of hygiene, sanitation, and cleanliness for youth globally to participate in and to urge others to do likewise.

Children's Mental Health and the Pandemic

"Schools in nearly every country in the world have closed due to the coronavirus, prompting concerns about students' mental health and well-being during the pandemic" (Galvin, 2020). According to UNESCO, nearly 1.6 billion students have been affected by school closure worldwide. Amid the unprecedented disruption of "normal" life, the immediate disturbance of daily routine, and the overwhelming fear of contracting the virus, life has drastically morphed into a new way of being in the blink of an eye.

Sara was a seven-year-old, confined to home with her self-quarantined family during the pandemic. She often had meaningful conversations with grandma during this complex and challenging time. Grandma and Sara had a ritual at the beginning of each talk. Grandma would ask, "Sara, what is the rose and what is the thorn of your day?" One day after many weeks of confinement, Sara surprisingly responded this way. "My thorn is the stress of living with my family, and the rose is the good feeling I have of being with my family." Sara's older sister Amy also had feelings about the quarantine. Her online class was reading the *Diary of Ann Frank* and she explained to Grandma,

> I decided to create a journal to write in every day about the isolation I live with, just like Ann Frank. I can't be with my friends, I can't go to school, I can't play sports, and I can't go to my prom. I stay inside a lot.

In research published by JAMA Pediatrics, April 2020, a study presented data on how Chinese children were faring after being confined to home. Huazhong University of Science and Technology in Wuhan research authors, Xinyan, Qi Xue, and Yu Zhou, explained, "The caution about protecting the mental health of children in home confinement is warranted. This study investigated depressive and anxiety symptoms among students ... which can help optimize intervention on the mental issues of children." Their research findings indicated that serious infectious disease may influence the mental health of children in the way other traumatic experience do. Students living in Wuhan experienced heightened depression and anxiety about their future that those in other communities where the lockdown was less pronounced (Dunleavy April 24, 2020).

The research was conducted with nearly 1,800 students in two primary schools in Wuhan and Huangshi, ranging from second to sixth grade that were locked down due to the virus spread. After a month, 235 showed signs of depression, and 19 percent of students reported symptoms of anxiety. "The heightened depressive symptoms overall may have been tied to the loss of outdoor activities and socializing, the authors said (Gavin, 2020)." Dunleavy April 24, 2020, reports that "20% of children on lockdown in China suffer from depression and anxiety ... and experts say that socioeconomic differences in the United States may only accentuate the issues."

This sentiment was echoed by Dr. Margarita Alegria chief of the Disparities Research Unit at Massachusetts General Hospital in Boston (Dunleavy, 2020) explained

> that in the United States, where there is greater income inequality, these problems could be more pronounced. Children in minority communities in the United States, may be particularly vulnerable, given some of the economic hardship experienced by these families in general, which may have been made worse by the pandemic. These children experiencing economic hardships may be open to more changes in the family relationship and parenting quality, as well as limited funds for food and housing, which may be circumstances that compound children's mental health issues already overburdened by social isolation and school closings.

A Kaiser Family Foundation survey (Kirzinger et al., 2020) indicates concerns are emerging about students in the United States. These concerns indicate nearly half of adults say, "their mental health has been negatively affected by the coronavirus." "The COVID-19 pandemic may worsen existing mental health problems and lead to more cases among children and adolescents because of the unique combination of public health crisis, social isolation, and economic recession," (Golberstein et al., 2020, US health researchers).

Figure 3.2 Impact of COVID-19.

Source: Photo by Michael Mimms on Unsplash.

Self-Quarantine: Loss of Privacy and Safety

Malia is nine-year old and lives in a two-bedroom apartment with her family. She misses seeing her grandparents and worries about their health during the pandemic. Malia built a fort in the living room behind the sofa and tells her mom it is her private space. She calls it her little apartment and brings snacks, stuffed animals, and her iPad charger.

"It is her go-to-place to FaceTime friends, relax away from her parents and baby sister, eat and sleep" (Margolin, 2020). Her mother explained the fort is a place where Malia can be alone and process the virus and all of its limitations on her. Ten-year-old Cory said his fort was a safe place where he can forget about what is going on in the world. Because many kids are confined to home, they have had time during the quarantine for fort building. It becomes a comforting and secure spot where kids can be alone and family members can leave them alone and know they are safe. Grayson, age 11, explained her view of living through the virus and the value of her fort. "Everything is wrong right now, but it's a safe space where no one worries about you. If you locked yourself in your room, people would worry but if you hide in your fort all day, no worries" (Margolin, 2020).

David Sobel, a child educator, explains in his book, *Children's Special Place 2001s*, that forts have always been a part of childhood, and he has researched the developmental function forts play in the lives of children across the globe. Sobel maintains that forts are universal and driven by "biological genetic disposition" that inspires kids to develop a sense of self as they separate from parents.

The development of forts begins around age four and it eventually leads to outside building around age six or seven. As kids get older, they build tree houses and fort like structures more independently. Sobel says, it's a "home away from home where a lot of magic happens inside. It's a place where you want to be just you, observing but unseen."

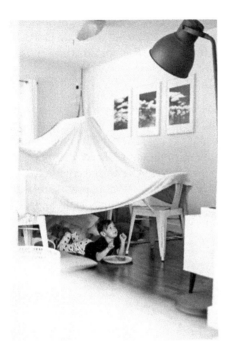

Figure 3.3 Forts.

Source: Photo by Nathan Dumlao on Unsplash.

Children have more time on their hands and forts are a creative home base that amplifies imagination and play and giving them a space to feel they have some control over their world. Emily King, a child psychologist, explains the reality of an intensified world for young people during the COVID-19 epidemic. "Everything is different. They are facing uncertainty – not knowing how long we are going to be doing this. With so much disruption, they are feeling what we are all feeling – great loss" (Margolin, 2020).

Projective Play Releases Stress

Often children reenact stressful events like the virus through play. Through role play with trusted toys kids can express anxiety and worry and then begin to normalize an uncertain event. Pelly's (2020) article speaks of a four-year-old who liked to pretend he was a doctor. Mom was shocked when she overheard his make-believe dialogue using a toy stethoscope to examine his toy. With a very serious tone, she listened to him say, "You are not well, you've got the coronavirus."

This little boy began exploring ways the virus might work, and soon told mom his idea about a vaccine. "What we need is a vaccine made of tiny alligators that could be injected into the blood to eat up all the coronavirus" (Pelly, 2020). His sister used projective play with a make-believe restaurant. She pretended with toys, squirting them with a hand sanitizer, and then having them wear masks and social distance before their imaginary curbside pickup (Goldman, Preface 2022).

Resilience through a Health Challenge

The COVID-19 virus pandemic has left many young people with a feeling of isolation, loss of the environment, loss of the daily routine, and loss of a future, loss of school and friends, and the challenges of living a changed life and a new normal. The following are attributes of resilience that many young people are working with during the pandemic. The crucial criteria for success in supporting the following resilience attributes is a responsive caregiver, one who recognizes the losses and trauma of a health pandemic and explores every opportunity for safety, compassion, and reassurance (see Chapter 12 for COVID-19 resources for kids).

- Flexibility
- Optimism
- Protection
- Generosity
- Compassion for ourselves and others
- Healthy hygiene
- Action
- Perseverance
- Conversations
- Faith in each other and the process
- Monitoring
- Fun

Role Models during COVID-19

Kids today are living in a hyper-connected world, an environment that makes it easier to spread infections like the corona virus. Ironically, climate change activist Greta Thunberg (see Chapter 8) very likely contracted the virus after a European trip. Greta models a key resilience attribute – taking responsibility. She warns her symptoms were mild to the point she almost did not feel ill and explained that is what makes it so dangerous.

Greta warns,

Many (especially young people) who might not notice any symptoms at all. Then they don't know they have the virus and can pass it on to people in risk groups. We who don't belong to a risk group have an enormous responsibility, our actions can be the difference between life and death for many others. (Reuters Staff, March 24, 2020)

Greta led the "school strike" for climate initiative. To avoid large gatherings that might increase the spread of COVID-19, she called for a digital protest. Greta asked March24climate activists every Friday to post photos of themselves with the word#climateStrikeOnline to avoid outdoor large demonstrations. The resilience of many teens rose to new heights as they bravely moved forward despite enormous obstacles during difficult times. The following are two examples of pioneering young people. Madeleine and Lulu were two innovative teens who demonstrated compassion for others and optimism during challenging times, enabling them to help others transform despair into activism.

Thirteen-year-old Madeleine exemplifies the resilience attributes of perseverance and action by converting an eighth-grade project into a healing experience for peers experiencing a death during the pandemic. Madeleine created the Covid Memorial Quilt and reached out to others through the Internet to join by adding a piece of the quilt in memory of a loved one. Madeleine reaches out to young and old wishing to honor a life lost to the virus to visit her website, http://www.covidquilt2020.com.

Figure 3.4 Covid Memorial Quilt.
Source: Permission K & M Fugate.

Lulu Sullivan, a high school sophomore, shines as model of communication and conversation during the pandemic. I participated in a podcast with Lulu Sullivan during the health crisis (June, 2020). Lulu explained she initiated this podcast, TEEN GRIEF, and the website during the pandemic to support grieving teens, provide information, create a forum for connection, and a platform for expression.

Lulu's dad died when she was thirteen. His death inspired her to create this resource at http://www.teengrief.com. "I created TEEN GRIEF because I knew it would help me through my grief. Talking to somebody my age who also knew true loss was something I needed (and still need). And I think others do too" (Goldman, Preface 2022).

Figure 3.5 TEEN GRIEF.

Source: Photo permission Lulu Sullivan.

Pope Francis and Scientists

Pope Francis (Barone, 2020) shared his insight into the connection between climate change and the COVID-19 virus as he asked for responses from world leaders to shift their focus toward humans and the environment rather than the economy. He appealed to everyone to realize the virus "could spur ecological conversion, the idea for people to lead more environmentally conscious lives through the understanding that the natural world is a creation of God" (Barone, 2020). He compared the COVID-19 pandemic to ongoing floods and fires as one of "nature's responses" to humanity's indifference to climate change and highlighted it as motivation for ecological conversion. The Pope stated, "I believe we have to slow down our rate of production and consumption and to learn to understand and contemplate the natural world. We need to reconnect with our real surroundings. This is an opportunity for conversion."

Brulliard (2020) in the *Washington Post* shares the interrelationship between the virus pandemic and the relationship human beings have to animals on the planet.

> As the world scrambles to cope with an unprecedented public health and economic crisis, many disease researchers say the coronavirus pandemic must be taken as a deadly warning. That means thinking of animals as partners whose health and habitats should be protected to stave off the next global outbreak.

She cites the following observation by Peter Daszak, a disease ecologist and president of EcoHealth Alliance, a public health organization that studies emerging disease. Daszak explains, "it's not a random act of God. It's caused by what we do to the environment. We need to start connecting that chain and say we need to do these things in a less risky way."

Sesame Street: Innovations for Young Children and COVID-19

Sesame Street has taken the three lessons to heart by meeting the needs of young children and families during the coronavirus crisis. They immediately placed online advice to parents, printable activities for children, videos to help them understand the need for hygiene in a fun and important way, and ways for families to take steps to prevent the spread of COVID-19. Since families are spending more time together in light of the contagion, Sesame Street went into action to create resources to help families stay healthy, find comfort, and learn playfully at home. This is part of the *Caring for Each Other* initiative – a long-term commitment to support families through crisis. They have provided words to use for family discussions about the coronavirus for young children through downloadable material. The following is an example of what parents can say to kids:

Figure 3.6 Talking to Kids about COVID-19.

1. Talk to kids about what they have heard about the COVID virus.
2. Ask them how they feel about the virus.
3. Explain the virus is like a cold and one way to protect ourselves is to protect eyes, nose, and mouth.
4. For protection, we eat healthy, rest, wash hands, and sneeze into elbows.

Handwashing

Sesame Street provides a solid foundation for young children to appreciate good hygiene at an early age and enjoy the process. Washing hands to protect against contagion is a first step and plants a seed point for future dialogue as kids mature. Sesame Street offers free downloadable resources at *Sesame Street and the COVID Virus* https://www.sesamestreet.org/printables/games-and-activities/talking-children-about-covid-19.

Handwashing: Step by Step is a downloadable printable coloring activity by Sesame Street to help young children, ages two to six, promote hygiene. Sesame Street provides a hand washing video for parents and children to view together.

How to Wash Your Hands

Color Elmo's handwashing steps below.
Hang this page by the sink to practice!

Figure 3.7 How to Wash Hands.

Source: © 2019 Sesame Workshop. All rights reserved. Sesame Street and all related trademarks, characters and design elements are owned and licensed by Sesame Workshop.

Sesame Street invites children to download the page, *How to Wash Hands*, color it in, then help them cut it apart and put the steps in order. Then kids are asked to post the cards in the correct sequence near the bathroom sink. The next time kids wash their hands, parents can help them do a good job by remembering Elmo's trick to sing the alphabet song to remember how long to wash.

Sneeze and Cough Safely

Sesame Street also offers a downloadable coloring book. It educates children about cleanliness, taking a bath, brushing hair, and sneezing and coughing safely to not spread germs or the virus.

Elena watched Sesame Street. Grover explained when you feel a tickle in your nose and throat, sneeze or cough into the bend of your elbow to stay germ free. Then Elena practiced the right way to use a tissue when she sneezes on her baby bear that had a cold. Projective play for children is not only an avenue to release feelings, but a practical way to reinforce important learning during COVID-19.

Figure 3.8 Sneeze on Baby Bear.

Source: Linda Goldman Photograph.

Mask Wearing

Children are also learning the importance of wearing masks to protect themselves and others from contagion. Francis wondered why everyone was wearing masks on TV. Her family was not wearing a mask at home.

Mom explained that wearing a mask helps protect the person wearing the mask and the other people in the room. Francis responded immediately and had a plan. "We have to put a mask on Mr. Lion, so he won't get the virus. Is that OK Mommy." "It sure is!" responded mom. Together they masked Mr. Lion and Frances felt much better.

Figure 3.9 A Mask for Lion.

Source: Linda Goldman Photograph.

Healthy Habits for Life

Sesame Street in Communities provides another response for kids and families called Health Emergencies. The website shares four videos, printable activities, articles for caregivers, and family home activities during the virus crisis (https://cdn.sesamestreet.org/)

Figure 3.10 Healthy Habits.

Sesame Street also partnered with CNN. Together they produced two town halls to answer kids' questions about the COVID-19 virus and help them cope on May 29 and June 13, 2020.

President Obama's Graduation Thoughts

President Obama (2020) gave a poignant graduation speech digitally to students graduating in the year of the pandemic quarantine. He summed up what these young people are living through during challenging times in the following words:

> Now graduating is a big achievement under any circumstances. Some of you have had to overcome serious obstacles along the way, whether it was an illness, or a parent losing a job, or living in a neighborhood where people too often count you out. Along with the usual challenges of growing up, all of you have had to deal with the added pressures of social media, reports of school shootings, and the specter of climate change.

> And then, just as you're about to celebrate having made it through, just as you've been looking forward to proms and senior nights, graduation ceremonies – and, let's face it, a whole bunch of parties – the world is turned upside down by a global pandemic. And as much as I'm sure you love your parents, I'll bet that being stuck at home with them and playing board games or watching "Tiger King" on TV is not exactly how you envisioned the last few months of your Senior year.

Conclusion

As the pandemic spread, skies become bluer, birds chirp more cheerfully, and distant mountains become visible in the absence of pollution. Nature is unmistakably singing a song of thank you for the rest that has been created for planet Earth by the virus. Children are learning to wash their hands carefully, sanitize their home and belongings, cover their sneeze into an elbow, and pick up liter wherever they may see it. The seemingly unrelated events of climate change and the pandemic have now merged into a new way of being ... in a cleaner, more caring world. These unprecedented occurrences are now emerging as teachers of hygiene, sanitation, and cleanliness for young people to participate in and urge others to do likewise.

The COVID-19 virus has become a huge overlay to those young people so concerned and frightened about their future regarding climate change. The virus has resulted in a myriad of losses, including economic downturn, isolation, abuse, and eliminations of in-person proms, graduations, and social interaction.

Yet the pandemic also represents a time of reflection and promise. It manifests new hope for a more collaborative world, more care for ourselves and others, and more concern and protection for our planet.

Figure 3.11 Isolation.

Source: Photo by Dragos Gonariu on Unsplash.

COVID-19 Resources for Children

Black, Heather. (2020). *Why did the whole world stop? Talking with kids about COVID-19.* Mindful Moments Publisher.

Chevalier, Dr. Tiffanny. (2020). *Baby put your mask on!* Independently Published.

Cheung, Catherine. (2020). *COVID-19 for kids: Understand the coronavirus disease and how to stay healthy.* Small Space Sprouts Publisher. Ages 2–6.

Luckey, Lindsey. (2020). *What is social distancing? A Children's guide & activity book.* Independently Published.

Morgan, Rob. (2020). *Madi goes to virtual school.* Independent Publisher.

O'Meara, Kitty. (2020). *And the people stayed.* TRA Publisher.

Quillen, Marylou. (2020). *Perry and Steve's new normal: Life during COVID-19.* Penguin Adventure.

Ross, Nicole. (2020). *Virtual First Day.* Independent Publisher.

Roumanis, Alexis. (2020). *What is COVID-19?* (Engaging Readers, Level 1). Engage Books. Ages 3–6.

Saunders, Rachel. (2020). *Going back to school during coronavirus.* Independently Published.

Thompson, Lisa. (2020). *Lucy's mask.* Independently Published.

Figure 3.12 Alone.

Source: Photo by Tong Nguyen on Unsplash.

Part II
Raising Awareness
Conversation, Activities, Practices

4 The Conversation: Creating Hope and Action through Dialogue

Children can be frightened if they don't know there are adults who care about climate change and are trying to fix problems. It can help battle the sense of helplessness and powerlessness.

–Wendy Greenspun, PhD (Shinn, 2020)

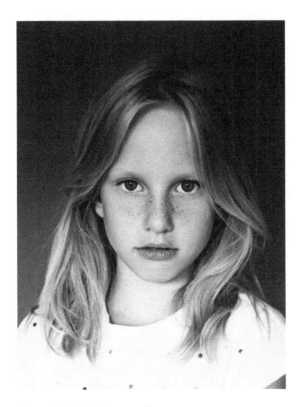

Figure 4.1 The Conversation.
Source: Photo by Lotte Meijer Oyy on Unsplash.

DOI: 10.4324/9781003051770-6

Introduction

As professionals and caring adults, it is often difficult to talk to children about death, sex, drugs, and violence. Yet, for Gen Z, Gen A, and millennials it is imperative we create dialogues about climate change. It has become the predominant challenge for these generations, provoking fear, loss, and sadness often without an avenue for young people to communicate how they feel and think to an older generation or peers.

As educators, therapists, parents, and caretakers of children we must strive to have accurate information and words to use to open conversations rather then close them. Communication with children is essential for developing trust. Similar to the approach of dialoguing with youth on any sensitive topic, the subject of climate change can be approached in a developmentally appropriate way.

This chapter establishes a foundation for conversations from preschool through high school that incorporates understandings at different developmental stages (see Chapter 2). It anchors factual and age-appropriate concepts and definitions of terms kids may need to know in order to discuss climate change openly and realistically. By creating words to use, we enhance learning. Using a common language to share ideas can plant the seeds for dialogue to grow and expand as children grow, as they voice thoughts and feelings in a respected environment. Terms include climate change, global warming, pollution, carbon imprint, fossil fuels, and so on, while underscoring accurate scientific data and offering solutions that diminish anxiety and support resilience and activism.

Too often young people are exposed to adult controversy about climate change, as many are divided on the idea that it may be real, a natural national phenomenon, or a hoax. Misconceptions and random media bombardment are a part of the discussion, emphasizing the continuous impact of social media, television, and film, which often creates an atmosphere of panic, grief, and anxiety that so many young people express as their greatest struggle and challenge. Several activities would be included with questions children may ask and possible responses to stimulate dialogue and listing myth versus fact about climate change.

Messages Kids Get

Do we want a community of grief, or do we want a community of hope?

Clichés too often reach young children that might inhibit their understanding of climate change, and actually add additional anxiety and worry. As mentioned in Chapter 1, Piaget speaks of cognitive developmental stages.

Children hear the message from parents, peers, professionals, and the media literally and form their world view around it. "It's up to you to save the planet," is an example of a charge given to kids that they cannot possibly achieve by themselves. The message carries an enormous burden of an unreachable demand to young children, teens, and young adults – that they are the saviors of planet Earth.

Figure 4.2 Save the Planet.
Source: Photo by Anton Lecock on Unsplash.

Too many of our youth have internalized this simple phrase, and it manifests itself in eco-anxiety and climate depression. They need to be motivated not out of fear – but out of common goals.

For the climate change movement to be most effective, and least harmful to mental health, we must communicate differently. Perhaps the following dialogue would create an environment whereby kids can be kids, teens can be teens, and young adults can be young adults. This dialogue would instill in children the promise that adults will take care of them, keep them safe, and join them in working together to create healthy lives for people, animals, plants, and Mother Earth. By honoring nature, the Earth, and the ever-evolving environment, we can convey a unity of purpose and a safe future for our children. We inspire this safety by stressing that youth are not personally responsible for the planet; but rather it is a community, national, and global responsibility.

The Conversation

When we can talk about our feelings, they become less overwhelming, less upsetting, and less scary. The people we trust with that important talk can help us know that we are not alone.

–Mr. Rogers, 2019, p. 15

It is always helpful to create an open environment whereby kids can explore and express their feelings. This dialogue is progressive as young children age, and provides an ongoing stream of concrete information, an avenue for teachable moments, a school lesson or a family time to promote healing planet activities, and a sense of confidence they are valued, respected, and loved.

Tips for Discussing Climate Change

- Provide age-appropriate truthful dialogue.
- Discuss challenges and positive changes.
- Reinforce responsible actions.
- Allow children to ask questions.
- Generate expression of children's feelings.
- Use art and writing to share feelings.
- Monitor TV.
- Create teachable moments.
- Be positive.
- Engage in family and school activities.
- Invite kids to continue the discussion.

Figure 4.3 Active Engagement.
Source: Photo by Joseph Gonzalex on Unsplash.

In Chapter 2, Piaget's cognitive stages of development are explained. Young children in the pre-operational phase rely on magical thinking, causality, and reversibility. They are aware of their surroundings, enjoy nature walks, notice seasonal change, and realize ongoing environmental cycles. This responsiveness to nature can create teachable moments to talk plants and animals, how they grow, and what we can do to help them. Activism can begin at an early age, stressing we all have a responsibility to keeping our world and ourselves healthy. Wendy Greenspun, psychologist explains,

> It's thinking about the impact you have – if you make a mess where plants and animals live, it can hurt them, and if you clean up, it helps them. Young children should be encouraged to share Earth's space with other living creatures. (Shinn, 2020)

Another spontaneous idea at an early age is to instill responsibility for cleanup activities. It helps create respect for the planet. Even saying thank you when a child turns off lights reinforces acknowledgment of a helpful act. Robin Gurwitch, a clinical psychologist at Duke University Medical Center emphasized, "when people most important to us notice our actions, we are more likely to do it again and carry it forward" (Shinn, 2020).

Develop Trust

Help youngsters trust the adults around them by being truthful, instilling confidence in taking care of them and their environment, and reassuring them that there is much we can all do to make our world better. Create teachable moments in early childhood. Build throughout growing up positive information about happenings in the environment and ways kids and families are keeping the Earth healthy. Parents and professionals can be aware of their own feelings about climate change concerns ... and be aware even young children are sensitive to adult feelings and may hear your conversations not meant for their ears.

In Piaget's concrete stage of cognitive development, kids want to know the facts. This is a good time to present vocabulary; different ideas about climate change in government and ask them what they have heard about climate change. Sometimes kids have misconceptions that an open discussion might dispel. Gurwitch suggests dispelling the myths about climate change by using the blanket analogy.

> Our world is protected by a layer surround the Earth, like a blanket that keeps it at just the right temperature. With global warming, there are more and more blankets being put around the Earth. We can't just toss them off. So, we're figuring out how to change back the right kind and number of blankets. (Shinn, 2020)

Instill Action for Change

Instill in young people there are challenges, and positive changes as well. An enormous number of adults are working together with kids to solve climate challenges and protect and prepare young people for the future. Children can compost, recycle and reuse, and choose paper straws. They can encourage parents to join them in riding bikes and walking instead of driving.

Youngsters of all ages can discuss their ability to make change by action. They can help decrease carbon emissions by promoting biking and car pooling to school, using energy efficient LED lights, and planting trees.

The urgency and stress teenagers feel today about climate change demands our attention, listening, and thoughtful responses to questions. If we cannot answer a question, we can let young people know we will work to together to find reliable information. This generation of young people is proficient in accessing media reports, and often those reports are contradictory, conflicting, and overwhelming on climate change.

Respect Youth Responsibility

Many young people feel a great responsibility to the environment and are seeking ways they can work together on the planet to dissolve present challenges. Whether kids are worried about the snails, air pollution, or melting ice caps, they can create projects for peers, use artwork and writing, or invite interested kids to rally or protest. Parents can attend protests with their children on Earth Day.

Younger generations may be more literate on scientific data and can actually teach older generations about climate change. They feel responsible for meeting the challenge of healing the planet. Their advocacy is contagious. Sometimes discouraged if change does not occur with rapid speed, it is important to remind them that by just being visible and speaking out, they are assuredly making change by creating global awareness of the problem.

Listen to Feelings

Adults can learn from today's youth, and parents can encourage dialogue on why their children feel climate change is a critical topic – what causes their outrage and what solutions are worthy of advocating. Discussion of youth movements through media and articles supports their quest for change and helps transform the anxiety, anger, and indignation into positive action. Greenspun emphasizes that for their mental health, "obsessing over all the things we don't know and can't do anything about often contributes to stress and anxiety" (Schinn, 2020). Help young people find the fine line between what is possible for them to do and what they can control, even if it is advocating for their future. Inherently talking and acting with passion about climate change can lead to anxiety and worry.

Parents can strategize with their children on ways to reduce these feelings. Just taking deep breaths, meditating (see Chapter 6), counting to ten, sharing with a trusted friend, or writing and drawing challenging emotions can help release them. Focusing on positive events at home, in school, in the community, in the nation, and globally can only reinforce positive outcomes. Many reports underscore we do have solutions to problems, and as scientists share these solutions, there is a huge generation of young people that are listening.

Student-Centered Learning: Carl Rogers

Educators, parents, and mental health professionals have been greatly influenced by the groundbreaking work of psychologist Carl Rogers, and his contributions to the student-centered learning movement and the development of trust and transparency through dialogues. Rogers theorized three core traits are necessary to develop relationships that lead to significant learning, congruence or genuineness, unconditional positive regard for students, and an empathetic understanding (Rogers, 1995). These conditions are genuineness, unconditional positive regard, and empathetic understanding.

Genuineness

Genuineness in actions and words forms the foundation to build relationship with young people. Adults must be authentic with children to establish trust. Young people need to feel safe to express themselves authentically in the classroom as real people that kids can relate to. We need to "enter into relationships with the learners without presenting a front of a facade" (Rogers, 1989, p. 271). Presenting true feelings and accepting those of students creates trust. Sharing interests, ideas, and life experiences with girls and boys opens with the doors for genuine student participation.

Unconditional Positive Regard

Unconditional positive regard for kids leads to greater self-esteem and increased ability to share and disclose. When kids are experiencing trauma, whether it be disaster from a flood or coronavirus, projecting total acceptance for the child can enhance mental health and learning. According to Rogers, this is a "warm, positive, and acceptant attitude" (1995, p. 62). "It is an atmosphere which simply demonstrates 'I care'; not 'I care for you if you behave thus and so'" (Rogers, 1995, p. 283). In this time of turbulence and abundant loss, young people are struggling with a myriad of feeling sometimes difficult to untangle. When kids know they are loved and valued, they more easily feel safe to reveal hidden feelings and thoughts. This can diminish ways kids hide feelings of shame, fear, and rage because they want to be accepted. They may act out as the only way they know to cry out for help. We cannot tell children enough that we care about them and love them.

Empathetic Understanding

To build relationships that create trust, safety, and continuity through growing up, we must establish with young people an empathetic environment that accepts thoughts and feelings without judgment. Feelings and thoughts about the environment that children share can only enhance relationships and move them toward a deeper space within themselves. This is why it is essential to find out who our students are as people, the barriers they face, and the resources they bring to school each day. Having empathy for our students also requires us to reserve judgment as we make every attempt to understand their worldview (Rogers, 1989).

Figure 4.4 Developing Trust.
Source: Photo by Mohammad Asadi on Unsplash.

Carl Rogers and his innovative understanding of relationships can motivate all caring adults to create an oasis of safety for expressing thoughts and feelings. The challenge of relationship building can be achieved by incorporating the three tenets' Rogers emphasized of genuineness, unconditional positive regard, and empathy. Whether the underlying feelings are a ten-year-old's concern about smoke inhalation, or a 16-year-old's fear of hurricane destruction, every young person needs adults around them that have their concern at heart, are steadfast in being present for them, and offer love and respect. We are growing the seeds for these children to evolve into caring and compassionate human beings.

The Discussion

> *There's absolutely no question that climate change is playing out before our eyes. We saw the heat dome event a few weeks ago. We unfortunately lost a lot of Oregonian through that event. In February we saw devastating ice storms. Over a half a million people lost power last fall ... We had unprecedented wildfires.*
> —Governor Kate Brown of Oregon (Sutton et al., 2021)

Sutton et al. July 20, 2021, reported the climate crisis in Oregon has solidified the reality that deadlier and more destructive wildfires have become the new normal. The entire west coast had been under serious threat of fire conditions due to excessive heat in July 2021. Nearly 650,000 people were placed under a heat advisory with temperatures remaining up to ten degrees above normal for days. These excessive drought conditions have produced fears and anxieties for kids who perceive their environment as unsafe, as they watch these climate challenges unfold with real time images.

An important aspect of addressing conversation with children and teens is an awareness of media representation of climate change and the ability of adults to process what children are integrating through these images and sound bites they see and hear. Lily was watching TV with her family when the news suddenly showed the devastating wildfires in Oregon. Their family lived in Southern California. Lily cried out as she watched the catastrophe virtually, "Mommy we have to move ... the fires will come to our house next." Lily's sister Jenny added frantically, "Where are the fire extinguishers. We need to be ready to put out the fires!!!"

Teachable Moments

This led Lily, her sister Jenny, and mom and dad to begin a discussion of climate change, exactly where these fires were happening, and what Lily imagined and spontaneously revealed through watching television. Lily's parents explained that hot dry continuous weather conditions fueled these wildfires in Oregon because prolonged drought can create fire conditions.

Watching the fires frightened Lily, and her parents used her reaction to incorporate a teachable moment for the children. They helped reduce

Lily's anxiety by bringing out a map to verify their home was far away from the danger. They honored Jenny's suggestion and formulated an emergency plan, with included locating where the fire extinguishers were, listing emergency phone numbers, establishing a family meeting place in case of an emergency, and storing emergency supplies.

NASA Climate Kids

The following is an explanation from an article by Allyson Shaw 2018, describing global warming as a process relevant to modern younger generations. Activities besides computers such as plugging in devices, driving cars, and cooling homes

> rely on energy sources such as natural gas, oil, and coal. Those energy sources release a gas called carbon dioxide into the atmosphere. When carbon dioxide and other greenhouse gases trap heat that would otherwise escape Earth's atmosphere, the planet's temperature rises. That's called global warming, which causes climate change. (Climate Reality Project. June 07, 2018a)

NASA's Climate Kids provides age-appropriate definitions for the following terms in a way that can promote dialogue and open meaningful discussion. They also share seven questions with age appropriate, concrete responses to create a dialogue about climate change. The following definitions and questions and answers are presented on the NASA's Climate Kids website with permission (Credit: NASA/ JPL-Caltech).

- *Climate:* The average pattern of weather conditions over a long period of time. Climate isn't weather – weather changes daily.
- *Global warming:* The increase in Earth's average temperature over a long period of time.
- *Carbon dioxide:* A gas released by the burning of coal, natural gas, oil, and wood that traps heat in the atmosphere.
- *Carbon footprint:* The amount of carbon dioxide one human releases into the environment in a year.
- *Fossil fuels:* Coal, oil, and natural gas, which come from the breakdown of ancient plants and animals over millions of years.

Children's Questions about Climate Change

1. What is global climate change?

Global climate is the average climate over the entire planet. The reason scientists and many other folks are concerned is that Earth's global climate is changing. The planet is warming up fast – faster than at any other time scientists know about from their studies of Earth's history.

2. Is the climate of the whole Earth really changing?

Yes! Earth has been getting warmer – and fast. Global climate is the average climate over the entire planet. And the reason scientists and folks like you are concerned is that Earth's global climate is changing.

Figure 4.5 Climate.

Source: Photo by NOAA on Unsplash.

3. What is climate?

"Climate" describes conditions over the long term and over an entire region. Climate is the big picture. It is the big picture of temperatures, rainfall, wind, and other conditions over a larger region and a longer time than weather. For example, the weather was rainy in Phoenix, Arizona, last week. But this city usually gets only about seven inches of rain each year. So, the climate for Arizona is dry. Much of Southern California also has a dry, desert climate. Brazil has a tropical climate because it's warm and rains there a lot.

4. What is weather?

TV weather reporters need all the information they can get to predict weather. Weather is local and temporary. On our Earth, we cannot control weather by turning a thermostat up to make it warmer or down to make it cooler. The best we can do is try to predict the weather.

Weather scientists, called meteorologists, try to foresee what's going to happen next.

5. Do we care if Earth is getting warmer?

Yes, we care! After all, Earth is our spaceship. It carries us on a 583-million-mile cruise around the sun every year. It even has its own "force field." Earth has a magnetic field that protects us from killer radiation and brutal solar wind. For its life-support system, Earth has all the air, water, and food we need. Just like astronauts on a long space voyage, we need to monitor all our "ship's" vital functions and keep our Earth "ship shape."

6. Does what we do matter?

Earth's fate is in our hands. Everything that happens here affects something over there. Earth has its own control system. Oceans, air, plants and animals, and energy from the sun all affect each other to make everything work in harmony. Nothing changes in one place without changing something in another place. The overall effect gives us our *global climate.*

7. What is making Earth's climate warmer?

Scientists have discovered that humans are causing this warming. But how do they know that? What are we doing that could cause the whole planet to get warmer? And how could warming happen so fast? What will happen to people and other living things if the planet keeps getting warmer? And what can we do to slow down or stop the warming?

Sesame Street and Nature

Introducing young children to a love and appreciation for nature and their role in caring for it can begin with simple activities that value plants, animals, and the environment. Sesame Street has been a forerunner in creating dialogue and activities to enhance a conversation that children can build on through their development.

Sesame Street provides the following downloadable activities (www.sesamestreet.org/parks) for children as well as vocabulary definitions for discussion. Activities include *Words are Here, There, Everywhere,* which include Nature Activity Cards and Nature Puzzles that broaden the young child's understanding through play.

Nature Words Definitions

Invite parents to engage children to explore nature vocabulary to help them learn and use new nature words. Use these words with kids to talk about and describe nature explorations in national parks, local parks, or their own backyards.

Amphibian: An animal, such as a frog, toad, salamander, or newt, that goes through a big change called a metamorphosis lives part of its life on land breathing through its skin and part of it in the water breathing through its gills has thin moist skin, four legs, and a backbone.

Figure 4.6 Nature Words.

Arachnid: A small animal, such as a spider, that has eight legs.

Binocular: A tool that helps you get a closer look at things that are far away.

Camouflage: To disguise or hide by blending into the background.

Compare: To figure out if things are the same or different.

Deciduous: A tree that loses its leaves once a year.

Garden: A place where plants, flowers, fruits, and vegetables are grown.

Habitat: A place where animals live and can find food, water, and a place to sleep.

Hibernate: When animals sleep for a very long time from winter until spring, when it's warm and easy to find food again.

Insect: A small animal that has six legs, two antennae, and usually two pairs of wings—such as flies, crickets, mosquitoes, beetles, butterflies, and bees.

Investigate: To do things that will help you find the answer to your question.

Journal: A book used to keep track of observations through writings, drawings, or photographs.

Magnify: To make something look bigger.

Metamorphosis: When something goes through a really big change, like when a caterpillar changes into a butterfly.

Migration: When animals move because the seasons change.

Nature: Plants, animals, and other things outside that are not made by people.

Observe: To use your senses to find out more about something.

Pollinate: When bees spread pollen from one plant, flower, fruit, or vegetable to another to help make more flowers grow.

Season: A time of the year that is characterized by a certain change in weather. There are four seasons in a year: winter, spring, summer, and fall. In winter it's cold and snowy, in spring it's warm and rainy, in summer it's hot, and in fall it's cool and windy. Depending on where you live the seasons might feel different.

Senses: What we use to experience everything around us. There are five of them: sight, taste, touch, smell, and hearing.

Texture: The way something feels.

Tool: Something used to do a specific task, like a magnifying glass, a shovel, or a flashlight.

Nature Puzzles

Sesame Street furthers and deepens the dialogue with young children about nature by providing nature puzzles.

Figure 4.7 Nature Puzzles.

Nature Activities

They also offer direct experiences activities for teachers in an *Educator View and Do Manual*. Each activity gives goals for what children will do, viewing a specific segment of Sesame Street, lists needed material information, and provides steps to create a project. The following is an example of one activity about seasons. It includes downloadable materials that can be used to create a nature journal and even an "explores national parks badge."

Educator Activity

GRAND CANYON: SEASONS CLASS NATURE JOURNAL

1. Once this has been done for all four seasons, it will be time to put the journal together to make a Four Seasons Class Journal!
2. Hole punch each page and use the yarn, string, or a binder ring to combine pages into a journal.
3. Children gather again in a large group and share and compare what was found during the four seasons.

How are the things the same and different?

Figure 4.8 Nature Journal.

Discussion/Activity Ideas

- Discuss what children found during the different seasons. Why were you able to collect more items during some seasons than others? What did you feel/smell/see/hear during each of the seasons?
- Talk about how the weather felt during each of the seasons and play a fun game figuring out the appropriate clothing to wear. Make pictures of different clothing (shorts, jacket, raincoat, snow boots, etc.) and pull them out of a bag, having the children guess which season they'd wear it in.
- How does your family adapt to the different seasons? How do you think animal families adapt to the different seasons?
- Talk about park rangers and why everyone should take care of their parks and nature. Earn nature explorer badges!
- Print out badges and give one to each child to color in. Then tape the badge to the child so they can wear it proudly.

Giving Voice to Young People

"A *voice* and a *choice* are the key that unlocks the door to empowerment for our children" (Goldman, 2017, p. 18).

Our youth have become a voice and a force!

Only then can a system emerge whereby young people, who otherwise might remain hidden, isolated, or voiceless, can become recognized individually for their voice, and collectively for their activism. By listening, honoring, and responding to these voices we can hear their fears, substantiate their truth, and provide activates that embolden their quest for safety and health for today and for the future.

Often adults are unsure of how to communicate with kids about climate change, so they remain silent fearing they do not have the correct words to use. They consciously or unconsciously restrain feelings by avoiding the topic. To reduce or extinguish eco-anxiety and climate depression, we need to create an oasis of safety for communication. Familiarizing ourselves with concepts concerning climate change and the environment, and the groundswell of fear, anxiety, and loss this generation is coping with is beneficial. The following figures drawn by young people can spark dialogues about climate change.

One elementary school girl explained her feelings in artwork when she drew these snails. She worried about them dying and did not know what do.

She said, "Snails are dying. Help!"

Figure 4.9 Snails.
Source: Permission Mother Earth Project.

Another youngster expressed loving feelings through artwork toward Mother Earth and explains her vision of how everyone can help the planet, "Treat the Earth like you want to be treated."

Figure 4.10 Treat the Earth Well.
Source: Permission Mother Earth Project.

A young protester at a climate change rally not only advocated for herself, but for her entire generation, as her poster relayed this powerful message and common fear, "I don't want to be the last generation."

Figure 4.11 The Last Generation.

Source: Photo permission John Hillegass.

Seventeen-year-old Emma-Jane Burian is a leader in the youth movement in Victoria. She explains that many young people are disappointed with the government's lack of action surrounding climate change. "Kids are feeling depressed that we might die and there might not be people to save us. Organizing helps combat that for me" (Egan-Elliott, 2019).

Rebecca, a 13-year-old organizer for the *Friday for Future* student strike in Victoria, explains sometimes she feels helpless when she thinks about climate change, "like everything is going faster... Organizing climate strikes is how I get more energy and how I say: 'Wow I'm actually making a difference. Maybe we can stop this climate crisis'" (Egan-Elliott, 2019).

In Canada, over 4,000 young people have agreed not to have children unless the government takes meaningful actions on climate change. Eighteen-year-old Emma Lim created this *No Future Pledge* movement. She very much wanted to be a mother. Yet she and those who signed the pledge are publicly expressing lack hope for a healthy future. Emma explains, "I am giving up my chance of having a family because I will only have children if I know I can keep them safe," she writes on the pledge website. "I am not the only young person giving up lifelong dreams because they are unsure of what the future will hold" (Egan-Elliott, 2019).

Children's Questions Create Dialogue

Children's questions are often a useful tool for therapists, educators, and caring adults. They are often a window into their soul and hold a mirror to see hidden thoughts and feelings. By honoring them, and responding to them with respect, we can use them as a key to unlock hidden emotions and anxieties.

What does extinction mean?
Why are the swans dying?
Why are the ice caps melting?
Why is the air polluted? (See Chapter 12 Climate Change Resources)

Our questions can help kids reveal hidden worries. One technique to help young children who are anxious about the environment is to ask them to list their top five worries about climate change. Tanya was a first grader that explained her number one worry was that dad would not recycle plastic. Tanya feared this would eventually hurt the Earth and nature. She sadly explained her dad did not think it was a big deal and kept throwing the plastic away.

I suggested Tanya to write dad a letter about how she felt about that, and then she could decide if she wanted to share it with dad. Tanya decorated the letter with pictures of trees and fish and birds and called the letter *Recycle for the Planet*. Tanya and her dad read the resource "*I can recycle*" and did many of the suggested activities together. Dad did begin to recycle with Tanya.

Recycle Paper Recycle Plastic Compost

Figure 4.12 Create Dialogue.
Source: Photo by Aaron Santelices on Unsplash.

Creative Arts Expression for Dialogue

A poem by ten-year-old Aria Jolie gives voice to her deep conviction to advocate for climate change. Aria's dialogue with her future self is an attempt to avert the crisis of today's world; her fear people are ruining the planet, and her description of an environment with pollution, dead fish, smoky skies, and distorted bird songs. This poem served as a catalyst for conversation.

> Dear future self,
> I want you to be better than me
> Can we break the never-ending cycle of trouble I see?
> Corrupt crisis constantly occurring
> White flags need to be waved
> Pollution problems are caused by the people ruining the planet
> Paradise not present
> Pufferfish perished and ponds polluted
> Peace signs need to mean something
> I can smell dead fish
> I see smoke soaring through soggy skies
> I hear birds' song distorted
> *Dear future self,*
> *What can I do before it's too late?*
>
> –Aria Jolie, Age 10

Republished with permission. Original published in *Hutch Magazine,* https://www.hutchkidsmagazine.org/

Aria ends her dialogue with her future self with the question – What can she do before it is too late? Her urgency is palpable, and she has chosen to become an elementary school advocate, meeting with peers for *School Strike for Climate* (see Chapter 8). Her originality in creating a conversation, a dialogue, a discussion, and a motivation for change with her future self is a dynamic teachable moment to share with others to keep the conversation moving forward.

Suggestions for Creating Conversation

Talking to children can be difficult and sometimes adults cannot find the age-appropriate words to use. Yet, if we begin in early childhood to create conversations about climate change, hygiene and cleanliness, and caring for the planet and other people, we build a paradigm that reflects the understanding that human beings are living on one planet together as a family. When the Earth is hurting, when people are hurting, when animals are hurting, it hurts all of us.

Adults can initiate discussion with kids on climate change by developing the following basic suggestions.

1. Be honest. Young children have a special sense when they are not told the truth and then begin to distrust the adults in their emotional environment. Teenagers also feel a sense of loss of trust if the adults around them are not transparent. They will research and find out information on their own.
2. Use age-appropriate language and limit responses to the question asked. Too much information can be overwhelming.
3. Ask kids what they already know. What do you think climate change is? What is the COVID virus? What is racism?
4. Honor children's questions. They are often a window to their soul, and a mirror to their inner experience.
5. Creating an environment of safety and non-judgment. In this way as the child matures, a continuous space for exploring deeper concepts and more advanced information is created.
6. Monitor TV and when possible, use it as a teachable moment to begin a dialogue on self-care, caring for others, and caring for nature and the environment. Look for climate good news.
7. Limit information to a child's understanding and concern. Validate their feelings are real and brainstorm on activities to make change.
8. Be open. If you do not know an answer, that is OK. Find the answers together.
9. Emphasize support networks available for children and families. Help is available (see Chapter 12).
10. Create an emergency kit with children. Let them participate in what items and ideas might be necessary in case of an emergency.
11. Provide a linking object. Kids often feel safer in participating when they have a special linking object such as blanket, stuffed animal, or picture.
12. Remind children they are resilient, they are safe, and families get through challenging situations. Be positive and share examples of all the good work being done for the environment and its inhabitants.
13. Discuss taking action. What can we do to help create a kinder, healthier world for people, nature, and the environment? Together families, teachers, caring adults, and young people can recycle, compost, plant a garden, or create a parachute for the planet (see Chapter 7).
14. Maintain a resource library (see Chapter 12). Have on-hand books like *Thank You Earth, I like to Recycle*, and *What Is Composting*? It helps to ignite a spontaneous conversation.

Immediate and Long-Term Conversations

Greta Thunberg, teen-age activist, has warned, "Our Earth is on fire!" (see Chapter 8). When kids hear this, they become afraid. Some wonder why should I go to school, do my homework, or play sports if we are not going to live?

Susan Clayton is a conservation psychologist and co-author of the American Psychological Association and ecoAmerica resource, "Mental Health and Our Changing Climate." Clayton presents the blanket analogy with children similar to Gurwitch's blanket dialogue as follows. "Our atmosphere is like a blanket and it keeps the Earth warm, which is a good thing. It's just that the blanket is too thick now because of gases we put in the air." Giving kids a simple metaphor helps them "have a better sense of what's actually happening" (Akpan, 2019).

There exists an immediate and long-term conversation about climate change with youth that can be addressed on several levels. Young people and families that live through disaster, such as Katie in Chapter 2, exemplify the trauma they endure and losses on so many levels that can lead to depression, anxiety, and prolonged grief over a life span.

Samantha Ahdoot, pediatrician, and lead author of the American Academy of Pediatrics policy statement on Global Climate Change and Children's Health, shared her educated outlook on conversations about climate change and its underlying stress. "I look at it through two lenses. Through the mental health consequences of extreme weather events, and through the effects of living in a world that is changing and the fear that it invokes in children" (Akpan, 2020).

Conclusion

Children and teens can also experience vicarious psychological trauma by constant mainstream media coverage of tragedies such as natural disasters of fires and earthquakes, environmental disasters including the COVID virus, and man-made adversities with images of murder, looting, and protesting. These occurrences viewed and absorbed into the psyches of our young people can indeed create a layer of mental stress that was not present before viewing. This additional catalysis for worry and fear creates more depression and anxiety for those girls and boys who witness these events from a social media distance.

Some adults argue we should not talk to young people about climate change. They believe discussions evoke fear. Can we hide the graphics that so easily flow out of our social media, can we eliminate the coverage of disaster and trauma which engulfs our television viewing, can we deny our weather is getting hotter, our air is more polluted, and our medical and emotional pandemics are something we are all living through together?

It is impossible to conceal the truth. Yet a line of delineation must be drawn between scaring kids and sharing with kids.

Clayton asserts some children may worry "when they feel like something's being kept from them because that means the problem is so bad that people aren't talking about it" (Apkin, 2019). Younger children take what they hear literally from adults, peers, and media. Spontaneous conversations about media images and sounds bites help kids discern truth and clarify misunderstandings. In middle and secondary school, it is almost impossible to insulate students from the climate change issues. School-based curriculums that include progressive information about climate helps generate dialogues that distinguish fact from fiction and build a concrete knowledge base to focus attention and action.

We can frame realistic circumstances happening on our planet through a positive, safe, healthy, and resilient landscape. Honest discussion motivates creative activism, self-worth, and confidence. Resilience is not just immediate gratification. It is the knowing and perseverance of climate goals that are ongoing and ever changing throughout a lifetime. The climate change conversation is continuous and enduring as well. It is a conversation younger and older generations can explore together for the collective good.

Figure 4.13 Safe Environment.
Source: *Photo by Markus Spiske on Unsplash.*

5   Environmental Activities for Young People: Counseling and Educators

The best way for peers to be on board about climate change is to engage them in simple ideas and activities.

–Ari Rubenstein, High School Student
Cofounder Mother Earth Project, Parachutes for the Planet

Figure 5.1 Environmental Activities.
Source: Photo by Ebony on Unsplash.

DOI: 10.4324/9781003051770-7

> *Young climate activists say they are motivated by feelings of eco-anxiety to organize strikes and demand action.*
>
> –Egan-Elliott, *Times* Colonist, September 27, 2019

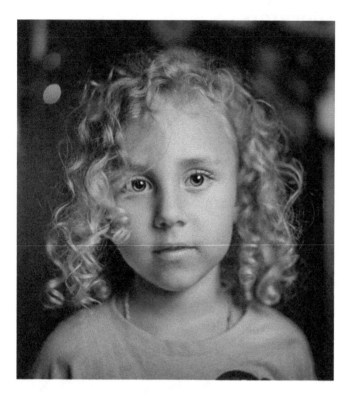

Figure 5.2 Recognizing Feelings.

Source: Photo by Janko Ferlic on Unsplash.

Introduction

This chapter provides activities to define and understand climate change, clear up misconceptions, and allow for dialogue about feelings associated with the well-being of the planet. Activities can be used in a therapeutic or classroom environment, focusing on children's worries, frustration, panic, sadness, and anger about climate change. By recognizing these feelings and providing activities that reduce fears and perceived loss, we can create a realistic platform for discussion to better understanding climate change and transform apprehension into resilience and hope.

The TV series *Big Little Lies* created an episode on climate change and children, third episode, second season 2019. Renato (Laura Dern) is a mom, furious about everyone talking about climate change, and she does not want to take it anymore. As the mother of a second grader in the show she rants to the teacher and principal that her daughter's little brain cannot handle it. Although mom thinks climate change is legitimate, she does not want the depressing topic brought up in school. "What possesses idiots like you to teach eight-year-olds that the planet is doomed?" she yells at the school's principal and teacher (Ivie, 2019). In this episode, her daughter actually had a panic attack as a result of the school discussion. Another mother argues with Renato we must talk about it even if it is depressing.

Some of the statistics are daunting, and adults have difficulty processing this accelerating world phenomenon of climate change. One is left with the question, "How do we talk to kids about climate change?"

What Is Being Taught about Climate Change?

I am proud to announce that New Jersey is the first state in the nation to incorporate climate change education across our K-12 learning standards – preparing our students for the future green economy.
Tammy Murphy, Governor of New Jersey Schugarman, 2020

"A recent NPR poll (NPR/Ipsos, 2019) found that eighty percent of parents in the US support the teaching of climate change in the classroom. The vast majority of teachers, (86 percent of teachers) agreed that they would like to address the topic, but only around 45 percent, said they actually did so. The most common response for why they were not teaching it was they felt it was "outside of their subject area" (McGough, 2019). This poll was conducted with over 1,000 US adult and 505 teachers separately. According to the results of the NPR/Ipsos poll: Whether they have children or not, two-thirds of Republicans and nine in ten Democrats agree that the subject needs to be taught in school. Yet the result of the poll indicated that fewer than half of parents have discussed the issue with their children, and fewer than half the teachers teach kids about climate change.

Many of the teachers worried if they taught about it, they would receive parent complaints. The poll also showed teachers felt they did not have the materials, did not know enough about the subject, or that their school will not allow it to be taught. Teachers wanting to teach about climate change state they would like state laws requiring it, they would need resources to answer student questions, which their students now bring up the topic in school, and their school to encourage them to talk about climate change. Erin Rowers teaches climate change to her fourth and fifth graders and explains, "If you teach from a problem-based learning style, students will repeatedly arrive at climate change as the cause and effect of many problems/issues in their world" (Kamenetz, 2019).

Many students do not need to wait to discuss climate change in school because they are experiencing the repercussions of a changing climate in their life. NPR Ed found in an analysis that in just one semester, the fall of 2017, for example, nine million US students across nine states and Puerto Rico missed some amount of school owing to natural disasters – which scientists say are becoming more frequent and severe because of climate change.

Teachers Weigh In

The NPR poll discovered the following common reasons teachers do or do not teach climate change:

Reasons Teachers Do Not Teach Climate Change

1. It's not related to the subject I teach.
2. Students too young.
3. I don't know enough about it.
4. I don't have the materials needed to teach the subject.
5. I don't believe in climate change.
6. State mandates it be taught at a different grade level.
7. My school does not allow it.
8. Students have already learned about it in school (Kamenetz, 2019, p. 6).

Teachers Who Cover Climate Change Differ from Those Who Do Not

1. I feel comfortable answering students' questions about climate change.
2. There should be state laws in place that require teaching climate change.
3. I have the resources I need to answer students' questions about climate change.
4. My students have brought up climate change in the classroom this year.
5. My school or school district encourages us to discuss climate change in the classroom (Kamenetz, 2019, p. 7).

Many teachers are very busy and must make decisions about what to teach. Other subjects seem more important to prioritize, and some teachers are concerned about parent complaints if they do teach about climate change.

Climate Anxiety Classes for Students

The University of Derby has introduced climate anxiety classes for students and faculty worried about the outcome of the planet and the anxiety they feel concerned about climate change concerns. The eco-anxiety workshops work with sadness, depression, and hopelessness associated with climate change and the enormous sense of loss felt about the future safety of the planet. Participants are encouraged to express feelings through art and eventually dance and drama.

Dr. Jamie Bird, deputy head of health and social care research at the university, explains young people suffer "climate grief" as they can see what they are losing, locally or abroad, like the fires in Australia (Williams, 2020). "Helplessness can underline a lot of the feelings and ... people don't know how to process them as it's something they have never felt before, and because many don't know how it will pan out" (Williams, 2020). One student explained (BBC News, 2020) that climate change "makes me very anxious because every time I look at the news and I rarely see any good news about the future. It just makes me think I'm not going to have a future."

The goal of these workshops is to tackle negative thoughts, share work together, and find solutions to issues. Words that arose for discussion were extinction, annihilation, threat, emergency, and catastrophe.

Giving Voice to High School Students

Joe Sachs is an environmental science teacher at BCC High School in Bethesda Maryland. Part of his curriculum is including information for students on biodiversity. Mr. Sachs, in a 2020 interview, explained the following to his students during a lesson that gave rise to much discussion. "We are now living in a time of a mass extinction event, whereby the rate of species being lost is growing." He shared percentages of 40 percent of amphibians becoming extinct, and 20 percent of mammals extinct or on their way.

Young people were amazed that elephants, rhinos, dolphins, seals, and more were not faring well. The rainforest has the highest rate of loss, which includes birds and monkeys. It is an area with a specific niche that needs specific food sources for the habitat. When conditions on which survival depends on are disturbed, species become very vulnerable.

The reaction to this standard lesson by the students surprised Mr. Sachs. The students were deeply upset that they were not aware of these facts until this lesson and did not know enough about the extinction crisis. They felt it was fundamental to their education to know if there are species dying on the planet, and how disturbed they were that they did not know.

At that point in the lesson, Mr. Jones *paused.* He stopped the lecture, moved away from the required curriculum, and opened the classroom to a much-needed discussion. This became a spontaneous, teachable moment!

The teens were spontaneous, and somewhat forlorn. They wanted to talk about the environment, and particularly bio-diversity loss. One student felt a great deal more communication about the subject was necessary.

Another teen wanted the environmental science class to be mandatory as part of the curriculum. She explained, "If young people don't know the details about climate change, it becomes very difficult to create the urgency we need to heal the planet."

Figure 5.3 A Voice.
Source: Photo by Wadi Lissa on Unsplash.

Realizing the arts is often an important and undervalued means of expression, he encouraged students to develop ideas to communicate through visual arts and poster presentations. They shared their anxieties about climate change, their disappointment in adults for not opening dialogues and sharing information, and how their newfound intellectual beliefs change to emotional expression. Students created a poster presentation of fears about climate change to display in their school and exhibited artwork in *The Museum of Contemporary Teenage Art* in their community. One group documented their work and created a presentation for third and fourth graders, sharing on their level of understanding. In turn, these elementary school children would process their understandings through art, writing, and activities.

Another student project concentrated on water issues in the environment. The students began to communicate with other peers around the world, creating a very visible display on *Water Issues in the Environment* in the hallways. One tenth grade boy decided to initiate a Compost Project and invited the student body to participate. The students created a composting service for the school and for BCC parents.

As Mr. Jones maintained *"pause time"* for discussion in the weeks ahead, classmates continued to explore feelings. Sophia felt hurt, almost horrified, that students were not informed about issues in the environment. She questioned the whole system of communicating information to young people. "I can't understand why everyone doesn't know these things about the changes on our Earth, especially parents and teachers!"

After many conversations and completions of projects, the teens began to ponder their role in this quagmire of communication. Many students mentioned Greta Thunberg (see Chapter 8) and admired her awareness that everyone is a part of the climate change problem, and that everyone is a part of the solution.

Greta used her voice to speak out and modeled how kids can speak out too. She stressed to younger generations and peers to *know* they are right when they voice concerns and ultimately act on them. In this way the despair and depression surrounding climate change can be transformed to resilience. Kids can be released from the angst associated with the environment by trying and doing. Eric voiced a strong opinion, "Our solution is activism. We can become the communicators and teach our parents and teachers." Mr. Sach's students yearned for a continued, age-appropriate, dialogue beginning at an early age within the school curriculum. His students were distraught about the lack of that conversation growing up – resulting in difficulty catching up with climate change information at their present age.

The Expressive Arts and Climate Change Conversation

The expressive arts provide children an opportunity to access their creativity to develop an understanding of challenging life events and feelings related to climate change. Play is part of a child's work, and an avenue to express unconscious projections through the arts that can release stored worries and fears. Expressive arts facilitated by a trained teacher, guidance counselor, or other mental health professional are generally viewed as a socially acceptable mode of therapeutic engagement that may alleviate emotional distress in children (Green & Drewes, 2013). Many play modalities such as art, projective play, sand play, letter writing, and music serve to engage school-age children's imagination, and empower healing through expression of feelings and problem-solving future outcomes.

The process of creating art can be a tool to assess the feelings and perceptions of children's internal worlds. Artwork permits communication between their inner and outer worlds of children. The expressive arts contain three predominant theoretical paradigms – psychoanalytic, developmental, and cognitive-behavioral therapy. Margaret Naumburg (1987) integrated aspects of both Freudian and Jungian psychoanalytic theory in practice. By focusing on uncovering unconscious material through spontaneous artwork, the door is open for free association without specific direction. Donald Winnicott's contribution to object relations theory has influenced art therapy by describing how children place greater value on particular objects than the item itself, which becomes a transitional object. Artwork created by a child in a safe, non-judgmental school environment can become a transitional object. It becomes a reminder of what a child was thinking and feeling during the expressive arts process. The following examples illustrate the power of the expressive arts in writing and painting to share ideas and imagery about climate change.

Riordan Writes a Letter

A third grader, Riordan, was invited with the rest of his class to commit to the "No Straw Challenge." This challenge was given at Summit Street Elementary School in Williston, Vermont, to a group of kindergarten students as well as third grade. Third grade teacher Timiny Bergstrom had designed and taught a lesson which left a big impression on Riordan. It included a video about turtles suffering from plastic straws.

She and her classmates were very touched by the video. Mrs. Bergstrom included in one expressive art lesson a writing assignment. She asked her students to compose letters to businesses to encourage them to stop using plastic straws. Riordan crafted a letter to Jeffrey, the owner of a nearby pizza restaurant, and very soon got a response. Riordan asked Jeffrey to rethink the use of plastic straws and here is what the letter said.

> Can you please stop using straws. Our class and the other classes had to see a video with a person had to pull a straw out of a turtle's nose because so much straws ended up in the ocean! It was soo sad. So, in conclusion please stop using straws. (Bilow, 2018)

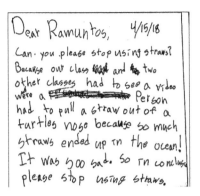

Dear Ramuntos,   4/15/18
Can you please stop using straws?
Because our class ~~had~~ and ~~to~~ two
other classes had to see a video
were a ~~~~~~~~~~~ person
had to pull a straw out of a
turtles nose because so much
straws ended up in the ocean!
It was too sad. So in conclusion
please stop using straws.

Figure 5.4 Letter.

Source: Permission Riordan and Kelly Redman.

Jeffrey, the owner, swiftly responded with gratitude. "I wrote an email back and thanked Riordan for opening my eyes, and that I had never even thought about straws being an issue. I love turtles too." He then acknowledged, "This letter that Riordan took the time to write meant the world to me. It made me realize we all have a footprint here and we're here to do the best we can" (Bilow, 2018).

This simple yet effective school lesson empowered Mrs. Bergstrom's third grade class, and especially Riordan that one person can make a difference. And they did! Jeffrey no longer uses landfill-bound plastic straws and has turned to compostable ones because of Riordan's request. Now Jeffrey uses reusable dishes and cups as well and donates food scraps to the local farmer. Mrs. Bergstrom also incorporated the Global UN Sustainable Development Goals in lessons.

Goals for sustainable development were incorporated into her lessons and she found the students to be appreciative and motivated to learn more from these objectives. She explained her third graders were the oldest in the school, and in their third grade they became the leaders of the *Green Team*. Their role was to sort and recycle the school recycling and educate and support younger children in the school to do the same.

Cooper's Painting of the Earth Melting

Cooper, a fifth grader from Belmont, MA, expressed feelings about climate change and what is presently happening to the Earth through artwork. Cooper is a sensitive student and well versed on the science of climate change. Through viewing this painting, one can visualize Cooper's concern about the melting Earth and carbon emissions.

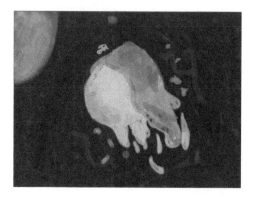

Figure 5.5 Melting Ice Caps by Cooper Bennett Burt.

Source: Drawing permission Steph and Cooper Burt.

After completing the painting, Cooper was able to verbalize these concerns illustrated in the artwork. Cooper explained, "When I was drawing the picture, I was thinking how carbon emissions from automobiles causes the atmosphere to melt the ice caps in the Arctic. So, sea levels are rising, making the Earth's surface closer to 80% water, instead of the 70% it is now."

Elena's Love for the Planet through Art

One creative student, Elena, was motivated to create her painting. She explained the following ideas were her inspiration.

> After seeing the ways that human interference has affected the turtles, like our use of plastic straws that often find themselves in the ocean, I was driven to create something that advocates for turtles. They don't have a voice themselves!
>
> –Elena

Elena also painted a vision of her optimistic future. She created a beautiful bird to represent her appreciation for the beauty in the world we live in.

> As a big advocate for animals, it pains me to see the natural ecosystems and habitats for wild creatures being affected and disappear because of our overwhelming inability to see the damage we as humans can cause and contribute to without so much as a second thought.
>
> –Elena

Figure 5.6 The Turtle.
Source: Permission Elena Peterson.

Figure 5.7 The Bird.
Source: Permission Elena Peterson.

Research on the Expressive Arts

The following is a compilation of research ideas and theories on the expressive arts and their ability to allow kids to share feelings, communicate ideas, and join together for solutions. The tools of projective play, clay, drawing, writing, and sand tables are vehicles that may unlock hidden thoughts and feelings that can be used with preschoolers and throughout the grades to release worries and develop strategies concerning the challenges of climate change.

Developmental art activity emphasizes the comprehensive understanding of the normative process of cognitive, emotional, physical, and artistic development of children and the precept that creative artistic activities offer normative experiences and promote increased social, emotional, and cognitive functioning for all individuals (Green & Drewes, 2014; Malchiodi et al., 2003). In contrast to the psychoanalytic approach to art activities, the cognitive-behavioral therapy approach implements techniques such as self-instruction training and stress inoculation training. Self-instruction training teaches behavioral techniques to students such as coaching impulsive students toward completion of drawing and coloring projects (Meichenbaum & Goodman, 1971).

> Goals and objectives are a consideration for working with young people through art. Teachers and counselors must consider how they will interact with students using art as a media of expression. Often some young people will need to be guided and encouraged during the art process, others require only a non-verbal adult witness. Adults need to stay tuned in to the needs of the individual student to assess the verbal and visual input required. Then, the teacher or mental health professional may observe the completed artwork and ask the student open-ended questions to help them describe their work. The discussion of the student's artwork enables adults to gain insights into the student's symbolic language represented within their art, without adults giving personal meaning to the content of the image.
>
> –Adapted from Goldman, 2017, p. 24

Somerset Elementary: Ms. Lewis's Art Class

Beginning the Conversation Early

Lynn Lewis, a 20-year veteran art teacher at Somerset Elementary School in Washington DC, has been accomplishing that conversation with kindergarteners to sixth graders in a fun, involved, and inspired educational forum. Ms. Lewis teaches children beginning in kindergarten and follows them through their educational journey. Her love for nature and the environment, coupled with her desire to inform and enlighten young minds and hearts about nature and their planet, transforms factual material about climate change into a living model of how kids can learn through art, and be motivated to recognize problems and be part of the solution.

These factors and research findings suggest authenticity in the way Ms. Lewis incorporates the expressive arts into giving children a tactile and intimate experience with nature and the environment that engages understandings about climate change in an age-appropriate way. She builds a developmentally fitting project each year she teaches students throughout their academic grade until graduation. Lessons are taught in a way that kids are not afraid of what they are learning, but rather voice their feelings about a concern, and then work together to find solutions. The expressive arts are apparent in children's posters, three dimensional models of the environment, helpful toy monsters to aid the planet, chalk drawings to help the bears, and The Green Kids Club.

The Green Kids Club

> *Green Kids Club is kids conceived and kids supported.*
> –Barbara Berlin, third grade teacher
> Somerset Elementary

The Green Kids Club is a group of third to fifth grade students at Somerset Elementary in Montgomery County Maryland. Spearheading the club is third grade teacher Barbara Berlin, who takes an active role in helping students promote beneficial ways to work with climate change within the school and community. Mrs. Berlin explained during an interview in 2020 the actual name of the club is SERT (School Energy Recycling Team) Green Kids Club. Every school in Montgomery County, MD, is encouraged to create a Green Kids Club and gain certification. The Green Kids Club has been certified by MAEOE (Maryland Association for Environmental Outdoor Education) since 2012. Certification was based on the following:

- Activities and projects at age/grade level
- School initiatives and support
- Connection to the community
- Helpfulness to the school

Students worked hard to meet the requirements. They planted a perennial school garden in the front garden bed of the school and eventually grew native plants. Kids promoted energy saving concepts by shutting down computers at night and turning lights off. They performed a play about recycling, and inspired classmates to clean the school grounds by presenting an annual micro trash cleanup for the school. This event highlighted the awareness that the tiniest pieces of trash are important to clean up. Green Kids Club members researched different aspects of climate change and presented information to the school with slide shows and presentation. They even had a Green Kids Moment at the beginning of the day announcements, telling an important understanding about climate change. Green Kid Ambassadors would visit younger students in kindergarten through second grade and teach them about recycling and litter.

Ms. Lewis explained that the Green Kids Club met each week to brainstorm activities to help their school and their world with climate change. Posters are displayed in the halls of the school with drawings and slogans on how kids can become involved in creating a healthy environment.

The following are a few examples of the slogans and posters:

Keep the future bright...
Give a hoot. Don't pollute!
Turn off the light.

What do you do when you see liter?

Figure 5.8 Litter Drawing Mila and Greta, Age 8.
Source: Permission Anita Sanchez & Pegg Hoffman.

These posters and slogans by the Green Kids Club illustrate the school environment supports positive change for climate related challenges.

Figure 5.9 Save the Bay! Drawing by Greta.

Source: Permission Pegg Hoffman.

When one enters the school doors, the commitment to nature, the environment is apparent. A visitor feels the presence of a true school team of students and educators giving voice to problems and solutions associated with climate change. The school postings for students, parents, and guests are visible reminders to recycle wisely.

Ms. Lewis creates art projects that are then converted onto products such as sweatshirts or T-shirts and then sold as a school project. The Green Kids Club used funds from the sale of art objects to purchase items that will help the school environment. They purchased hand blowers to put in bathrooms as replacements for paper towels, and a special attachment to school water fountains that continually display the number of plastic water bottles not used because of the fountain.

Climate Change and Art Class

The art class is also a forum for learning about environmental challenges and what can be done. Ms. Lewis presented a PowerPoint presentation including polar bear pictures to her kindergarten class. This generated the following lively discussion about how kids felt and what they thought they could do.

A Kindergarten Lesson: What Is Happening to the Polar Bears?

Ms. Lewis began her lesson with the following poster. "Is ice melting too fast for POLAR BEARS to thrive and enjoy the Northern Lights?" Their collage and chalk art activity were displayed in the Somerset Halls. She explained that in class discussion each idea was honored and recorded, no matter how inconsequential the response may have seemed.

The following information was presented to these students about the polar caps melting and how it impacts the polar bears. Then the children were asked, "What can we do?" The following are their responses.

Global Warming Is Causing Ice Sheets and Icebergs to Melt in Artic Regions

Figure 5.10 Polar Bear.

Source: Photo by Jacqueline Godany in Unsplash.

- Polar bears are threatened by ice melting because they are losing sea ice habitat.
- Polar bears hunt seals from floating sheets of sea ice. Seals are their favorite food. But as the Artic has warmed in recent years, the ice is melting earlier. This gives the bears less time to hunt. So, some bears might not be able to build up the fat they need to survive the rest of the year. The time and space they have to hunt is shortened by warming temperatures. Seals also need the ice to raise their young.
- Pregnant females build ice dens in the winter, where they hibernate to store energy and give birth to cubs. These dens can collapse with melting temperatures.
- Warming temperatures can make polar bears sick. More diseases thrive in warmer temperatures.

What Can We Do? The Kindergarteners Responded with the Following Ideas

- I will help my polar bear by cooking his seal. Charlotte
- I will help the polar bears search for seals. Ariya
- Don't litter because that doesn't help the environment. I will put less trash and plastic in the ocean. Mae
- Drive less. Walk more. Scotty
- I will walk everywhere. Lucy
- I will bike anywhere I want. Sienna
- I will put soil in my car's exhaust pipe, so the gas is absorbed when it comes out. Caleb
- I will tell my mom, don't drive the car.
- I will tell my mom and my dad not to use their cars too often they will walk and walk and walk all weekend. Sarah
- I will ride a scooter. Audrey
- Go walking to go shopping. Rafael.
- I will drive my car less. I will hug my polar bear more. Isba
- Put snow where polar bears live. Kanta

The kindergartens used collage and chalk to illustrate lessons involving the bears and Artic ice melting. This image illustrates concern about animals under the beautiful northern lights.

Figure 5.11 Artic Melting.

Source: Permission Lynn Lewis.

Projective Play in Art Class

Play is considered a fundamental aspect of early life, and it has been shown to improve the social, emotional, cognitive, and physical domains of children (Green & Drewes, 2014). Play helps young people understand their world and release stresses from traumatic events. Play serves as a route for children to express emotions and feelings through imagination, symbolism, and fantasy (Russ, 2007). Play therapy allows the counselor to enter the child's experience, which can facilitate growth and healing in a way that is congruent with the developmental age of the child (Goldman, 2017, p. 247).

In Ms. Lewis's art class, the conversation about nature and the environment continues in second grade. Children are encouraged to use projective play to express ideas and feelings about climate change. Kids create helping monsters for the environment and brainstorm the ways this little stuffed animal could help plants and animals.

Figure 5.12 Helping Monster.
Source: Permission Lynn Lewis.

The Tree of Life Art Project

Another one of Ms. Lewis's art classes was inspired by the story, "Tree of Life, Home of the African Baobab" by Barbara Bash. Third graders wrote and illustrated a personal tree of life.

The tree contained symbols which had special meaning. Kids were encouraged to create paper trees and share gratitude for the trees that give so much joy in life. Bash explains in her story that *The Tree of Life* is a universal motif found in every culture: new and old. It is often seen as a symbol for universality, spiritual nourishment, and enlightenment.

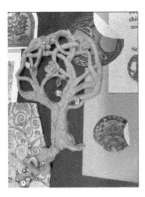

Figure 5.13 Paper Tree.
Source: Permission L. Lewis.

Fourth Grade Bay Sculpture Project

Mrs. Lewis gave students the option of sculpting an underwater or above water view of the Chesapeake Bay. They were invited to roll, pinch, carve, and join the clay in order to create this sculpture. Part of their sculpture was to include something from their previous Bay Food Chain Watercolor.

Figure 5.14 Bay Sculpture.
Source: Permission Lynn Lewis.

Students were asked to address this question, "What do I need to know to set an achievable but challenging goal?"

Fourth Grade Farmscape Project

Miss Lewis gave another assignment entitled Farmscape, asking students the question, "How can farmers protect the Chesapeake Bay?"

In conjunction with their bay studies in fourth grade art, Ms. Lewis challenged her kids to brainstorm possible ways farmers in the watershed area can prevent nutrients from running out into the bay.

Figure 5.15 Farmscape
Source: Permission Lynn Lewis.

Here is what they found out:

*   Contour plowing – crops follow contour of hillside so that rainwater will be absorbed by crops rather than directed into streams.
*   Rotate planting and ploughing times.
*   Dig ditches to direct runoff into thick vegetation which will absorb nutrients.

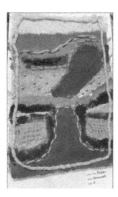

Figure 5.16 Farmscape Yarn.
Source: Permission Lynn Lewis.

- Rotate crops.
- Build some fences to direct runoff.
- Do not over fertilize.
- Use environment-friendly fertilizers.
- Practice organic methods of farming.
- Dispose of animal waste immediately.

Students were then required to use some of these possibilities in their artwork when painting farmlands. They used pastels and/or oils. Yarn was used to show ideas about runoff.

Somerset Elementary School: Mother Earth Project

The town of Somerset presented an Exhibition Grand Opening of artwork sponsored by the fifth grade "micro, macro, and me project" at Somerset Elementary. It was held at Somerset Town Hall, Chevy Chase, Maryland. The artwork was the product of a collaboration with Somerset School.

Teacher Lynn Lewis explains in a video the work of Jeremiah, and cofounder Ari Rubenstein (pianist) and Simon Diesenhaus perform Michael Jackson's *Man in the Mirror*, The Mother Earth Project's theme song. Mother Earth's cofounders Ari and Barton Rubenstein gave a presentation to a middle school. Congressman Jamie Ruskin came to visit and listened and participated in discussion with the students.

The following image is an example of a young person's artwork inspired by their love and protection for Mother Earth. AB shares the love for the environment through artwork and what it gives us. AB also writes about ways that all of us can help in keeping Mother Earth healthy, such as picking up trash and cutting down fewer trees.

Figure 5.17 Care for the Environment.

Source: Permission from Mother Earth Project.

I care for the environment, and you should too since the environment gives us lots of things, like water to drink and trees for oxygen. But our environment is already in danger. Floods, people cutting down trees, and people leaving their trash on the floor are not helping the fact. But we could do better than that, we can make our environment clean by picking up the trash, cutting less trees down. Remember we can make a difference! (AB)

Environmental Service and Science Club Acts: Bethesda Chevy Chase High School

In an interview with organizer Hank Greeves on March 18, 2021, Hank explained the Bethesda Chevy Chase High School (B-CC) Environmental Science Club's mission is to directly impact other students to act. These students are committed to engaging peers in a more physical and immediately rewarding kind of way, seeking to create awareness of issues and teach young people to take action for the environment. Hank felt if students could realize they can be a catalyst for change, they can carry this realization throughout their life.

Hank highlighted the focus of the environmental club was on science and service. Each weekly meeting club members may have been exposed to a science documentary about the planet or endangered species. They may also use that time to make and display posters in school that educate classmates on what do for the environment. Here is an example of one of the posters the club made and displayed on the three rules of recycling.

Figure 5.18 Three Rules

Source: Permission Hank Greeves.

The Tree-Plenish Project

On April 18, 2021, the students at B-CC presented an event to offset the high school's use of paper by requesting a tree be planted in as many yards in they can in the surrounding area. Sponsored by the Environmental Service and Science Club at Bethesda-Chevy Chase High School, this student-based project enabled classmates to become agents of change by researching environmental issues that impact our local community and translating these into action.

The goal of the tree project was to plant 240 trees on April 18 to offset the impact of the school's paper usage of 2.4 million sheets of paper used during the 2018–2019 school year, the last full, uninterrupted academic year before the pandemic. The Environmental Service Science Club has partnered with the nonprofit Tree-Plenish Project made up of college students from around the country.

Figure 5.19 Actions.

Source: Permission Hank Greeves.

Students asked for volunteers to help plant trees on the day of the event, April 18, 2021, or by signing up to have a tree planted in your yard. Visitors to the website https://www.tree-plenishevents.org/ Bethesda choose their tree of choice after viewing information about the three trees that are options. The Tree-Plenish Project is a student/ community-based effort to increase sustainability. It is one of three club projects inspiring young people to become an agent for change. Other motivating activities included canvassing area restaurants to promote low- and no-cost practices to support a healthier planet and conducting weekly stream cleanups.

Lobbying for Local Businesses on Environment-Friendly Practices

Service participation includes lobbying for local businesses to maintain more environment-friendly practices. After cold calling local businesses to address environmental concerns, the students created a pamphlet that explained climate issues and what businesses could do. One restaurant agreed to stop giving out plastic straws unless requested. Another agreed to limit the flow of faucet water and to allow club members to place posters about activities for the environment in their building.

Stream Cleanup

Stream Cleanup was another service project. Hank felt this endeavor was the most engaging activity. About 45 students hiked for a day in a nearby sprawling creek, filling bags, and bags of trash. Here are the before and after photos of the cleanup.

Students spent the day cleaning litter at near-by Rock Creek Park. Hank commented it was both fun and engaging.

Figure 5.20 Before Cleanup.

Figure 5.21 After Rock Creek Cleanup.
Source: Permission Hank Greeves 5.20 & 5.21.

Figure 5.22 Club Members Cleanup.
Source: Permission Hank Greeves.

Once a year students held a huge Club Fair that was chaotic and fun. Most of the student bodies were there, and many gave their emails to be contacted to volunteer for the third service project, The Tree Planting. The event was helpful in recruiting participation. The tree project also served as an avenue for students to gain service hours and help the community.

At the completion of the interview with Hank, he again reiterated it was crucial to let people know why the project was important. Although the school used over two million sheets of paper in one year – when learning went online during the pandemic year not a single piece of paper was used by students during the quarantine.

This knowledge serves to embolden the idea that a serious reduction of paper in schools is feasible. A partial reason for this reduction is the growth in the power of technology and the knowledge that trees serve a real purpose. Hank contemplated his final ambition about the goals of the Science Environmental Club in the following way.

"Before I graduate this year, I want to write a letter to anyone that will read it – stressing the ideas and projects created by the club, and the ability we all have to continue these activities in future years.

We did the paper project to show we don't need to use so much paper, and we can make up for all the paper used. People need to be asked, "'How can you do your part?' I want to leave the school with a legacy of power and the idea that we are ultimately here to do something!"

Figure 5.23 Trees Are Important.
Source: Photo by Tim Leitzkus.

Climate Kids Activities

NASA's Climate Kids has fun activities that are freely downloadable for activities about the environment that can be done in a classroom, at home, or in a counseling situation. This hands-on project allows kids of varied ages to use expressive arts while learning a concept and also have fun! The following lesson is an example of a downloadable project given with permission from NASA Climate Kids from the website http://climatekids.nasa.gov/make.

Lesson 1: NASA Climate Kids – Make a Terrarium Mini Garden

Credit: NASA/JPL-Caltech

A terrarium is like an aquarium, but for plants instead of fish. It is made in just about any glass container. It is planted to look like a miniature garden or forest enclosed in its own little world.

You can easily make a beautiful terrarium yourself.

First, you want all the plants to thrive in the same kind of environment. For example, you could plant all succulents (including cactus), because they need very little water. Or you could plant all ferns, because they like it moist. You could put moss with the ferns, because moss likes it moist too. If you put a fern with a cactus, one or the other might not do well (the fern if it gets too dry, the cactus if it gets too wet).

You can use an open container or a closed container. An open container is best for succulents and cacti. They like lots of air. A closed container (with a lid) might be best for ferns, ivies, and begonias. They like it humid. But if you see a lot of water condensing on the lid, remove it for a while, then replace it. For any terrarium, you need:

Materials

- Clear glass container. For example, aquarium of any size, goldfish bowl, cookie jar, pickle jar, vase with a broad bottom, brandy snifter, or even a shallow dish with a glass bowl turned upside down over it.
- Rocks (around marble sized, depending on the size of container).
- Activated charcoal to filter the water and help prevent growth of fungi.
- Potting soil (sterilized).
- Small plants of different colors, shapes, and textures. Try to get miniature plants that aren't going to grow too big for the container (optional).
- Moss.
- Decorative rocks or pebbles, or both.
- Fun decor, like tiny pinecones, shells, ceramic animals, or a garden gnome.

Make sure your glass container is clean and shiny. The layers of rock and soil are part of the beauty of your terrarium.

Instructions

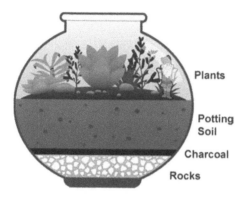

Figure 5.24 Plant.

Source: NASA/JPL-Caltech.

1. Start with a layer of rocks, about one inch or so, at the bottom of your container. These will help the soil drainage, so the roots of your plants won't get water-logged.
2. Add a 1/2-inch-thick layer of charcoal.
3. Fill the container up to half-full of potting soil.
4. Plant your plants. When you remove them from their little pots, carefully tease the roots apart and remove some of the old soil so they will fit nicely in the terrarium. Arrange them to look nice. Leave some space for them to breathe and grow. Pat down the soil so they don't get uprooted easily.
5. Add decorative pebbles, rocks, pinecones, or whatever to make your terrarium look like a little garden world.
6. Water the plants, but not too much.
7. Place in indirect light.

A terrarium holds warmth, just like the Earth's atmosphere. A terrarium has its own mini climate. The container has just a small opening or sometimes even a lid to completely enclose the container. That makes a terrarium like a greenhouse.

Figure 5.25 A Terrarium.
Source: NASA/JPL-Caltech.

Sunlight enters through glass and warms the air, soil, and plants the same way that sunlight coming through the atmosphere warms Earth's surface. The glass holds in some of the warmth, just as Earth's atmosphere does.

Lesson 2: Resource Provoking Activity: Mother Earth Thank You

Write a thank you note to Mother Earth. The following books can be used as motivators for a classroom discussion on climate change. The ideas can be modified for different age groups, and spark lively conversations about the climate, the environment, how kids feel, and what they can do.

Figure 5.26 Thank You Earth Cover, 2018
Source: Permission April Sayre.

Thank You Earth by April Pulley Sayre is a beautifully illustrated book that speaks to children about Mother Earth and motivates them to consider what they are thankful for. *Thank You Earth Cover* explains,

> Water, sun, light.
> Patterns, curves, shapes, colors.
> Things that crawl, fly, float, run, bloom, ripen.
> Think of everything Earth gives us.
> What are you most thankful for?

These words can motivate discussion in kindergarten through 12th grade. All students can easily discuss the virtues of planet Earth, writing or drawing age appropriate thank you messages. Mary, age 6, was thankful her plants were growing.

Author April Sayre suggests that kids share their thank you notes to the planet, because there is no mailbox for Mother Earth. She encourages them to communicate letters at school, to newspapers, and with community and national leaders. Then she offers ideas that young people can use to put their thank you notes into action.

Figure 5.27 Thankful Plants Grow.

Source: Photo by Jonathan Borba on Unsplash.

Lesson 3: Things to Help My World Discussion

This activity can lead to a new lesson for all ages about activities to help the world.

Another motivating resource for children is *10 Things I Can Do to Help My World* by Melanie Walsh. These activities include turning off the lights, feeding the birds, and throwing trash away.

Family activities such as composting, and planting seeds are also suggested. This book can spark lively discussion, encouraging kids to create new ways to help their world, share their ideas with others, and transform these ideas into action.

Other ideas for action include promoting no plastic straws in school or creating a campaign to recycle and compost in the community. A.J. Retaleato is a six-year-old who spent his summer cleaning up the environment. He spoke about his mission in this way "I want to clean the park; I feel bad for the Earth" (Smith, 2020, p. 29). Retaleato, with his dad, has cleaned nine parks and schools. He was even awarded a special citation for his service to the environment by his town. He sums up his personal reward in cleansing the planet in this way. "I don't want kids getting hurt on broken glass. And I like how clean it looks when I'm done."

Draw or Write the Following

The following questions can be modified according to age group and promote a safe and open discussion on climate change, the future, and what kids can do! This can lead to an action plan of ideas and events within the school and community.

What is your biggest worry about climate change?
What do you wish your teacher or parents would do?
What scares you about climate change? What makes you sad?
Do you have questions about climate change?
What can you do to help the environment be healthy?
Do you have a family plan to help the environment? Does your school have a plan?

The Importance of Climate Education in Schools

In an analysis of dozens of middle school and high school textbooks, we found that descriptions of climate change were superficial and contained errors; some did not discuss the topic at all.
–Klein and Preston, the Hechinger Report, 2020

In the United States, many of the textbooks used in classroom learning barely scratch the surface knowledge about the environment and the tremendous obstacles generations of kids will face on this issue of climate change. High school students have become an increasing force in climate change activism; in 2019, hundreds of thousands of young people skipped school and took to the streets to protest the climate crisis in a global strike in September 2020" (Klein et al., 2020). Chanting from demonstrators in New York City could be heard as they marched, "You had a future, and so should we. We vote next" (Sengupta, 2019).

On June 3, 2020, New Jersey became the first state in the nation to require that climate education be taught in all grades, K-12. This groundbreaking ruling went almost unnoticed between the pandemic and upheaval occurring in the country. Climate change will be taught in seven subject areas (Fallon, NewJersey.com, 2020) that include:

1. Twenty-first century life and careers
2. Comprehensive health and physical education
3. Science
4. Social studies
5. Technology
6. Visual and performing arts
7. World languages

This is empowering for students, parents, and educators to join in a dialogue that begins with early ages until graduation, with developmentally appropriate information and conversation at each grade level. New Jersey will be implementing teacher training and curriculum development that raised the bar for the rest of the states in America.

> At the same time, the connections between pollution, negative health impacts, and the zip code you are born into are clear – and are now even clearer for all to see. If these connections seemed hidden before, COVID-19's direct and disproportionate impacts on communities of color and low-income communities in close proximity to sources of pollution like power plants, incinerators, and industrial centers are being proven through peer-reviewed studies. Teaching these connections, in social studies, in technology, and in twenty-first century life and careers opens up incredible learning opportunities. (Schugarman, 2020)

Scott Fallon explains on www.NewJersey.com that New Jersey will not only be the first state to implement climate change into K-12 curriculum, but the new standards implemented September 2021 and 2022, will "offer a broad outline that will allow school districts to craft instruction based on why the planet is warming and what can be done to mitigate it" (2020). New Jersey has been heavily impacted by rising sea levels and extreme heat.

Generalizations about what is possible in the climate change curriculum for each grade level are presented. Younger children might incorporate ideas needed to improve plants, animals, and humans in terms of global warming around their school. Resources from NASA and other federal agencies can help middle school kids take action on the impact of climate change in their communities. Negative health effects from extreme heat can be a focus for high school students through scientific study and models of the impact of high temperatures (Fallon, 2020).

Governor Phil Murphy emphasized the importance of student learning about climate change in the following statement, "This generation of students will feel the effects of climate change more than any other, and it is critical that every student is provided an opportunity to study and understand the climate crisis through a comprehensive, interdisciplinary lens" (Fallon, 2020). A survey in 2019, IPSOS, found 80 percent of American parents and 90 percent of teachers supported climate change being taught in the schools. In Katherine Martinko's article in TreeHugger, Tammy Murphy, wife of Governor Phil Murphy, was an advocate for this curriculum development. She explains the new updates incorporating climate change will be "a partnership between generations" (2020).

The New Jersey Department of Education stated the new standards will provide students with the "knowledge and skills to succeed in our rapidly changing world." It recognizes students' desires to learn more about climate change, saying the updated curriculum will "leverage the passion students have shown for this critical issue and provide them opportunities to develop a deep understanding of the science behind the changes and to explore the solutions our world desperately needs" (Martinko, 2020).

Teaching UN Global Goals for Sustainable Development

We only have one planet. We have nowhere else to go. If we use our creative powers properly, we don't need anywhere else. If we take care of it, and each other, everything we need is right here.
                                    –Sir Ken Robinson, Global Goals, 2021

Global Goals for Sustainable Development were instituted by the United Nations and consist of the framework and the foundation for any lesson involving Climate Change. These goals are a part of the *World's Largest Lesson* (see Chapter 11) and include a downloadable printout of the 17 goals formulated by almost 200 countries to global care for the planet and people of and on Mother Earth. Here are the goals which can remain visible for students during a lesson.

1. No poverty	7. Renewable energy	13. Climate action
2. No hunger	8. Good jobs and economic growth	14. Life below water
3. Good health	9. Innovation and infrastructure	15. Life on land
4. Quality education	10. Reduced inequalities	16. Peace and justice
5. Gender equality	11. Sustainable cities and communities	17. Partnerships for goals
6. Clean water and sanitation	12. Responsible consumption	

Figure 5.28 Downloadable UN Sustainable Development Goals.

Source: "The content of this publication has not been approved by the United Nations and does not reflect the views of the United Nations or its officials or Member States." Link to UN Sustainable Development Goals https://www.un.org/sustainabledevelopment/.

The United Nations (UN) has created and partnered with others to provide resources for each developmental level children are growing up in. The first is titled *The Sustainable Developmental Goals 2017* written and published by the United Nations. With the simplest of pictures and words, it allows preschoolers exposed to the goals and creates a foundation of learning that can be built upon. The additional information provided for each goal allows children of every age to gain a basic understanding of the Global Goals.

This resource presents practical lessons for each goal in a way kids can become involved with meaningful activities. It details lessons for grade one through twelve in relationship to the UN Global Goals. The youngest kids can learn about the UN Goals through age-appropriate language and understandings. They build on this knowing throughout their educational development.

The second book by the United Nations, *Frieda Makes a Difference* 2019, continues to develop concepts about the UN Sustainable Development Goals for kids and what actions they can take as they grow older.

Frieda explains on page one that "these goals are part of a plan of action that world leaders agreed will make the world a better place by 2030 – The Goals call for all countries to help protect our planet." Throughout the storyline Frieda explains we all deserve to eat good foods and have proper medicine, and equality in all of our communities. She emphasized the right for everyone to have clean air, water, sanitation, and good jobs. "All people deserve a life of the highest quality" (United Nations, 2019, p. 28).

Frieda ends her journey with a request for kids to take action to help the planet. Recycle, reuse, and reduce are some suggestions. Advocating for fishes in the ocean and animals on land is important. Her final words for healing the planet are encouraging. "Everyone must work together to make the world much better for all" (United Nations, 2019, p. 42).

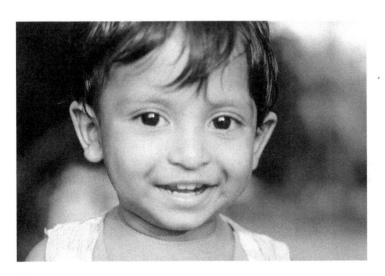

Figure 5.29 Teaching UN Goals Early.

Source: Photo by Iqram-O-dowla Shawon on Unsplash.

Teaching UN Goals to Third Grade

Third grade teacher, Timiny Berstrom, had student view the following videos to stimulate conversation about the UN Goals – What is The United Nations (UN)? Video We the People for Global Goals, Video 1 and 2, and Just a Kid Global Goals video as well as The World's Largest Lesson video (see Chapter 11).

This led to many stimulating discussions involving the goals, and together the class formulated responses to their Global Goals Chart. One third grader joined with an eighth grader to make posters for Goals 3, 4, and 7. The class brainstormed many projects they could do, including a clothing or art supply drive for recently resettled refugees in their town, a persuasive letter to legislatures and local businesses, and monetary donations to charities.

For middle and high school students Rebecca Sjonger has created a resource, *UN Sustainable Development Goals, Taking Action to End Poverty 2020.* In the chapter on Goal 6, clean water and sanitation, Sjonger explains to young readers that people living in poverty are also drinking water that is not clean, creating health issues and sometimes more death and disease. Challenges are presented that include cooking with polluted water and in some regions the shortage of rainfall limiting water supply. Lastly, is a resource for teachers to develop lessons within the structure of their curriculums to expand information and understanding about the *Global Goals: Empowering Students to Improve the World in Sixty Lessons* by Reimers et al. (2017).

Conclusion

Learning and education are no longer limited to a school building, especially when the learning involves climate change and nature. All generations need to exercise flexibility and innovativeness to reach beyond the school walls to enlarge ideas, engage businesses, reclaim communities, create green schoolyards, visit natural parks, and provide role models.

Expanding minds to include outdoor learning at the earliest of ages helps plants the seeds and cements the foundation for the intimate bond a child can experience with nature, the beauty of nature children can carry with them, and the commitment through loving nature to care for the planet and all that live on it.

> We need to recognize the outdoor classroom that exists throughout time in our natural environment, waiting for enough people to appreciate the abundance of learning it holds for all of us.

Figure 5.30 Inspire Children.

Source: Photo by Taylor Smith on Unsplash.

6 Mindfulness and Meditation: Stress Reduction, Yoga, School Gardens, Nature

Mindfulness helps us to come back to the here and now, to be aware of what is going on in the present moment, and to be in touch with the wonders of life.

–Hanh, Thich Nhat 2008, p. 7[1]

Figure 6.1 Yoga.

Source: HLF. All photos and materials pertaining to Holistic Life Foundation (HLF) are adapted with permission from the HLF website www.holisticlifefoundation.org.

DOI: 10.4324/9781003051770-8

Mindfulness is the combination of awareness, centering, and being present. It is the awareness of your thoughts, emotions, actions, and energy. It is the ability to get centered and stay centered in all situations. And it is the ability to be present, not letting internal and external distractions take you from the current moment. This leads to the development of empathy, compassion, love, balance, and harmony.

–The Holistic Life Foundation Website HLF

Figure 6.2 Meditation.
Source: HLF.

This definition of mindfulness is shared on Holistic Life Foundation (HLF) website, with a suggestion for all to read, hear, and embrace. The following information and photos are adapted with permission from HLF website www.holisticlifefoundation.org.

Introduction: Holistic Life Foundation Program

The Holistic Life Foundation (HLF) empowers communities through a comprehensive approach to develop the inner lives of children through yoga, mindfulness, and self-care practices. It is a Baltimore-based non-profit organization committed to nurturing the wellness of children and adults in underserved communities, and is deeply committed to learning, community, and stewardship of the environment, providing a high-quality evidence-based programs and curriculum to improve community well-being. For kids to be able to deal with stressful events in their life, self-regulation skills and coping mechanism are required.

Youngsters are faced with stressful events for which self-regulation skills can prove helpful. These childhood stresses include anxiety, fear, and depression surrounding climate change. This community does not have direct access to a green environment, which can be very important for a child's stress reduction (see Chapter 10: Benefits of Green Schoolyards). The practical techniques discussed by the HLF, in this chapter, and other initiatives can assuredly reduce challenging feelings related to the environment and support resilience and hope.

Holistic Me: Robert W. Coleman Elementary School Mindful School Program

The Holistic Life Foundation after school program, Holistic Me, was piloted in 2002 at Windsor Hills Elementary School. Now it is facilitated at Robert W. Coleman Elementary School. The program serves over 100 students from grades Pre-K through fifth grade. This multifaceted after school program incorporates many enrichment activities such as woodworking, environmental projects, team building, art and entrepreneurship, basketball, martial arts, dance, and steel drums.

Students in Holistic Me benefit and grow in many ways from their participation. They learn a combination of yoga, mindfulness practices, meditation, centering, and breath work that empower them with skills for peaceful conflict resolution, improved focus and concentration, greater control and awareness of thoughts and emotions, improved self-regulation, anger management, as well as stress reduction and relaxation. In the fitness and sports fundamentals portion of the program, students learn the fundamental sports skills as well as learning exercises and skills for overall fitness, developing teamwork and leadership skills, and building the foundation for leading a healthy lifestyle.

Students learn about their interconnectedness to the entire world and not just their neighborhood in the environmental education program. Learning the importance of stewardship, environmental justice and sustainability, students see how the environment impacts them and vice versa. Students also receive supplemental instruction in their core classes including math, language arts, and science through homework assistance and one-on-one tutoring.

Holistic Me maintains an 85 percent average attendance. Students who have graduated out of the program into the Holistic Life Foundation Mentoring Program come back to volunteer as tutors and yoga instructors. The students planned and facilitated several community cleanups, set up greening projects in their homes, and constructed a raised-bed vegetable garden at their school (see Chapter 10).

They love the children, they love the community, and they are an asset to Robert W. Coleman. There are some children who have anger management problems. The yoga program has enabled those children to do meditation techniques and instead of them reacting and getting angry, they've learned how to meditate and redirect their anger.

–Carlillian Thompson Principal, Robert W. Coleman
Elementary School

Students made a bulletin board explaining why they practice mindfulness. It was displayed in the hall at their school and titled, "We Practice Mindfulness Because." Each child displayed their picture and the reason why they practiced mindfulness. Here is what some students said.

Meditation calms me down and stuff.
–4th grade girl

Figure 6.3 Calm.
Source: HLF.

When I first started, I was kinda bad...now the breathing has calmed me down.

–7th grade boy

I learned how to control myself doing yoga.
–2nd grade boy

It's like karma. If I do something bad like punch somebody in the jaw, something bad is gonna happen to me. But if I do something good, good stuff will happen.

–5th grade boy

Figure 6.4 Control.
Source: HLF.

Figure 6.5 Breathe.
Source: HLF.

The program has helped me because now I know different routines and exercises that I can do at home that helps me lower and reduce my stress. So, whenever I get stressed out, I can just do a pose and sometimes I can show my mother and my family.

–4th grade girl

The most important thing I learned in the program is that it's all different ways to deal with your stress instead of like fighting and stuff.
–5th grade boy

It helps you relieve stress when you really feel stressed out or you're really mad and focus on what's inside of you and just make sure that you stay calm.
–5th grade girl

Figure 6.6 Pose.
Source: HLF.

Mindful Moment

The Robert Coleman School is an elementary school in an urban setting in Baltimore City. The school has incorporated the Mindful Moment program as an integral part of the day of a student. The Mindful Moment recording is played twice daily at about eight am and two pm. Staff members are present in a classroom for the duration of the 15-minute practice making sure that student engagement is high. Each staff member has three or four assigned classes that they are responsible for visiting daily and give two engagement scores daily to each class weekly.

These engagement scores are also used to acknowledge classes that have outstanding participation, through the weekly presentation of "Mindful Masters'" trophies. For these purposes, classes have been split into three groups using an engagement score tracking chart. Average scores are also calculated over the year to determine the winners of the end of the year Mindful Masters' party.

Students became increasingly competent in the practices used during the Mindful Moment. They easily applied these practices when asked to do so during the day.

Figure 6.7 Mindful Masters.
Source: HLF.

Classroom Visits

During the morning periods after the morning mindful moment to the beginning of the first yoga classes at 11 am, staff members visit their assigned classes to check in with students who teachers and administrators have identifies as needing special attention, and otherwise support teachers in the classroom. Examples of staff duties during this time include:

- Checking in with students for signs of emotional issues early in the day
- Removing students who are upset or otherwise disruptive out of class for brief conversation and mindfulness practices
- Helping to integrate mindfulness practices into student's daily, in-class experiences
- Assisting teachers with classes while embodying the core concepts of mindfulness

Implementing these classroom visits noticeably reduced referrals to the Mindful Moment, suggesting early morning interventions and staff visits have helped prevent later issues.

Mindful Moment Room

This room serves as a cool down or calm down room for children who are upset, or otherwise disruptive in class. Teachers and other staff refer students to the room, and students can self-refer with permission of their supervising adult.

Once brought to the Mindful Moment room, students are taken through centering practices such as belly breathing and the bell game to help them deescalate emotionally. The Mindful Moment staff engages students in dialogue about the incident that led to the referral, emphasizing the emotions the student is feeling. Finally, staff and students develop a plan to help use mindfulness technique to address similar situations in the future or to reset emotionally to continue with the day. These visits are usually 20 minutes but can be longer if needed.

Students usually show visible signs of emotional de-escalation after guided practice in the Mindful Moment room. Teachers and staff continue to bring children to this room, commonly referred to as the "calm down" room. This is a first step when dealing with upset or disruptive students, a visible endorsement to the value of this service.

Daily Yoga Classes

Throughout the year, three 45-minute yoga classes a day, five days a week are taught. These classes take place in the school library, and each of the schools 15 classes attends one yoga class a week. The structure of these classes centers on breath practice, special breathing techniques, Asana (pose) practice, and concluding with silent reflection.

During these classes "mindful masters" are identified as students who demonstrate high engagement. They are then allowed to practice in front of the class on their own yoga mats. This serves as an incentive for students to remain engaged throughout the class and encourages leadership behavior.

Occasionally there are special activities that are considered a reward for getting through class with high participation. An example of this is "pizza pose" where students use a yoga pose, straddle forward bend, and their imaginations to make a pizza step by step. These interactive exercises are especially useful with younger classes from Pre-K through second grade.

Mindful Moment Program: Patterson Park High School

Patterson High School is a comprehensive community high school with over 1,000 students, grades nine through 12. Patterson has a very diverse student population, which includes students from a variety of ethnic groups and backgrounds. Most of today's students are challenged with an unparallel amount of stress and anxiety. According to the National Institute of Mental Health (2017), over 31 percent of adolescents ages 13–18 had experienced an anxiety disorder.

Mindful Moment Room

The Mindful Moment room is an oasis of calm that is always available during the day. Students can self-refer to the Mindful Moment room, or teachers may send distressed or disruptive students for individual assistance with emotional self-regulation. Holistic Life Foundation

Figure 6.8 Mindful Moment Room.
Source: HLF.

Workforce Development participants staff the room, some who are graduates of the Holistic Me afterschool program.

Partnerships have been formed with the school social workers, nurse, and school psychologists who often refer students to the Mindful Moment room regularly for assistance with anxiety, stress, headaches, stomach issues, or emotional distress.

When a student enters the Mindful Moment room, they sign in the visitor log and are assigned a mindfulness instructor. Many students have built relationships with these instructors and may request a specific instructor who is already familiar with them or their situation. The structure adopted for best practice for handling student referrals has been five minutes of targeted discussion, and 15 minutes of mindfulness practice.

The mindfulness practice is chosen based on the needs of the student at the time of referral or by student request. Most often students are led through a series of breathing exercises, but some scenarios may call for yoga. After 20 minutes in the Mindful Moment room, students are given a pass to return to their class. On occasion, students are kept longer depending on the severity of their situation.

Full Classes

To foster a culture of mindfulness within Patterson High School the staff began offering 60–90-minute mindfulness classes. Initially this was offered to a teacher with a particularly difficult and rowdy class to give them the opportunity to bring their class into the Mindful Moment room for an introductory class in mindfulness as a concept and practice. The overwhelming responses to these classes were positive, and then these classes were offered to everyone.

The full classes gave students tools and skills for peaceful conflict resolution, improved focus and concentration, greater control and awareness of thoughts and emotions, improved self-regulation, as well as stress reduction and relaxation. The curriculum for these classes is based on yoga, meditation, breathing, tai-chi, centering, and other mindfulness techniques. Through these classes and increased awareness of mindfulness as a practice, the culture of Patterson has changed noticeably. Students who have attended full classes report that they have used the techniques to help with sleep regulation at home, anxiety before testing, self-regulation, and conflict resolution.

Mindful Moment Effectiveness

The Mindful Moment program has demonstrated its effectiveness in supporting social and emotional well-being and academic performance. Demonstrated impacts at Patterson Park High School included:

- Suspensions for fighting dropped from 49 in the 2012–2013 school year to 23 in the 2013–2014 school year.
- Students in the halls were referred to the Mindful Moment room, this helped reduce suspensions in the hallways and stairwells from 62 in the 2012–2013 school year to 35 in the 2013–2014 school year.
- Students getting into verbal or physical altercations in the classroom were referred to the Mindful Moment room, this helped reduce suspensions in the classroom from 36 in the 2012–2013 school year to 17 in the 2013–2014 school year.
- The attendance rate went up from 71.3 percent in the 2012–2013 school year to 74.2 percent in the 2013–2014 school year.
- The number of ninth graders being promoted to the tenth grade increased from 45 percent in the 2012–2013 school year to 64 percent in the 2013–2014 school year.

Ambassador Training

The Mindfulness Ambassador Training Initiative began in December 2014. The purpose of this initiative was to progressively train students to be able to lead Mindful Moment, build a confident mindful ambassador through encouragement and training, teach students to lead the Mindful Moment under guidance of staff, encourage ambassadors to lead the Mindful Moment alone consistently, and foster a student-led culture of mindfulness within Patterson High School.

Mindful Moment Ambassadors as well as staff partnered with Patterson for Peace in Violence Prevention Week. Ambassadors began tracking their own engagement within their first period class. Efforts began to focus on the ninth-grade classes and ambassadors joined staff in visiting ninth grade classes to model the practice as the Mindful Moment recording played in the morning. Ambassadors led faculty in breath work and meditation within their faculty meeting. When tracking attendance and progress reports for ambassadors, most ambassadors had either maintained their grade level or increased their grades.

Environmental Programs

The Holistic Life Foundations Environmental programs focus on education and advocacy. These programs provide students with opportunities to increase their knowledge and awareness of the Chesapeake Bay watershed as well as the larger global environment. Then, that knowledge is used to show the interrelatedness and interconnectedness of the entire global environment, to expand students' outlook from the neighborhood level to the biosphere level.

Youth participating in Holistic Life Foundation environmental programs have facilitated community cleanups, growing community vegetable gardens, building a park on a vacant lot, constructing worm-composting bins, and coordinating recycling programs.

Students testified in front of the Baltimore City Council in support of the Baltimore City Sustainability Plan and received Presidential

Figure 6.9 Planting.

Source: HLF.

Environmental Youth Awards for outstanding youth environmental stewardship from President Obama. Kids participated in Earth Day tree plantings, as well as other environmental activities. They also attend environmentally themed field trips, as well as go hiking and camping.

Holistic Me Community Garden

The Holistic Me after School program created and managed two raised bed community gardens at Robert W. Coleman Elementary School. Many of the children in urban communities are disconnected from nature and this initiative is meeting that need (see Chapter 10).

Figure 6.10 The Garden.
Source: HLF.

One little girl was proud of her drawing. She explained, "I love the Earth."

Figure 6.11 I Love the Earth.
Source: HLF.

Vernal Pool Hike

For the past four years the Holistic Life Foundation annually has taken participants from its Holistic Me and mentoring programs to Big Gunpowder Falls in Monkton, Maryland. This allows children to connect to a habitat filled with tadpoles, frogs, salamanders, and insects that they would not encounter in their urban environment.

Children seem to become more and more enthusiastic with each visit and anticipate the experience. This project was supported and made possible by the Natural History Society of Maryland.

Figure 6.12 Connect to Nature.
Source: HLF.

Research on Mindfulness

Understanding the Population

Growing up in urban communities, such as East or West Baltimore, that are characterized by having few resources, high rates of unemployment, homelessness, and crime, there exists a population of traumatized students. Living in urban poverty brings increased exposure to crime and violence, particularly for adolescents. A growing body of research has documented those children and adolescents who grow up in low-income neighborhoods do less well on a range of developmental outcomes, social, emotional, and cognitive.

Traumatic and stressful experiences, which may range from major life events like abuse and divorce, to chronic interpersonal stress such as ongoing family conflict to daily challenges that could include money for transportation or school supplies, have been established as risk factors for a range of psychological problems. The risk of academic failure, school-dropout, internalizing as well as externalizing psychological problems, school bullying, and aggression in response to the exposure of traumatizing events is significantly higher to youth growing up in low-income neighborhoods. Even though urban youth have an increased risk of suffering from psychological problems, they are less likely to receive help. To be able to deal with such stressful events, self-regulation skills, coping mechanism are required. Each day, children living these stressful events need regulation skills to help them cope.

Positive Outcomes for Youth at Risk

Contemplative exercises such as mindfulness, meditation, breathing exercises, and yoga are tools young at-risk kids can acquire, use, and share in school, and continue to practice them throughout their lifetime. The field of research on contemplative practices, such as mindfulness and yoga, is growing rapidly. Interventions targeting several areas suggest many positive promising effects that include resiliency and optimism, self-worth, social competence, and pro-social behaviors, reducing stress and increasing executive function such as increased focus and emotional regulation. All these positive outcomes from mindfulness programs lead to improved academic success and less punitive issues in school.

Dr. Marilyn Wedge states in *Psychology Today 2018* that "there are seven evidence-based ways that kids can benefit from mindfulness techniques." Wedge explains that "because mindfulness can promote skills that are controlled in the prefrontal cortex of the brain, like the ability to focus and concentrate, it is especially useful for children" (2018). The following benefits from practicing mindfulness are adapted from the Wedge article:

1. Gives kids the habit of focusing on the present and ignoring distraction
2. Teaches calmness in the face of stressful times
3. Creates good habits for the future – meditating when faced with a life challenge
4. Promotes happiness by lowering stress and anxiety
5. Fosters patience
6. Improves executive function in the brain by improving cognitive control, memory, and thus achieving better grades
7. Improves attentiveness and impulse control

In 2014, the Erickson Institute had received a multimillion-dollar grant which they used to create the Calm Classroom Program, a mindfulness-based program that creates a Calm Spot in school (Sirola, 2019). Calm Spots are safe places within a school where students can go to calm themselves and renew their emotions and focus by watching and listening to videos about nature and animals. The study done by the Institute included two thousand students from kindergarten through second grade. The Erickson Institute focused on kids growing up in low-income families, with an understanding of the long-term stress they may feel growing up in poverty. Often these kids have a higher percentage of acting out in school with emotional outbursts, tantrums, or defiance, resulting in punishment and even expulsion. With 15 minutes of daily classroom mindfulness sessions, educators report less angry, emotional explosions, and suspensions.

On April 30, 2015, after the Baltimore riots, Holistic Life Foundation planned an event for the entire community that included a meditation and open discussions about the anger and frustration the community felt and how, as a community, they can work together to redirect that energy into positive goals. Again in 2016, when Baltimore was threatened with more community violence, Patterson High School stepped up its mindfulness game with 15 minutes of breathing exercise and meditation instruction each morning for all the students over the school intercom. Baynard Woods (2016) states that Baltimore City had reached over 300 murders and 1,000 non-fatal shootings by the end of 2015.

"Inhale all the love the universe has to offer ... and exhale anything that doesn't benefit you." This was the instruction given a high school class. Principal Vance Benton explained,

> The program is intended to help students cope with the prevalence of death, violence, and turmoil in their lives... When you look at our children and you compare their situations every day, they feel like it could be their last day. Every day they feel like they may have to take some else's life if it came to it. Every day they are dealing with a close friend or comrade or family member that is killed senselessly. (Woods, 2016)

Benton reveals most of the students are African American or Latino, and many are immigrants that have escaped from disaster in other countries, and he likens their life in Baltimore to the experience of soldiers at war.

The Mindfulness Curriculum: Research and Outcomes

The Holistic Life Foundation has created, developed, and piloted a 24-week mindfulness curriculum, based on the structure of their successful after-school program. The curriculum empowers students with tools and skills for peaceful conflict resolution, improved focus and concentration, greater control and awareness of thoughts and emotions, improved self-regulation, as well as stress reduction and relaxation. The curriculum is based on yoga, meditation, breathing, tai-chi, centering, and other mindfulness techniques. The curriculum consists of two sessions per week each lasting 40- minutes and taking place during resource periods.

Sessions begin with a brief centering exercise, then yoga and tai-chi exercises, followed by breathing, then a discussion on a selected topic, and ending with a meditation. Participants are given assignments between sessions to reinforce lessons.

The Holistic Life Foundation has partnered with The Johns Hopkins Bloomberg School of Public Health and The Prevention Research Center at Pennsylvania State University to facilitate a randomized control study on the curriculum in four Baltimore City Public Schools. This was also the first ever-randomized controlled trial of a school-based mindfulness and yoga intervention for urban youth. Preliminary results a have been obtained and a scientific paper by Mendelsohn et al., October 2010, was published in the *Journal of Abnormal Child Psychology*.

The curriculum was studied, with the same partners, as a part of a larger, three year, federally funded trial in six public elementary and middle schools in Baltimore City. Findings from the study showed that students participating had a positive impact on problematic responses to stress, including rumination, intrusive thoughts, and emotional arousal. Participants also showed a reduction in involuntary stress reactions, which leads to improved social, emotional, and behavioral development.

Mendelson et al. (2010) maintain in their research that underserved urban youth often experience a very high degree of stress, trauma, and relational challenges, resulting in poor academics and behavioral difficulties. Using a 12-week intervention they assessed the acceptability and outcomes of a school-based mindfulness and yoga program with fourth and fifth graders. These interventions were well liked by students, teachers, and administrations who found they created a positive impact on otherwise problematic student response to stress that would have previously created greater emotional arousal and intrusive thoughts. Mendelson et al. conclude that "mindfulness based approaches may improve adjustment among chronically stressed and disadvantaged youth by enhancing self-regulatory capacities" (p. 1).

Mendelson's 2010 of HLF Stress Reduction and Mindfulness Curriculum showed that implementing the curriculum in the school context was attractive to students, teachers, and school administrators. Positive effects were observed on problematic behaviors, including rumination, intrusive thoughts, and emotional arousal. A qualitative assessment with middle school students following our intervention showed experiences in improved impulse control and emotional regulation.

Angela Haupt confirms in her 2016 article that mindfulness in schools is essential, emphasizing meditation can replace detention. She presents the discussion that breathing, and movement exercises, and quiet time not only belong in the classroom but that they are paramount tools for learning and well-being. The Mindful Moment room at the Robert W. Coleman Elementary School models a safe and inviting space for kids to practice breathing, meditation, and talk about their feelings in a protected and comfortable environment of pretty colors, inviting chairs, herbal tea, and soft scents. This room becomes a positive alternative to punishment and detention, by equipping students with techniques to strengthen coping with stressful situations, resolve conflicts, and maintain an ability to nurture themselves and their peers.

"You see kids dealing with a lot of anger and frustration that they were taking out on their peers physically, and now they're able to manage that anger," says Ali Smith, cofounder of the Holistic Life Foundation.

> They can feel anger rising, and they say, "OK, this is what anger feels like, and I can choose to express that anger or to re-center myself and get back to that place of inner peace and calm." Because once they learn it, that's something no one can ever take away from them. (Haupt, 2016)

A Reciprocal Model is used by The Holistic Life Foundation that extends mindfulness practices in the classroom to outside of the classroom. Smith explains that some students become leaders may eventually become staffers. "And that's a cool way to get the practice out into the neighborhoods."

> If we can't reach everybody, the kids can. They get empowered by it because they understand how and when to use it, and a lot of them use it with their parents and the people in their neighborhoods. With the kids being young teachers, they're able to go home and affect everyone around them. (Haupt, 2016)

Discipline Reduction

In too many schools throughout the country emotional outbursts, aggressive behaviors, and defiance are met with punishment, detention, suspension, and shaming. Other reactions to acting out could be extra work and loss of special activities like art and recess. In Denver's Doull Elementary School, the implementation of assigning an after-school activity of yoga is a new by-product to misbehaving. Doull's version of "alternative discipline is part of the school's embrace of social-emotional learning and is emblematic of the growing trend of K-12 schools to cultivate school environments that are attuned to the social and emotional well-being of children" (Jones, 2019).

Before they can be assigned a yoga class for a behavior, their teacher will address the situation that occurred and then send the child to the schools "cool down room" where the child can practice breathing techniques and talk to a caring staff member about their feelings. Many kids wanted to join the yoga club after school. The interest was so great that the principal added an extra yoga club day for those children who wanted yoga as a club activity. Principal Carrigan explained, "What we love about yoga is that they (students) leave with some actual skills that can help them in life" (Jones, 2019).

> Yoga helped me to deal with my issues using positive ways instead of going back to my old ways of handling things.
>
> –Holistic Life Foundation Student

Figure 6.13 Yoga Helped Handle Things.
Source: HLF.

Mindfulness Practices for Young People

Mindfulness is a powerful tool for children and adults. Quieting the mind, remaining in the present, and relaxing the body can only serve our young ones during extreme planetary stressful events, involving climate change, a pandemic, and disruptive politics.

These external challenges amplify difficult conditions at home, such as loss of income, heightened anger, abrupt school changes, and quarantine confinement. Girls and boys can learn to practice loving kindness each morning or before bed by saying the follow for themselves and others.

A Living Kindness Practice

> *May I be safe*
> *May I be free of feeling scared*
> *May I be happy.*

May my body be healthy and strong.
May I feel peaceful inside.
May I be thankful for help.
And may I feel love in my heart for
myself and for other people in my life.
May all beings everywhere be happy.
–Adapted from Carter, 9/10/2020 &
Ruth Berlin, 2021

Figure 6.14 Lovingkindness.
Source: HLF.

Carter (2012) explains kids can be invited to also give living kindness to someone they feel thankful for, someone they feel neutral toward, and someone they are having a hard time with like a school bully. They can end their practice by sending love to all these people and wishing happiness for everyone.

Cognitive Defusion

Steven Handel discusses cognitive defusion, acceptance, and commitment therapy (ACT) as an avenue that supports reducing anxiety in young people by creating distance from troublesome thoughts. In Acceptance and Commitment Therapy (ACT) mindfulness-based tools help kids to manage their thought. Cognitive defusion is a part of the ACT techniques used. Handel defines cognitive delusion as, "the process of accepting our thought while at the same time distancing ourselves from them and not clinging to them" (2018). He relays metaphors that help children detach from their thoughts to create a feeling of well-being. They help kids to distance from thoughts, recognize they may not really be a part of them, and diffuse their power. The following metaphors are adapted from Handel's *Seven Metaphors for Cognitive Defusion*, 2018.

Clouds in the sky. Pretend the sky is your mind, and the clouds are just thoughts that float by.

River stream. The mind is a river and thoughts flow.

Passenger on the bus. Visualize yourself being a bus driver and the passengers are your thoughts. You can stop and let passengers on and off the bus and the kids are in control.

Suggestion box. The mind is now a suggestion box, but we don't always have to accept the thoughts that go in. They are just suggestions, and we have the power to say yes or no to them.

Destroying your thoughts. There is great power in writing down negative thoughts and then tearing them up in a safe place, symbolic of dissolving negativity and empowering transformation.

Feeding the wolves. This is a well-known parable about two wolves that live inside all of us. One is light and hope, the other is darkness and anger. Ask kids, which wolf do you want to feed. That's the one that will grow.

Imagery

Another mindfulness technique is the use of imagery. Ruth Berlin, a skilled and empathetic therapist, created an imagery that can be used with young people. Ruth calls this original process "My Theater." Children envision a theatre where they can see their life drama on the screen. Sometimes young people cannot see the forest through the trees. That might be what the first row feels like. In this row it is usually difficult to see the stage because it is so close up it hurts your neck. It is too loud and scary, and too overwhelming to even pay attention. Youngsters become blind to understanding the drama. We can ask them to describe what the front row feels like and decide if they want to move or stay.

Kids can move back row by row in their mind to see a more realistic view that holds less attachment and more ability to solve a problem. The further they move their seat, the greater wisdom and perspective they attain. The middle rows are less personal and more objective. There are 100 rows in this theatre, and kids need to find the right threshold for themselves. The 100th row is very distanced, enabling a child to view their drama from a keenly impersonal position to move away from a very toxic experience. As they travel and change seats in this imagery of watching their drama at a theatre, they are gaining the ability to move from the very personal to the very impersonal.

Tapping

Kindergarteners at Chatsworth Elementary School in New York had learned the technique of tapping to begin the day in a calm way.

In Liz Slade's class, a student mindful leader was chosen and came to the head of the class. She began tapping her thumb on each of her fingers and repeating, "I am calm now." Her peers did the same. Then the children took out their feelings journal. Slade explained, "They are learning the experience of settling their body. What used to be a wild time now becomes a charming, sweet moment when we all take a pause and come back to being present" (Gerszberg, 2021).

Teachers are very aware of a student's inability to focus and control their impulsivity. Slade explains one little girl in her class seemed ready to knock over a building made by a classmate. She watched the girl begin to knock the blocks down but took a very deep breath and walked away instead. "The kids can learn to notice distraction, self-regulate, and ask themselves, 'What do I need?'" (Gerszberg, 2021).

Movement

When I first began teaching second grade in 1968, not many people were practicing yoga nor had they even heard of it. I found myself loving yoga and wanting to incorporate it into the classroom. I had a classroom of 22 second grade repeaters with emotional, social, and learning issues. We began a journey of yoga movement using a children's resource, *Be a Bird, Be a Frog, Be a Tree* (1973) by Rachel Carr. Children would pick an image from the book and become it in a yoga pose, and the rest of the class would follow suit.

Sometimes when children got restless, we would stop the lesson, stand up, and begin to do a few of their favorite yoga postures together. It settled their emotions and helped them become more focused to begin learning.

Figure 6.15 Yoga Pose.
Source: HLF.

The Silent Sigh

Gerszberg maintains the Silent Sigh is a technique that works well in school. Sighing can be an expression of relief, disappointment, sadness, hopelessness, or exhaustion. The Silent Sigh is intentional way to release big emotions and retune the body and breath, bringing students into the present during times of transition. The quietness of the silent sigh can happen in a classroom when classmates are not even aware of someone using this practice to stabilize themselves. Just taking a deep, deep breath in silence and then breathing it out slowly helps kids to regulate and shift their mood and energy (Gerszberg, 2021).

Breathing

Breathing is the very foundation of mindfulness in the classroom as it allows students to reset their emotions in a calm way. Christopher Willard explains that breathing can be used to create more focus and silence. "Resetting the breath with a deliberate practice can regulate, shift, and stabilize energy and mood" (2016). The 7–11 breath is an easy and popular way to have children bring themselves into the present, especially if they feel panic, rage, or sadness with any emotional struggle. Students easily breathe in for seven counts and out for eleven counts. Beginning with five breaths at a time, kids learn to exhale longer than inhale. It helps to raise the energy and relax the nervous system.

Resources on Life's Meaning

Children of all ages can benefit by the resource, *The Three Questions* (Muth, 2002). This is a storybook that has a young boy ask his animal friends the following questions: When is the best time to do things? Who is the most important one? What is the right thing to do? The old turtle Leo explains the only important time is now, the most important person is always the one you are with, and the most important thing is to do good for the one who is standing at your side.

The response to a child seeking answers for the meaning of life places all the answers in the present, remembering who you are with and how important each person is. The wisdom of the three questions and responses can serve as a fertile ground for discussion on the meaning of life, the quest for inner peace, and the mindfulness practice of living in the present.

The following is a list of resources that can be used in the classroom and at home. They are simple, yet effective in their presentation of the ideas about mindfulness, empathy, and compassion that kids can learn easily. The resources also include apps for stories before bedtime, visualizations, guided meditations, and mindfulness practices.

Resources for Mindfulness and Life Meaning

Books for Kids

Hadessa, Maria, & Ekere Tallie. (2019). *Laylas's happiness*. New York: Enchanted Lion Books. Ages 5–10.

McGhee, Holly. (2017). *Come with me*. New York: G.P. Putnam's Sons. Ages 5–10.

McGhee, Holly. (2019). *Listen*. New York: Roaring Brook Press. Ages 5–10.

Meiners, Cheri. (2013). *Be confident!* Minneapolis, MN: Free Spirit Press. Ages 4–8.

Meiners, Cheri. (2013). *Be positive.* Minneapolis, MN: Free Spirit Press. Ages 4–8.

Meiners, Cheri. (2014). *Bounce back*. Minneapolis, MN: Free Spirit Press. Ages 4–8.

Muth, Jon. (2002). *The three questions* (Based on a Story by Leo Tolstoy). New York: Scholastic Press. All ages.

Hanh, Thich Nhat (2008). *Mindful Moments: Ten Exercises for Well-Being*. Berkeley, California: Parallax Press. All ages.

Hanh, Thich Nhat (2012). *A Handful of Quiet*. Berkeley, CA: Plum Blossom Books. All ages.

Apps for Kids

Headspace – breathing, visualizations ages 6–8 and 9–12.

Calm Kids Features – sleep stories for bedtime.

Breathe, Think, Do with Sesame Street – bilingual app (English and Spanish), ages 2–5.

Mindful Family – guided meditations for the whole family (four years and older).

Smiling Mind – classroom friendly practices, ages 3 and up.

Dreamy Kid Meditation – guided journeys and sleep stories, ages 3–17.

Mindful Powers – guided meditation, ages 7–10 (Courtney Sullivan, 2020).

Conclusion

Mindfulness is the awareness that emerges through paying attention on purpose, in the present moment, non-judgmentally.
–Jon Kabat Zinn (Gerszberg, 2021)

In conclusion, research and practical experience supports the paradigm that stress related techniques acquired and reinforced in school are powerful engines for self-love and empathy for others. Studies confirm children improve behavior, reduce stress, increase attentional capacity, progress in academics, and even sleep.

Meditation, breathing techniques, yoga, and guided imagery are a few of the many tools that students acquire though a mindfulness school program. These techniques become allies and friends to youth experiencing trauma. This model serves climate justice challenges found in underserved, low-income, urban environments without nature to commune with, without gardens to grow food, and without a safety net to escape the abuse, violence, or death that surround them.

Principal Vance Benton of Patterson High School underscores this idea about his students.

> When they're under situations outside the school building, sometimes difficult situations, hopefully, they will be able to take a breath, reconsider, and possibly walk away from death... And when I say walk away from death, that means either death themselves or them killing someone based on a situation that exploded. (Sreenivasan, 2017)

Mindfulness in school is an innovative model for achieving student success instead of shaming, isolating, or punishing. Reduction in detentions, suspensions, and aggression are documented by many school systems working with mindfulness as a part of their day. Replacing detention with a mindfulness option in response to emotional overwhelm can become a key transformation in the school environmental climate.

Creating urban school gardens helps reduce environmental injustice by providing a space to enjoy nature, clean the environment, and grow food. Whether it be yoga, deep breathing, planting, or enjoying in a nature walk, students can acquire techniques that quiet their mind and body as they learn to be present and focused.

Seven-year-old Anthony experienced nightly temper tantrums followed by nightmares. He began to learn these meditation and mindfulness techniques in his classroom. One night Anthony surprisingly said to his father as a reoccurring tantrum was brewing, "Daddy, let's do some mindful breathing that I learned at school."

For a few minutes they breathed together and then Anthony hugged his dad and said, "I love you Daddy." Anthony had transitioned his school learning to home and successfully regulated his emotions and de-escalated overwhelming feelings with a loving result.

Note

1 Hanh, Thich Nhat Moments of Mindfulness, Parallax Press 2013.

Figure 6.16 I love you Daddy.
Source: Permission Jon Goldman.

Part III

The Goal

Transformation for a
Healthy Planet

7 Globally Inspired Projects: Parachutes for the Planet, Fridays For Future, Global Youth Strike, Climate Live, Global Coordination

Humanity is now standing at a crossroads. We must now decide which path we want to take. How do we want the future living conditions for all living species to be like?

–Greta Thunberg, Extinction Rebellion in London,
Eco-age, April 2019

Figure 7.1 Parachute for the Planet.
Source: Permission Mother Earth Project MEP.

DOI: 10.4324/9781003051770-10

Parachutes serve as the global visual language for committing to sustainable actions. They bridge communities and countries with a common goal, to live more sustainably and to demand better climate laws.

–Barton Rubenstein, Mother Earth Project (MEP) Cofounder

Figure 7.2 Parachutes around the World.

Source: MEP.

All images and materials from Parachutes for the Planet adapted with permission from the Mother Earth Project (MEP) https://mother earthproject.org/parachutes/.

Introduction

I am beginning this chapter with the project, Parachutes for the Planet, because of its simplicity and ability to seamlessly reach out to young people and gain participation throughout the globe. This project lays the foundation for understanding climate change in a comfortable, enjoyable way needed to promote action to help serve the environment. Ari Rubenstein is a youth activist highlighted in Chapter 8 and cofounder of the Parachutes. He stated in a January 2019 interview, "There is a very fine line between educating the ignorance of the public that might be unaware of facts and discouraging young people not to join activities because of peer pressure or judgement." The Parachutes project is a gentle way to invite kids to participate.

Ari wants everyone to understand this parachute program is the "glue" that can bind many youths to become involved in a global community by expressing feelings and sharing ideas about Mother Earth. Ari invites everyone to join in a community conversation as parachutes are being developed in schools and other programs. Young students from Charlotte, North Carolina, are decorating their community parachute in Figure 7.3 while they share ideas.

Figure 7.3 Building Dialogue.
Source: MEP.

In this way, kids' bond with others, creating a common goal of making a parachute together. Then they display it for all to see.

This chapter progresses in a gradual development of action-based experiences for young people. Another exciting program inviting a global response is Climate Live. This is a music program geared to climate change that is open to the entirety of planet Earth.

Next on the ladder of climbing activism is the movement, No Future, No Children, where young people have joined together and decided the environment is not safe to have children grow up in. The Sunrise Movement is a youth-based California movement that meets with public officials for action on climate issues. Fridays for Action, Global Action Strike is highlighted as an urgent global action to transform minds and hearts on climate change.

These movements provide youth involvement from kindergarten through college, creating the opportunity for kids to become a part of the worldwide solution. The landscape for participation is boundless and can range from drawing a picture to protesting at the nation's capital.

Parachutes for the Planet

Parachutes for the Planet is a part of the climate revolution happening now throughout the world. Barton and Ari Rubenstein, cofounders of Parachutes for the Planet, had previously initiated the Mother Earth Project, an idea to raise awareness and make a difference for the planet. The parachute program became a mechanism to expand the Mother Earth Project to the next level, by unifying young and old alike to unite for a healthy environment.

Communities are encouraged to begin their own parachute collection for future climate demonstration events worldwide. Children decorate parachutes with writing and artwork that exemplifies feelings and concerns about climate change. The following are ideas expressed by students on their school parachutes about recycling and trash collection. They also participated in active advocacy with political leaders and displayed parachutes to create awareness of climate challenges.

Figure 7.4 Recycle Plastic.
Source: MEP.

Figure 7.5 Trash.
Source: MEP.

One child drew an idea on her parachute, "Recycle plastic, live fantastic!!" Another little boy posted the following suggestion on his parachute: "Adopt a city block and keep it clean weekly (I do) and you will clean an average of 3 TONS of trash yearly."

Figure 7.6 Youth for Climate Law.
Source: MEP.

Young people organized meetings with local politicians with parachutes to focus on attaining better climate laws. This figure shows high school students sharing their parachute with US Senator Van Hollen to encourage better climate laws.

Youth activists post on social media. They also display parachutes in the community to increase awareness of climate change for the people living there. These parachutes were displayed in Washington DC with the message, "Transform Our World."

Figure 7.7 Parachute Display.
Source: MEP.

Examples of sustainable action in the community inspired by the project include a student organized campaign for Indianapolis restaurants to phase out plastic straws. The students at Indianapolis Public School 913 organized a Zero Waste Program. In Indianapolis, Mayor Joe Hogsett proclaimed June 21 as "Dump the Pump Day" in Indianapolis. This holiday was designed to encourage the use of public transportation, biking, or walking, instead of using a car.

National Involvement

The following are examples from some of the hundreds of United States parachutes and those from other countries globally whereby children and teens have participated in the project. There are over 36,000 thousand parachutes now displayed worldwide. Youngsters have been given voice to fears, sadness, hope, and activism through the media of art and words on these parachutes. Kids and families are contributing to a planetary movement by joining together to heal the planet when and where they can.

Salem High School, 2018, The Environmental Club New Jersey.

The young people in Salem High School Environmental Club have visually created a platform for saving many species on the planet by the artwork on the parachute.

Figure 7.8 Salem High School.
Source: MEP.

Figure 7.9 Save the Birds.
Source: MEP.

High School International Baccalaureate, Salem New Jersey 11th Grade

The motto for this International Baccalaureate Program is clearly expressed on their parachute. Preserve – Conserve – Protect. Preserving wildlife, conserving energy, and protecting species are paramount for this group.

Figure 7.10 Preserve-Conserve-Protect.

Source: MEP.

Native American Parachute

The following is the Native American Collaborative Inter-Tribal Parachute in Santa Ana California. This vibrant parachute was a part of the Road for Climate Action trip. As the parachute traveled across the country, each tribe added their own messages regarding environmental issues and action they would like to convey. The Acjachemen Nation hoped for everyone to pray for healing Earth and honoring water (Figure 7.11).

The parachute began its journey at Chief Lookinghorse's World Peace and Prayer Day, a sacred three-day gathering in Southern California, June

Figure 7.11 Prayer for Healing the Earth.

Source: MEP.

2018. Then it was worked on by other local tribes, the Acjachemen Nation and the Southern Cal Indian Center, journeying to the Las Vegas Indian Center, the Paiute of Southern Utah in Cedar City, the Denver Indian Center, two Lakota tribes (Oglala and Rosebud), the Seneca Nation in NY, and concluding with a two-day pow wow in Massachusetts. It is the only cross-county inter-tribal collaborative parachute.

This parachute was then carried across the country by On the Road for Climate Action, a scientist/educator team traveling through over 36 states advocating for climate solutions. On August 1, 2018, the journey began in California in a low-emission vehicle. The team traveled east through the great plains, New England, Florida, and then back to California in an 11-week trip.

Along the way, the Parachute and the On the Road for Climate Change team visited different communities to speak with city councils, community groups, and college campuses on the important issue of climate change and solutions. They engaged in door-to-door activity and administered a climate survey aimed to assess climate sentiment around the country and how it differs by region, with hopes to use this data to develop effective strategies of climate communication.

A pinnacle of their voyage was a visit to Capitol Hill, where they welcome fellow citizens to join them in meeting with members of Congress – "A Day of Congressional Climate Action!"

This is a very special cross-country collaborative, inter-tribal youth project that was initially presented at the conclusion of World Peace and Prayer Day, a special ceremony dedicated to peace and harmony among all living beings as well as gathering in prayer for the healing of our Earth.

Sunnyvale Parachute

Younger children have voices too! Elementary school children shared feelings about the environment. In Sunnyvale, kids decorated their parachute as part of the Parachutes for the Planet activity. Each dot on the parachute represents a child's feelings.

Bring your bags home and do not use plastic bags.

Teach kids about climate change and eating vegan.

Use less electricity and pick up more trash that I find.

My dot is that I will always turn off the lights when I leave the room.

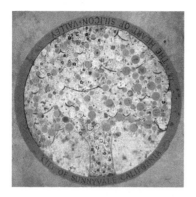

Figure 7.12 Sunnyvale Parachute.
Source: MEP.

Figure 7.13 Save the Bees. Be Nice to the Animals.
Source: MEP.

Figure 7.14 Don't Throw Trash in the Water Because an Animal Could Eat It and Die.

Source: MEP.

Girl Scout Troops #3602 Cabin John Maryland

The sixth-grade middle school girl scout troop in Bethesda, Maryland at Pyle middle school contributed a parachute to the Mother Earth Project. The parachute's artwork expresses feelings about lowering the use of fossil fuels and looking to see what is being destroyed in nature.

Figure 7.15 Look What You Are Killing.

Source: MEP.

Climate Camp

Earth Charter Indiana exists to inspire and advance sustainable, just, and peaceful living in Indiana by promoting the values and principles of the Earth Charter. The Earth Charter is a declaration of fundamental ethical principles for building a just, sustainable, and peaceful global society.

Figure 7.16 Climate Camp.
Source: MEP.

Company Overview Earth Charter Indiana cofounders John Gibson and Jerry King have been friends and collaborators on Indianapolis neighborhood projects for nearly two decades, including a Climate Camp for young people. In 2001, they teamed up to convene a community assessment of the Earth Charter; an assessment which led to the formation of a new nonprofit organization that would promote the Charter's integrated approach to sustainable community development.

Kindergarten Class of Cesar E. Chavez Elementary School: Oregon, United States

The following are two letters from kindergarten teachers, Lynn Bridge and Erica Dunn, at Cesar E. Chavez Elementary School in Oregon. They express activities that these preschoolers participate in to create a love of nature and a respect for Mother Earth. They compost, plant flowers, and use sustainable materials. The involvement of the children is palpable as is their excitement in joining with others for the parachute project.

Hello World,

We were happy to participate in the parachute activity. We work as a whole class to recycle properly, and limit/properly use the resources we are privileged to have at school.

We recently planted sunflower seeds as a learning about gardening and life cycles project. In Science we have learned about trees and worms. We draw and learn in our school garden. Sincerely,

Mrs. Lynn Bridge's Kindergarteners

Another kindergarten teacher, Erica Dunn, explains her students' involvement in climate change and the parachute project as follows,

My students had an absolute blast participating in parachutes for the planet! We compost all our food waste at our school, and we are a green school, so this was an excellent way to highlight. And talk about the ways that our students are working to take care of the earth every day. We have been collecting cans to plant flowers in for Mother's Day instead of buying plastic or cardboard pots in

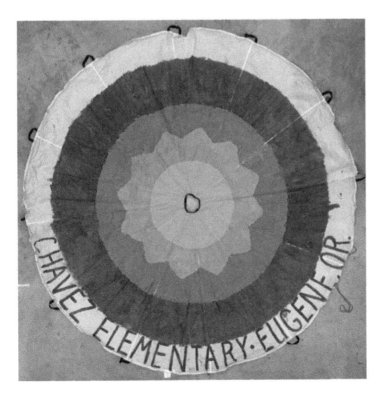

Figure 7.17 Chavez Elementary.
Source: MEP.

an effort to recycle and use more sustainable materials. We chose to participate to have another way to highlight how important it is to take care of the Earth with our young learners.

This school and 39 others in Eugene Oregon's School District 4 J created 40 parachutes in 2018, which were sent to our headquarters and were displayed on the National Mall and at the US Capitol during climate strikes. They were the first large contribution to our collection and gave the Parachutes for The Planet project its original burst of energy. Tana Shepard was the school official responsible for activating this project in Eugene.

International Involvement

Sierra Leone Vocational Agricultural Secondary School

The vocational agricultural secondary school in Sierra Leone felt it was important to share in their artwork on their parachutes and requested they do more parachutes in other areas of Sierra Leone to create a greater understanding throughout the country for World Environment Day (June 5th). They offered to create national exhibition to catch the attention of the new government and invite media houses. They were excited that this was the first time Sierra Lone had hosted a program like this. Part of the artwork on their parachute emphasized environmental concerns in their country. One important message posted on their parachute was a plea to stop building houses under the mountains and stop taking sharks teeth.

Shandong China

Mary Klug was a facilitator for the Pachamama Alliance. She brought the symposium, The Awakening the Dreamer (ATD) to China. The ATD symposium was given on July 7th in Dezhou, Shandong, China. Mary explained, "The purpose of the ATD Symposium is to bring forth an environmentally sustainable, socially just, and spiritually fulfilling human presence on our planet." Mary came back from China with this parachute made by a kindergarten and Pachamama Alliance attendees.

The Parachute has delicately placed drawings of sunflower and hands. In the drawing, intertwined with nature are the words "Thanks My Home!"

Figure 7.18 China Parachute.
Source: MEP.

Nigeria Secondary School Parachute

Figure 7.19 Nigeria Parachute.
Source: MEP.

Panama City: Pope Comes to Panama City and Takes Parachutes to the Vatican

Founder Bart Rubenstein explains, "Sustainable actions bring communities together in intimate ways that are unexpected." This was personified in the Pope's visit to Panama City in January 2019 for the World Youth Pilgrimage. Many Catholic parish schools were given parachutes to decorate for the planet. Over 40 decorated parachutes were displayed that January. These parachutes were displayed during the final Pope gathering with 15,000 volunteers inside the stadium (Permission Mother Earth Project). The Pope took one parachute decorated with a large hand and handprints back to the Vatican. He declared a Climate Emergency for the Catholic Faith soon after his trip, sending a powerful message to over one billion followers. The parachutes could have been a catalyst to bring about this strong declaration.

Figure 7.20 Parachutes and the Pope.
Source: MEP.

Rosemont Elementary School British Columbia

Judy Betts, a retired teacher and volunteer with Citizens' Climate Lobby, went to Rosemont Elementary School to help students contribute to Parachutes for the Planet. Betts said the kindergarten to fifth grade students surprised her by how much they already knew about climate change. "Unfortunately, I do get kids who say to me, 'I'm scared.' I find that a hard thing to address," she said.

Because it is scary. 2030 is when these Grade one students will graduate, and that's when we're supposed to have met the carbon emission standards as written out in the Paris Accord. I sure hope we make it. I don't know. Their feedback is a curiosity about the planet. I hope a deeper appreciation of the need to take care of the planet as well. (Planet's website)

The four parachutes made at Rosemont are each divided by elemental themes – earth, fire, water, and air – and include students' messages about how to protect each element. Betts said the parachutes were displayed locally before being taken to Victoria along with approximately 30 more locally made parachutes. There they then were laid out on the grounds of the provincial legislature.

Nelson British Columbia Community

This parachute was made in Nelson, British Columbia at a lakeside local park in 2019. Children and their parents, aunts, or grandparents sat alongside each other to contribute, create, and share in conversation about what makes a healthy planet.

The parachute then went to Victoria British Columbia with a local Climate Change lobby group. The children shared the following sentiments of so many young activists – as it reads on the parachute.

Figure 7.21 Nelson British Columbia.
Source: MEP.

When the last tree has been cut down,

When the last fish has been caught,

The last river poisoned,

Only then will we realize that one cannot eat money.

Concerts Launch: Climate Life for 2021

Can you hear us yet?
–Leaders of Climate Live, 2021

The following is adapted from the press release about the worldwide project, Climate Live. Dominque Pastor is one of the spokespersons for this huge event. She is an activist highlighted in Chapter 8.

On April 24, 2021, simultaneous youth-led global climate concerts in 43 countries will be held on April 24, 2021, by members of FridaysForFuture youth climate groups. Many in these groups have organized the global school strikes, and now they are bringing artists, activists, and scientists to the global stage to fight for climate justice.

In September 2019, 7.6 million young people in over 7,000 cities across the world took to the streets to demand climate action. Yet many youths felt disappointed that leaders had still failed to act with the necessary urgency required.

Thus, Climate Live was created. It is a movement to harness the universal language of music and use the power of music to unite people.

Music Goals for Climate Change

The goals for using music as a catalyst for change are the following:

1 *Engage:* Enlarge the global movement by engaging a new audience through music.
2 *Educate:* Raise awareness of the challenges faced by people on the frontlines of ecological breakdown, as well as those forecast by scientists for the future.
3 *Empower:* Pressure world leaders to take action to combat the climate crisis with a focus on the UN Climate Change Conference (COP26) in Glasgow on November 2021.

A top priority for each concert is planning with sustainability. Professionals, venues, artists and local authorities are working together with Climate Live to strive to make the events as sustainable as possible. "The race to safeguard the future of this planet has begun, so now we must come together." Explains Climate Live. Activist Greta Thunberg reminds everyone that, "To change everything, we need everyone."

Frances Fox, 19, from the United Kingdom, is the founder of Climate Live. Frances explains on the press release (2021) that,

> I started *Climate Live* in the spring of 2019, after being inspired by an interview in which Brian May said there should be a Live Aid for the climate crisis. I thought this was a brilliant idea to engage more young people in the movement, with our own spin, so immediately started messaging activists from all over the world!

Leaders of Climate Live are hoping audiences attending Climate Live Concert will leave with a newfound feeling of empowerment, accompanied with tools to engage in the climate movement. 2021 is a key year for climate action. Climate Live initiators feel they have exactly one year until the UN COP26 conference, when governments will have to renew their Paris Agreement pledges. Therefore, their concerts call for these to be more ambitious in line with necessary 1.5°C targets. As climate activists they have listened to the science and then treat every crisis as a crisis. Each participating country is planning concerts adhering to social distancing guidelines and essential contingency plans.

Our major question to world leaders is – "Can you hear us yet?"

Climate Live Leaders Speak Out

Many climate activists have voiced their concerns and future goals and are hopeful these concerts will embolden young people to speak out and take action. They feel it is an opportunity for young people across the world to have their voice heard. Here are their voices, their hopes, and their frustrations.

Christiana Figueres, former executive secretary of the United Nations Framework Convention on Climate Change (UNFCCC), who played a key role in the 2015 Paris Agreement, stated:

> There is no doubt that young people, informed by science, have brought the climate crisis to the attention of leaders from all sectors. It is now our generation's responsibility to protect what we love from the damages of climate change by following up on promises with the necessary actions in this decade, to fulfil the goals of the Paris Agreement. I applaud our brilliant young people for stepping up again to hold leaders to account in the lead up to COP26 in 2021, when countries must come together to show we are on track for a resilient future. Our young people have asked whether we can hear

them. It is time to demonstrate that we are truly listening. (Climate Live Press Release 2021 with permission)

The following are statements by participants in Climate Live with permission. *"*Time is running out for the planet as we know it. We must act now if we're going to save it. The youth activists who are standing up need help and those with a voice have a responsibility to use it."

–Joe Seaward, Glass Animals artist

We have just experienced four typhoons in the span of a month. I had to sit in the dark without electricity, not able to go home because the roads to our house were flooded up to the second floor of houses. This is the climate crisis; this is why we need action. We are the second most vulnerable country to the impacts of the climate crisis in the world. It's a scary thing and we desperately need more people out on the streets if we want to see change. Climate Live is the perfect way to do that.

–Mitzi Jonelle Tan, 23, The Philippines

Climate Live is beyond just music. The climate crisis isn't just an issue of the far-off future, it is today, and we are experiencing the impacts right now. We need to act now.

–Kevin Mtai, 24, Kenya, Founder of Kenya Environmental
Activists Network

Climate Live will give a voice to those most affected by climate change and to the millions of young people concerned about the future of our planet.

–Timi Barabas, 17, New Zealand

Climate Live is critical in a time when the climate crisis has become less prominent in the public eye.

–Andrea Manning, 22, USA

Hope is in the people, in the movement, which is getting bigger and bigger, but we need more people, and Climate Live is the opportunity for this to happen.

–Nicole Becker, 19, Argentina

Creating Movements

The Global Youth Climate Strike took place on September 20, 2019. It was the largest global demonstration ever in the fight against climate change. This truly global event was inspired by activist Greta Thunberg and her group FridaysForFuture. Young people throughout the planet organized to skip school and protest in their countries over what they feel is a

Figure 7.22 Strike for Change.
Source: MEP.

threatening climate crisis, inspired by their disappointment that adults are not doing enough to transition off of fossil fuels.

Youth were joined by caring adults and companies such as Amazon and Google to amass a population of citizens demonstrating for change.

No Future, No Children

A movement of young activists taking a more personal approach to climate changed by that refusing to have kids until there is action on climate change. Some children have also taken more personal approaches. The "#NoFutureNoChildren" movement was begun by Canadian Emma Lim, 18, on an issue that impacts many young people very personally. Participants pledge not to have children until the government takes serious action against climate change. Emma explains, "I am giving up my chance of having a family because I will only have children if I know I can keep them safe," she says on her website. "It breaks my heart, but I created this pledge because I know I am not alone... We've read the science, and now we're pleading with our government" (Miller, 2019). Fifteen hundred young people signed the pledge that week.

The Sunrise Movement

The Sunrise Movement is a California youth group that met with Senator Dianne Feinstein about climate policies. At 29, Alexandria Ocasio-Cortez of New York is the youngest representative in Congress. She is vigorously moving climate issues included in the "Green New Deal" to the forefront. Andrew Winston suggests "we are in the middle of a major re-alignment of values around climate. It is now unacceptable to young activists and the millions of people they inspire, to espouse climate denial or play the "let's go slow" card. They don't appreciate being handed a disaster movie for them to live with for 70 or 80 years. Winston encourages companies to listen to these advocates as the tide is changing and our young people are profoundly dedicated to make change with climate, especially in policies for today and the future. Winston maintains,

> It might take the youngest Americans to get companies to take a real and public stand for aggressive global action on climate change, after all, if they don't, they risk getting out of step with an entire generation of employees and customers. (2019)

Zero Hour (adapted from the ZEROHOUR Website http://thisiszerohour. org/our-platform/)

Zero Hour was birthed by a group of young people who were frustrated by the inaction of elected officials on climate change. Jamie Margolin, Nadia Nazar, Madelaine Tew, and Anagee Artis gathered with several friends to organize against being ignored and make a difference through action. Their vision is to act on climate change, "holding adults and elected officials accountable for their legacy of destruction...We believe in harnessing the power of youth-led organizing and leadership" (Zero Hour website, 2021). The Zero Hour platform "specifies the need for climate justice, including equity, racial justice, and economic justice." Their platform was carefully prepared after reviewing the requirements in the Our Children's Trust. Jamie is one of 13 plaintiffs suing Washington State for not acting on climate change (see Chapter 11). Jamie also wrote *Youth to Power: Your Voice and How to Use It* (2020) whereby she describes how young people can act to protect planet Earth.

Global Day of Action

These young Americans challenging business and government policies on climate change were strikingly present on the path to action. Thousands of students took to the streets throughout the world to boldly voice their concerns, refusing to go to school one day a week. Their goal was to draw attention to the magnitude of fearful issues facing this generation about climate change. The Global Day of Action was March 15, 2019. Teenagers were represented in locations ranging from Chile, Canada, and Iran to the United States.

Berrigan (2019) characterizes these kids on strike in America in the following way.

This clarion call comes from teenagers, the crew we characterize here in America as eye-rolling creatures suspended in a helpless state of consumerism, hyper-sexualization, and crushing academic pressure. Of course, there are kids in the streets and assembling at congressional offices for climate change and a host of other issues here, too.

With the overwhelming and complex layers of issues these youth face daily, their perseverance to move forward with the creation of a healthy planet for themselves, others, and the environment is palpable.

Mark Hertsguaard (2011) calls these girls and boys *Generation Hot*. "Some two billion young people, all of whom have grown up under global warming and are fated to spend the rest of their lives confronting its mounting impacts." Berrigan (2019) maintains too many adults have a denial reflex about climate change. Her article voices concern for her two young children and teenager and for all children as well. She initially wondered if talking to kids about climate change would unnecessarily worry them, but as she watched the future generation flood city streets to make a statement to their elders, she decided families need to learn information together. In this way, the family is united in the fight against climate change and in the preparation for a different future. Berrigan concludes, "We need to live collectively, not just individually, as if the planet matters." And it does.

One sign summed up the perceived inaction and priorities of government reading, "If the climate was a bank, you would have saved it already!"

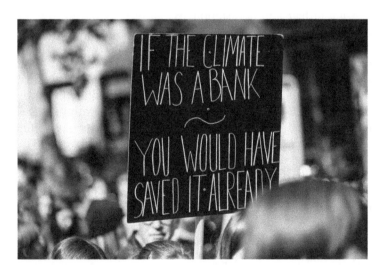

Figure 7.23 If Climate Was a Bank.
Photo by Markus Spiske on Unsplash

The Youth Strike for Action Movement: FridaysForFuture

Swedish activist Greta Thunberg put a face on the global movement to fight climate change and become a global environmental visionary. Skipping school on Fridays as a protest to the inaction on climate change, led to a Global Climate Strike (https://globalclimatestrike.net). This event emerged from a groundswell of worry on the part of young people and evolved into a movement to strike Friday attendance at school as a protest about the future survival of the planet. This is a youth created movement in a global cooperative effort to inspire transformation.

The Youth Strikes for Climate Movement is a tremendously growing crusade involving school students across the world united in demanding action on climate change. The striking students engaged with FridaysFor Future.org had registered over 500 events throughout 51 countries. These students skipped school on March 15 to make their voices heard. They issued an adamant open later which began with the following: "We are going to change the fate of humanity, whether you like it or not." *The Guardian* published this letter with the following,

> United we will rise on 15 March 2019 and many times after until we see climate justice. We demand the world's decision makers take responsibility and solve this crisis. You have failed us in the past. [But] the youth of this world has started to move, and we will not rest again.

The letter continues, "We are the voiceless future of humanity ... we will not accept a life in fear and devastation. We have the right to live our dreams and hopes."

Participants from over 150 countries inspired 2,500 events around the world. Youth activists from Afghanistan, Australia, Bangladesh, Indonesia, China, Chile, El Salvador, France, Germany, the United States, and many more countries stood in protest of the failure to act by adults to help the health of the planet. They carried signs with messages of fear, depression, and hope that merged with one voice to say young people want to be heard in supporting a healthy and safe world. The following are examples of messages on posters from protesting youth worldwide. The similarity of purpose and resolve that these global initiators expressed that day is an indicator to adults and peers that this movement is united, cohesive, diverse, and energized.

Australia – "How you live today will affect my entire future."

Bangladesh – "There is no planet B."

Greece – "No one is too small to make a difference."

Japan – "Save the earth."

Nigeria – "Youth rise for climatejustice."

Philippines – "Cancel all mining and logging companies! Save the earth."

Poland – "The end is near. My future is in your hands."

South Africa – "Say no to air pollution." "You will die of old age. Your kids will die of climate change."

Kiev Ukraine – "Protect our Earth Yes. No."

United Kingdom – "We speak forthe trees."

(Resnick & Scruggs, 2019)

Parachute and ArtsForClimate supporting #FridaysforFuture was presented for senior secondary schools in Abuja, FCT. The following flyer explained their activism and demand for change. Parachute and art would be displayed for public viewing with dates and times and information for contacts. This project was powered in part by the Mother Earth Project.

Figure 7.24 Abuja.

Source: MEP.

The poster reads as follows:

We demand that our local leaders commit to building a fossil free Africa that puts people and justice before profits. Africa must follow the Climate Vulnerable Forum pledge made by sixteen African governments in November 2016 to accelerate the transition toward an economy powered by 100% renewables.

Youth activist Leah Namugerwa (see Chapter 8) explains in the following Instagram post, the urgency and bravery of her activism, and her dedication, resilience, and commitment to keeping her work alive and moving it forward through FridaysForFuture.

Figure 7.25 Leah and FridaysForFuture.
Source: MEP.

"In three weeks I'll be making 100 weeks of #schoolstrike4climate. My climate activism journey hasn't been smooth. It involved arrests, intimidation, police blocking, mocking, racial abuse, and some injustices."

Instead of getting discouraged, I've got more courage to fight on.
(Leah Namugerwa Instagram Post, December 21, 2020)

Young people are exhibiting an urgency that appears far greater than the impatience of youth. In their own words they feel compelled to save the planet. Our youth have gone far beyond mainstream complacency, and now strive to create a new environmental world one step at a time. They seem determined to build a better, if not brand-new world. They fear the old world of adults has disappeared, and the denial to act on scientific fact now makes their pleas for help often vacant to meaningful change.

The Letter: Global Coordination Group Youth Led Climate Strike

For people under 18 in most countries, the only democratic right we have is to demonstrate. We don't have representation...To study for a future that will not exist, that does not make sense.

–Jonas Kampus, a Swiss 17-year-old student activist
(*The Guardian*, 2019)

Seventeen-year-old Swiss Activist Jonas Kampus was one of the 150 students in a coordinating group that created this letter, along with Swedish activist Greta Thunberg and 17-year-old English activist Anna Taylor. The letter not only speaks to truth for these young warriors, but also legitimizes this movement as being a global phenomenon. The strikes would not end, Taylor said, until "environmental protection is put as politicians' top priority, over everything else. Young people are cooperating now, but governments are not cooperating anywhere near as much as they should." *The Guardian* itself explains to its readership that on planet Earth, "We've never had a better chance to make a greener world" (2019).

Student activists felt betrayed by an older generation that lives in climate denial vacuum and will not acknowledge children are deeply concerned, sometimes to the point of depression and anxiety, about their future being dimmer than preceding generations. These youth promoted protesters state their views are being ignored. The following is an open letter published by *The Guardian* (March 1, 2019) in its entirety, written by *the global co-ordination group of the youth-led climate strike.*

We, the young, are deeply concerned about our future. Humanity is currently causing the sixth mass extinction of species and the global climate system is at the brink of a catastrophic crisis. It is devastating impacts are already felt by millions of people around the globe. Yet we are far from reaching the goals of the Paris agreement.

Young people make up more than half of the global population. Our generation grew up with the climate crisis and we will have to deal with it for the rest of our lives. Despite that fact, most of us are not included in the local and global decision-making process. *We are the voiceless future of humanity.*

We will no longer accept this injustice. We demand justice for all past, current, and future victims of the climate crisis, and so we are rising up. Thousands of us have taken to the streets in the past current and future victims of the climate crisis, and so we are rising up. Thousands of us have taken to the streets in the past weeks all around the world. Now we will make our voices heard. On 15 March, we will protest on every continent.

We finally need to treat the climate crisis as a crisis. It is the biggest threat in human history, and we will not accept the world's decision-makers' inaction that threatens our entire civilization. We will not accept a life in fear and devastation. We have the right to live our dreams and hopes. Climate Change is already happening. People did die, are dying and will die because of it, but we can and will stop this madness.

We, the young, have started to move. We are going to change the fate of humanity, whether you like it or not. United we will rise until we see climate justice. We demand the world's decision-makers take responsibility and solve this crisis.

You have failed us in the past. If you continue failing us in the future, we, the young people, will make change happen by ourselves. The youth of this world has started to move, and we will not rest again.
–The global coordination group of the youth-led climate strike 2019

Figure 7.26 Global Coordination.

Source: Photo with permission John Hillegass.

8   Youth Activists for the Environment

We are striking because we have done our homework and they have not.
                                    –Greta Thunberg, 2018 TEDx speech

Figure 8.1 What Can You Do?

Source: Photo by Markus Spiske on Unsplash.

DOI: 10.4324/9781003051770-11

> *When it comes to one of the biggest global problems, the default message from older generations to younger ones is silence.*
> –Kamenetz, 2019, p. 3.

Introduction

Young people feel the urgency to speak out for their health and the health of the planet. They are frustrated, enraged, and disappointed in politicians, educators, and parents who appear disinterested in the subject, uneducated in the Earth's happenings, and ill-informed and uncaring about how to take part in promoting well-being. Their silence is deafening, and their apathy unconscionable. The fear of adults not caring about the future, the apprehension that there will not be a future, and the anger that this generation feels they shoulder the burden for change drive our young people to speak out and act.

And a Child Shall Lead the Way...

This chapter highlights the ability of young people to commit to weekly sustainable actions at home, school, community, and planet. Examples of these actions may be planting trees, sharing the Parachutes for The Planet project with other schools and clubs (see Chapter 7), changing light bulbs to LED, picking up ten pieces of trash daily on the streets, switching to renewable energy, asking restaurants to change their plastic cups to paper, composting food scraps, and using bicycles more. There are many actions youngsters can do to support a healthy environment.

With this background of unrest so eloquently stated by youth activists in the previous chapter, we clearly see the urgency for action and hear soundly the plea for help in order to move forward for the welfare of the planet and all of its inhabitants. Young people throughout the world are rising to the present moment to educate, model, protest, strike, and persevere in passionate pleas and fervent movements to make this world we live in and on better for ourselves, each other, and the planet. Among the many youths exercising immense energy and determination are the following leaders of their generation.

In this chapter, young people like Luna and Aria work for climate change in their homes, schools, and communities. Other representative youths are soaring to the heights of speaking out for Mother Earth and creating movements. They are Greta Thunberg, Ari Rubenstein, Jerome Foster II, Licypriya Kangujam, Leah Namugerwa, and Dominique Palmer highlighted in this chapter. There are many, many more kids of all ages working equally as hard to lovingly care for our planet. These highlighted activists serve as role models and pioneers leading the way to a better Earth for themselves and their future selves.

Greta Thunberg: 17-Year-Old Swedish Activist

Greta Thunberg is a young activist from Sweden that has transformed the climate change movement, inspiring young people to give voice to their planet and their future. Greta, a teenager with autism, speaks with great eloquence and honesty about the concerns her generation faces about the future of the planet and those who live on it.

Figure 8.2 Greta for President.

Source: Photo by Markus Spiske on Unsplash.

Greta's words have touched the minds and hearts of kids, parents, and political and spiritual leaders throughout the world. Some even carried posters of "Greta for President." Greta Thunberg was part of the global coordination group and furthered her message by speaking to many nations, including the United Nations. Greta began the School Strike for Climate protests and has achieved celebrity recognition placing her on the cover of the *Time* magazine, December 2019, as the young face of the Climate Change Movement. Millions of school age children and adults across the nation and around the world join Greta in demanding politicians, corporations, and governments to create change through action by promoting #fridaysforfuture. Greta spoke passionately to the United Nations and sparked young people to do the impossible ... change minds to movement on climate change. Greta inspired the Friday Climate Strike on September 20, 2019 (#fridaysforfuture). Over seven million people joined the climate strike #weekforfuture, becoming one of the biggest global demonstrations in history.

Greta serves as an inspiring pioneer and folk hero for her generation. Her panic and urgency to heal the environment has motivated a groundswell of youth to join her work that has been recognized for a Nobel Peace Prize. "Greta's protest, all alone, sparked a worldwide children's march. Her quiet voice, joined by thousands of voices, became a roar" (Winter, 2019). Greta is a trailblazer for her generation and a leader in terms of advocacy for youth on climate change issues. She openly shares she has been diagnosed with Asperger's and Obsessive-Compulsive Disorder (OCD). At her young age she was persistent in speaking out for climate change to world leaders and youth as well. She began by engaging her parents in the battle to save the planet, convincing them to only use an electric car and eat vegetarian. Then Greta moved forward to the rest of the world, leading a sit out in Stockholm Sweden in 2018 in front of parliament. Every day for two weeks during school time, Greta sat with her sign reading "School Strike for Climate." She insisted Sweden reduce carbon emissions in line with the Paris Agreement. Greta quickly rose to popularity on social media, and instantaneously became world renown for her deliberate strike on prevailing norms for climate change. Soon she was joined by millions of climate change activists which included a significant part of our younger generation. Her global strike on May 24, 2018, engaged 1.8 billion participants residing in over 100 countries.

The following is a glimpse at Greta's resounding voice in the years 2018 and 2019 that has inspired a generation of climate activists. She has met the Pope, assembled almost five million dedicated followers on Instagram and Facebook (Davies, 2019), and won the GQ "Game Changer of the Year" award. Greta spoke at her TEDx Stockholm Sweden 2018, COP24 (24th Conference of the Parties to the United Nations Framework Convention on Climate Change), Poland, December 2018; World Economic Forum, Davos, Switzerland, January 2019; EU Parliament, Brussels, April 2019; Extinction Rebellion Non-violent Protest against climate change breakdown, London, UK, April 2019; House of Parliament, London, UK, April 2019; R20 Austrian World Summit, Vienna, May 2019; UN Climate Change Summit NY, September 2019; the US Congress, Washington DC, September 201; and the COP@% Madrid, December 2019.

Best of all, Greta is revered by followers as a mentor, role model, and voice for her generation. Several of the activists in this chapter stated Greta was their role model, and Licpriya, Ari, Leah, and Jerome have shared activities with Greta. Many of Greta's words are highlighted throughout the book because she has become the spokesperson for her generation. Here are a few inspiring quotes by Greta Thunberg.

> *This is the year 2019. This is not the time and place for dreams. This is the time to wake up. This is a moment in history where we need to be wide awake.*
> –US Congress, Washington DC, September 2019 (Davies, 2019)

For way too long, the politicians and the people in power have gotten away with not doing anything to fight the climate crisis and ecological crisis. But we will make sure that they will not get away with it any longer.
–Extinction Rebellion, UK April 2019 (Davies, 2019)

You say you love your children above all else and yet you are stealing their future in front of their very eyes.
–COP24, December 2018 (www.eco-age.com)

Since our leader are behaving like children, we will have to take the responsibility they should have taken long ago.
–COP 224, December 2018 (www.eco-age.com)

Ari Rubenstien

Ari Rubenstein is a high school student and cofounder of Parachutes for the Planet, which began with the Mother Earth Project. Ari began his activism at age 12. He explained it began as a family project that evolved into a global, international community. The goal was to create one powerfully large voice of young people speaking out for the health and well-being of the environment. Ari explained that "hope comes through action. We strike every week to educate and activate change." The following ideas explain the objectives Ari strives to balance and achieve in his activism throughout every field of study. These three objectives include:

1. *Striking* with middle school students and young adults to get their voices heard.
2. *Lobbying* to politicians to create change in government policies.
3. *Physical work* with frontline communities to combat challenges and create positive future plans for the environment.

Ari was thoughtful when asked the question, "What is the hardest for you about your commitment to activism for the planet. "Burnout," he responded. "I get frustrated, angry, and have less time for school work. I wish parents understood it is OK to tell kids to take breaks, sometimes do nothing to refresh our minds – it gives us more energy."

Part of Ari's activism is motivated by his perseverance and his strong will not to be complacent, and dissolve complacency in those around him. Sometimes peers can be frustrating, watching them waste food or refuse to recycle. "The best way for peers to be on board is to engage them in simple ideas and activities. Attacking them only pushes them away" (Interview, 2020). A compost service was initiated by Ari to serve families in his high school community. It became an environmental project that grew in momentum with volunteers and family users.

Figure 8.3 Ari Calls for Action.

Source: MEP.

Both Greta and Ari share a common thread of resilience. Their authenticity in their struggle to generate awareness to peers and adults, and their determination to be an integral part of the solution in creating a healthy planet is palpable. As Ari described Greta, he explained, "She is unique in her ordinariness!" And so is he.

Aria Jolie

Fourth grader Aria asks herself and others, "What can I do as a ten-year-old to help climate change?" She speaks for many children her age, still in elementary school, so dedicated to climate change and the health and well-being of her environment.

The following is an interview with Aria on May 1, 2020, about her feelings on climate change in the mid of the coronavirus pandemic. She immediately explained. "I feel the virus is good for climate change. Factories are closed, not as many flights, people are not driving, and China is seeing its first clear skies."

Aria continues with a hopeful outlook. "If we are able to get through this horrible time without factories and airplanes flying around, why can't we do it without a pandemic." She warned, "If we don't pull ourselves together, the environment is going downhill!!!" During the interview I asked Aria if she felt she was an activist. "Yes" was her immediate response. She continued, "There are a few types of activists. As a ten-year-old I feel I am doing a lot for the environment, but I could do more." She listed some of her environment saving activities.

1. *Litter:* Picking up trash no matter how tiny. She remarked how unbelievable it was to her that people could throw trash out of their car window.

Figure 8.4 Aria.
Source: Permission Aria and Lauren Redmond.

2. *Family projects:* As a family, emphasis on carpooling and sharing rides for any activity and limiting travel on airplanes.
3. *Protesting together:* Aria and her mom and dad, Lauren and Eric, attended the sustainability event, Black Youth in the Climate Movement for MLK Celebration Event at the Carver Recreation Center for young people K-12.

Aria was inspired by the activists at the conference, and the admonition of one of the speakers that "people may be staying away from plastic straws, but we need to do more, and step up our game for big changes to happen." During a question and answer period, Aria asked, "What can I do as a ten-year-old to help?" The response was to raise awareness of climate change, make posters, educate about recycle bins, and so on.

Self-quarantined at home during the pandemic of 2020, she was motivated to share her feelings about climate change in poetry and art work. Aria's poem written during quarantining is about herself, her feelings during COVID, and her inner strength that enables her to be an advocate for climate change. Her emotions run the gamut of uncertainty to confidence for attributes she contains that are not always as apparent as appearance.

See Me by Aria, age 12

Like a peacock

Able to fly despite being held down

I am walking around with only half a crown 'cause I'm scared to own it.

I deserve the throne, but I am thrown out of my zone every time I am called pretty.

High self-esteem is just a dream to me.

But do not underestimate me because there has been an update

I love myself like nobody else

I am not just pretty, I am witty

I am not just cute, I am astute

Do not put a lid on me

'Cause I'm so much more than you can see.

Aria Jolie, with permission

Aria explained in the following way her painting of the Earth and a person trying to save it from global warming with a rope from going downhill. "This is a person that represents everyone that is trying to save Earth. The person is pulling the Earth with a rope (away) from global warming."

Figure 8.5 Aria's Painting.

Source: With permission Aria and Lauren Redmond.

Aria's introspective message of her underlying inner strength is apparent in one of her many climate change projects. Her determination to save the bees led her and her grandfather Len to work together on a bee saving enterpise, whereby Aria got bravely "suited up" to become a junior bee keeper and bee savior.

Figure 8.6 The Bees.

Source: With permission Aria and Lauren Redmond.

Jerome Foster II

Rather than debating whether this crisis is real, we need to be finding solutions to solve it.

–Jerome Foster II (Alexander, 2020, p. 63)

Jerome Foster is an organizer and striker with Fridays for Future, working hard to demand legal action on climate change. Jerome is the founder of OneMillionOfUs, an organization dedicated to getting out the youth vote. He maintains every person needs to change habits and behaviors to ensure a healthy planet as well as advocating for far reaching change through government and legislation. At the age of 19, Jerome has fought hard for climate change during his growing up years. A few of his many teen activities was founder and editor-in-chief of the *Climate Reporter*, a global news blog, and a Smithsonian Ambassador. He is also the founder and CEO of TAU VR, a virtual reality company that recreates climate change impact.

Jerome lives in Washington DC and demonstrates much of his activism there. After joining Zero Hour, he began striking Friday mornings in front of the White House for climate change. On Friday afternoons he would strike again at the Capitol Building, holding a handmade sign that read "School Strike for Climate." At the same time he was interning with US representative John Lewis. Jerome feared his striking could create difficulties for him. However, the opposite took place. He was actually invited by the House Select Committee on the climate crisis to speak at an event. His organization One Million of Us strove to gather youth voters to become educated on climate change issues and be sure to vote. As Jerome explains, "Change starts in the streets and ends at the polls" (Alexander, 2020, p. 63). He actually joined Jane Fonda in raising awareness in the Fire Drill Friday on social media. He has spent hours testifying for the Clean Energy DC Act of 2018, a revolutionary decarbonization bill.

Jerome and his peers advocate strongly for the Climate Change Education Act, which is a bill that would mandate climate topics be incorporated into science curriculum for students in K-12 grade. In this way, early education on climate and nature would build developmentally through the school years. Chapter 5 highlights New Jersey as the first state to create and incorporate this kind of curriculum in their school system.

The software Jerome invented for his company TAU VR was instrumental in explaining climate change to many in Washington DC that were apathetic to or unschooled on his cause. His virtual reality software allows users to experience the challenges involved in climate change and the consequences these challenges might produce. Viewers can watch glaciers melt, move through plastic-filled oceans, and travel to oil refineries pumping carbon dioxide in the air. Jerome hopes this technology will better help onlookers gain a visceral understanding of planetary issues presented at this time.

Jerome is a strong believer that his generation, Gen Z, will get the job done for the environment. "We've got to be united in how we act as a generation, and how we act as a human species as a whole" (First-Arai, 2019). However, he is inclusive of all ages and races to join in the movement for climate change. "We need a truly diverse and multi-generational movement made of people from all ages and backgrounds, not just the youth" (Smith-Janssen, 2020).

Foster sees Greta Thunberg as a key influence on his activism and realized how alone and brave she was to reach out to young people. He initially received an email from her, an invitation to join the strike. And he did. After 56 weeks of Greta's striking, Jerome had the opportunity to join Greta at a White House Strike in 2019.

Licypriya Kangujam: Nine-Year-Old Activist in India

Licypriya Kangujam is a nine-year-old Indian climate activist who is a powerhouse of energy protesting for immediate action to combat climate change. Licpriya is the founder of the Child Movement and one of the youngest activists in the world. She does not want to be known as the

Indian "Greta," but rather for her desire to strive for a healthy planet Earth. Her focus is her home country India, which is the fifth most vulnerable country to climate change as reported in the Climate Risk Index 2020 (IANS, 2019).

Licpriya explains as the world warms, climate-fueled extreme weather events will increase enormously and with greater regularity … to fight this future prophecy, she explained in her speech at the Climate Summit in Spain 2019 that we want "a system change, not the climate change" (*Economic Times*, 2019). When she was six-years-old, she began her strong activism by pressing the Indian government to rethink climate policies to create a cleaner Earth. In July 2018, Licpriya attended the Asian Ministerial Conference for Disaster Risk Reduction in Mongolia and realized her mission was activism for the planet.

The future is the children. The world needs to make a better planet for us. Our leaders need to act now before it's too late (Caruso, 2020).
–Licypriya Kangujam

Figure 8.7 Action.

Source: Photo permission Licypriya Kangujam.

This child prodigy activist has called on world leaders by speaking at the United Nations Climate Conference (COP25) in Madrid in 2019. Her demands for the Indian government are specific to climate justice and climate education, and they are presented with an urgency. She has spoken in over 32 countries on climate change, with a fierce resolve to urge world leaders to "act now against climate change" (*Economic Times*, 2019). Licypriya mesmerized her audience at the the COP25 with her enthusiastic perserverence as she boldly stated her goal. "I have come here to tell the world leaders that this is the time to act as it is a real climate emergency" (*Economic Times*, 2019).

Here are a few actions she feels must be achieved. These actions support the realization of her goal of a healthy environment with healthy people (Caruso, 2020): (1) government regulation of fossil fuel and carbon emissions and (2) every student in India must plant a minimum of ten trees each after passing their exams. With 350 million students in the country, doing this would result in the planting of 3.5 billion new trees every year.

Her activist journey began when she was six years old and attended the Third Asian Ministerial Conference for Disaster Risks Reduction 2018 (AMCDRR 2018) in Mongolia. "It was my life changing event." During the conference, she met many world leaders and also thousands of delegates from various countries of the world. Many had highlighted various issues of disaster.

Figure 8.8 Global Plea.

Source: Photo permission Licypriya Kangujam.

"I cry when I see children losing their parents and people becoming homeless due to danger from disasters. My heart feels sorrowful for people who can't help themselves when disaster strikes. Many root causes are the impact of climate change" (Panache, 2019, *Economist Times*).

After returning from Mongolia in July 2018, Licpriya established an organization called The Child Movement to engage global leaders to take immediate action to make changes in the environment to ensure a healthy world for the children. Licpriya Kangujam continues to discuss climate issues with political leaders, especially air pollution that plagues India and is associated with poor health and illness. Her voice has been amplified by a large presence on social media, spreading her message across the globe to young people and world leaders as well. The United Nations has also created a platform to educate the public and increase awareness about her future, the future of others, and the future of the planet.

Licypriya explains, "I'm pressuring the government to ensure the health of every child in India. I will continue to put more pressure on our world leaders." She joins Greta in advocating for the planet.

Figure 8.9 Greta and Licy.

Source: Photo permission Licypriya and Greta Staff.

Leah Namugerwa

Leah Namugerwa at 15 years of age became the leading youth advocate for climate justice in Uganda. She was also inspired by Greta Thunberg.

The preponderance of drought, the inability to grow crops, and other climate-related issues related to the environment motivated Leah to appeal to young people to join her in global initiatives to help her country and the planet.

Figure 8.10 Leah Grows Crops.

Source: Permission Leah Namugerwa.

Leah became extremely aware of the difficulties in Uganda due to climate change. Haider Sarwar presents the following information in his rising article. Twenty-four million people from 2004 to 2013 were impacted by the drought and in one year, 2010–2011, these droughts created damage of 1.2 billion dollars. It is estimated that by 2030, Uganda will be very susceptible to environment degradation because of an estimated 1.5-degree increase of temperature (Sarwar, 2020).

Leah did not stand by silently to watch Uganda's environmental decline. Instead, she called out to everyone for action against ecological breakdown. She began actively protesting for climate action every Friday and encouraged her peers to do likewise (see Chapter 7).

Leah was determined to get her message to others despite major opposition, and she began missing school on Fridays. Her actions encouraged many other students to follow suit and be absent for Friday class and heighten the focus of climate change on the world stage.

When questioned about her personal safety because of her outspoken advocacy, Leah responded boldly, "My safety? I think that will make more climate awareness, if they try to (arrest me). If that happens, (the media) will have to come" (Sarwar, 2020).

Leah received valuable support from family for her efforts. Her uncle is part of the organization Green Campaign Africa that supports Fridays for Future Uganda.

Figure 8.11 School Strike.
Source: Permission Leah Namugerwa.

Leah understands environmental education and communication of environmental challenges is essential for her younger peers to understand the immediacy and scope of climate change difficulties in Uganda. Leah Namugerwa is a beacon of light, shining onto the planet to help restore and replenish Mother Earth.

Dominique Palmer

As climate activists we must continue standing together during these difficult times and advocate to protect our planet and our lives.

–Dominique (2020)

Dominique Palmer is a 21-year-old climate activist and striker in the UK Student Climate Network and Fridays for Future International, youth-led movements discussed in this chapter. She is an activist for climate justice, attending the Global Climate Strike in London, 2019. She was voted one of the top 100 leading UK environmentalists in *Forbes* magazine, UK. Dominque has established Launch video featuring artists and activists @climatelive2021 (see Chapter 7).

Dominque (2021) explains that because of COVID-19 "the world is facing a crisis, the COVID-19 pandemic, at the same time the world is facing another crisis – a climate and ecological emergency." She points out dramatically that climate change contributes to pandemics like COVID-19, and if left unaddressed, life-threatening infectious disease will increase and become stronger. Thus, the urgency for climate change.

Figure 8.12 Dominique.

Source: Permission Dominique Palmer.

Because of the health crisis, it was unacceptable to strike on mass in the streets. Dominique and fellow activists displayed flexibility in transitioning from outdoors to a digital forum. This allowed them to virtually continue to pressure. Their flexibility during crisis allowed these young people to continue to pressure governments, spread education, build strong connections, and embrace new people. The following photo is part of Fridays for Future, whereby young people around the globe participated in a Zoom climate strike.

Figure 8.13 Zoom Climate Change.

Source: Permission Dominique Palmer.

Dominque holds a firm stance that systemic change is not only possible but can evolve into a large-scale action on climate change. She stresses the pandemic and online advocacy had created a window in time to transition from a zero-carbon economy to adoption of economic reforms like the Green New Deal.

She has become a motivator for unity in the digital age and spreading the word to maintain connections, solidarity, and momentum to move forward. Emailing public officials, creating digital platforms, and disseminating information through social media channels conquer many of the challenges presented by the pandemic and helps mobilize young people throughout the globe for climate justice. We the Planet is an online youth-led campaign for Earth Day April 22. Dominque hosted a webinar with activists, scientists, and journalists who streamed weekly on YouTube, Facebook, and Twitter.

This global zoom with youth activists protesting for Fridays for Future is holding up individual mandates for creating change. Dominique was protesting from home in Figure 8.13 with a poster on twitter for an online climate strike.

Dominque's following words on Instagram bring home her immense passion and perseverance to inspire the world and inhabitants of all ages to join together to co-create a healthy planet Earth.

The race to safeguard our future has already begun, and it can feel overwhelming to look at the action we must take for intersectional climate justice, but moments like this remind me just how many of us are fighting for this – and we're getting bigger every year!

Figure 8.14 Climate Justice.
Source: Permission Dominique Palmer

"This truly is not just a moment, but a movement, and collectively we can achieve so much. I will always fight for true climate justice, an equitable future, a system that places people and planet at the heart of it. Let's keep fighting until we get it" (Dominique, Instagram).

Luna – Fourth Grade

Luna is a fourth grader, speaking out through painting and writing about her activism for the planet and its well-being. Her emotional intelligence is wise beyond her years, and her depth of understanding for the needs of others and her planet is profound. In an interview with Luna and her mother Kirsten on October 27, 2020, she expressed disappointment in older generations. "Parents say they care about their children, but they don't see they are ruining their future right in front of their eyes. They throw trash in the street, use plastic straws, and drive cars instead of riding bikes."

Luna continued to share her feelings:

Last week I felt I was at a breaking point. I was worried about the California wildfires. I was upset with adults. We have compost collections in our neighborhood with a compost crew that picks it up on garbage day. Our compost is filled with leftover food, shells, egg, and so on. Some of my neighbors refused to join in. Adults say they care, but they are not aligning with our future! Then I remembered the words of Greta, reminding young people they can transform their anxiety into action.

Luna decided to post on her mom's Facebook page because she felt it could be a forum for social action. Here is what she wrote:

Hey Mommy's Friends – 10/27/2020

It's Luna

Over the summer I visited some amazing natural places, and I realized how much I want to help save the Earth. Also, my grandma gave me a book called WE ARE ALL GRETA about saving the planet. Her words are inspiring me.

I've chosen a picture with water and nature to remind us just how beautiful our planet is. Instead of being scared because our planet is heating up and burning. I WANT TO ACT. WE NEED TO ACT!

Today I ask everyone my mommy knows on Facebook to stop using plastic water bottles. Please start drinking tap water and carrying your own reusable bottles.

Last night I was feeling fearful after seeing footage of the California wildfires, but Greta says, "swap fear for action to save the future."

LET'S DO THIS.

We can make a difference!

Figure 8.15 Luna's Post, 10/27/2020.
Source: Permission Luna and Kirsten Darling.

Luna explained she did not have a lot of money to travel around the world and share her beliefs and ideas, she only had the area she lived in, her home, her school, and her community. As our dialogue deepened, she began to realize that every action she took was a brave stand for caring for the planet. She remembered when her friends were selling lemonade in plastic double cups. She asked for just one cup, and the other girls looked questioningly at Luna. "I know they think I'm crazy, but it is important not to use too much plastic!"

Another scenario of activism occurred when Luna was visiting her aunt. She asked for some water. Her aunt responded there is a cup right there for you. "I'd rather have the water in a glass," she explained. "I'm thirsty, I want water, I have a reusable cup." Her aunt said, "Well if that is what you want," with a sigh and disgusted voice. Still Luna felt it was the right thing to do.

A third moment of activism was with her six-year-old brother Bret. They were crossing his soccer field in the rain, and Luna felt compelled to pick the trash up no matter how wet they got. It just made her feel good, and she did not want a dirty park.

Luna realized these three spontaneous acts of courage may have created a spark for others to become aware of the importance of creating a clean environment and eliminating waste. She was capable of creating change wherever she went and whatever she did. She could make a difference.

Figure 8.16 Cleaning Up.

Source: Permission Luna and Kirsten Darling.

The following drawings share Luna's willingness to promote a healthy planet and her heartfelt wishes for a healing environment. The first drawing is of planet Earth. Luna explained that the rainbows in the picture get lighter as they go up because people are not improving because people still use plastic straws and throw away fast food wrappers on the ground.

> The middle is the Earth and it gets sad. I made a circle to show that we are all connected. We are a human family. We share a circle of responsibility.

Figure 8.17. Luna's Artwork

Source: Permission Luna and Kirsten Darling.

The next two drawings are Luna's self-portrait. In the first self-portrait, Luna explained she was looking out toward the Earth and used beautiful vibrant earth colors of green and orange and brown found in nature.

The splattering of color can be seen in different ways. The eyes are circles that can view things differently. The splattering can be seen as trash or a recycled belt. It could look dirty or beautiful, flowers, or garbage. "We have to make a conscious effort to see and create the best we can."

Luna explains the second self-portrait in Spanish by writing, "Quiero salvar la tierra." It is translated as "I want to save the Earth." Luna drew herself and said she was a superhero here to save the planet.

> "That's the power!", she explains. Instead of feeling sad and anxious, I posted on Facebook, stopped using plastic using, recycling, and compositing. I even shared my bathwater with my brother!

Figure 8.18 Self-Portrait 1.

Source: Permission Luna and Kirsten Darling.

Figure 8.19 Self-Portrait 2.

Source: Permission Luna and Kirsten Darling.

Luna sent me a video of her standing next to a tree in a beautiful wooded area with this message. "Hi Linda. I'm in nature. This is my happy place!" with a big smile on her face. Then she cheerfully skipped away.

Luna used the creative arts (see Chapter 5) to again express her feelings of advocacy in a cut out collage. She beautifully made the collage with bees, flowers, a tree, and sun adding the words, "Save the Earth."

Figure 8.20 Luna's Collage.

Source: Permission Luna and Kirsten Darling.

Luna's sensitivity to her social environment of peers as well as her natural environment earned her a special award at school, The Kindness Award. She was noted for her kindness to her classmates, especially one boy who found noise of any kind hindered his ability to read. One beautiful example of Luna's kindness, not only to her peers but also to those she doesn't know, was her top wish on her list for Christmas. Luna wanted to donate 12 inches of her cut hair to make a wig for a kid with cancer, and that is just what she did!!!!

Luna's big heart spreads to the environment, her friends, and everyone on the planet.

Figure 8.21 Luna's Hair.

Source: Permission Luna and Kirsten Darling.

Conclusion

Together we must demand a different way, a life-giving system that defends the natural world on which we all depend.

–Monbiot, 2020

This quote exemplifies the need to join with young activists to their immediacy in a call for action for every inhabitant of the planet. As Monbiot declares in his quote, together we can affirm our natural life and join our youth in educating ourselves, acting upon that education, and moving society forward to a global perspective of what a healthy Earth would and could be. The advocacy of those cited in this chapter and the hundreds and hundreds of youths they represent globally gives new meaning to the phrase, "And a child shall lead the way."

Assuredly, there is little doubt this generation has stepped up to the plate and hit a home run in terms of becoming an educated voice that all ages can learn from and admire. Together as one universal agent of change, we can seek new understandings and innovations to secure the well-being of our environment and all who live on it.

President Obama's Graduate Advocacy Advice

Former President Barack Obama sends a powerful message to young people on their digital graduation day (May 17, 2020) during the COVID-19 quarantine. He calls on the youth to recognize that "if we are going to save the environment and defeat future pandemics, we are going to have to do it together – and in many ways you have already taken the lead."

Obama sums up the advocacy these young people possess and their ability and perseverance in educating older generations in his closing advice at graduation.

If the world's going to get better, it going to be up to you. That realization may be kind of intimidating. But I hope it's also inspiring. With all the challenges this country faces right now, nobody can tell you "No, you're too young to understand" or "this is how it's always been done." Because with so much uncertainty, with everything suddenly up for grabs, this is your generation's world to shape.

And as the Pope so beautifully states a way of life to choose, his words seem to resonate with the words of President Obama.

> *We are all born to help each other. No matter how difficult it is… Life is good when you are happy; but much better when others are happy because of you.*
>
> –Pope Francis, 2017

Figure 8.22 Helping Each Other.

Source: Photo by Patty Brite on Unsplash.

9 Family Activities to Support a Healthy Planet

Parents can help children find ways to move toward action, from hopeless to hopeful.

–Child Psychologist Dr. Jillian Roberts (Egan-Elliott, 2019)

Figure 9.1 Healthy Family.
Source: Photo by Limor Zellerm on Unsplash.

DOI: 10.4324/9781003051770-12

Introduction

Parents can become a part of a cohesive and consistent conversation when they begin to educate themselves on the facts about climate change and share common, age-appropriate language for dialogues. Helping their children take action is a positive outlet for anxiety and a step toward making a positive difference in their lives.

This family discussion can begin to dissolve misconceptions and share evidence-based facts about the environment. Family teachable moments include a basic dialogue about how a simple plant at home "breathes," and eventually concepts can expand with age and develop deeper understandings such as the carbon cycle on a global scale.

For children ages eight and under, Scholastic encourages conversation with kids eight or under and parents to "strive to strengthen his or her relationship with the environment so that when the time comes, he/she will have already developed a passion and appreciation for nature." Family gardening, camping, and sharing books about nature, animals, and climate will imprint ideals to "help your child become a protector of the planet and a better learner" (Scholastic Parents and Staff, 2020).

Families can work together to create change and help the planet become healthy. Examples of family activities include shorter showers, turning lights off, not wasting food, using paper straws, recycling, etc. Parents can participate with kids in climate change events.

Being with other kids helps them feel they are acting, and they are not alone. They gain a sense of hope and empowerment when they form a group with other young people and can inspire change in the community and government itself.

Even family pets can become a symbolic part of a united home front to share advocacy for the environment. Parents can encourage kids to attend rallies for climate change.

Figure 9.2 Family Pets.

Source: Permission kellybdc, CC BY 2.0, https://creativecommons.org/licenses/by/2.0, via Wikimedia Commons.

One family decided to take part in a strike for climate change. Their dog wore a sign as he marched with them, "Climate Change is REAL DOGGONEIT!" Another puppy marching with his family during a climate action strike wore a sign that read, "I am striking for climate change. No obedience school on Fridays."

Enjoy Nature in Family Activities

Nature is a family activity. Whether it is hiking for the day, a walk with the dog around the block, gazing at the stars, or bird watching at a sanctuary, a child's interaction with nature and their family is an integral part of youngsters learning the benefits and appreciation of their environment. With their children, moms and dads and grandparents can enjoy watching the change of seasons, the growth of flowers, and the beauty of their surround in color and sound. The vibrancy of nature energizes kids, and the many lessons of nature serve as teachable moments for children and parents.

Relaxing in Nature

Nature quiets the mind, and often stills thoughts in a meditative way. Allowing kids to relax, enjoy the moment, and drink the wealth of the nectar of nature available to all is a secret gift of the environment that offers well-being and solitude.

Figure 9.3 Nature Hikes.
Source: Photo by Juliane Lieberman on Unsplash.

Having Fun

Another gift of Mother Earth is fun in nature. Playing ball, looking for birds, listening to the wind drifting through the leaves, and spotting a squirrel scampering from tree to tree can be so enjoyable as a family.

Figure 9.4 Fun in Nature.

Source: Photo by Robert Collins on Unsplash.

Just Being

Just the quietude of family time outdoors, freed of the restraints of schedules and *to do lists,* emboldens the entire family. Chapter 10 describes in greater depth the researched principles of attention restoration and stress reduction that nature showers on our children.

Figure 9.5 Relaxing in Nature.

Source: Photo by Janko Ferlice on Unsplash.

Timiny Bergstrom has two children, five-year-old Palmer and nine-year-old Hudon. This family has very important goals that include enjoying environmental activities, such as cleaning liter off the street and telling family and friends about the dangers of plastic straws. The entire family has joined the 1000 Hours Outside movement that they each have committed to as a family unit. Every family member tracks time spent outdoors, all seeking to reach the thousand hours and communicating in a lively fashion daily on how far they have gotten. The goal of this movement is the following:

> The entire purpose of *1000 Hours Outside* is to attempt to match nature time with screen time. If kids can consume media through screens 1200 hours a year on average, then the time is there and at least some of it can and should be shifted towards a more productive and healthier outcome. (Yurich, 2021)

They underscore the concept that the amount of time kids and family members spend outdoors is important and engaging together in nature is a memorable family experience. The benefits of breathing fresh outdoor air and integrating the beauty and splendor of nature into daily family activities are its own reward.

A Model of Family and Nature Interaction

Timiny expresses her love for nature to her research findings (see Chapter 10) on the positive impact of a nature experience 2020. In her introduction, she shares her experience of nature and its benefits as follows:

> Nature experiences have always been very powerful to me. Growing up in rural Vermont, I used to spend hours wandering around my yard, collecting berries, examining our garden, inhaling the fresh air, and imagining running a school or a summer camp in my backyard. I have very fond memories of my dad taking me camping and canoeing in the moonlight on our local reservoir.... To this day, I continue to experience those same feelings when I immerse myself in the natural world. Experiences in nature feel powerful, almost magical to me. (Bergstrom, 2020)

Timiny and her husband have transformed this love of nature and its positive outcomes to their children as they all work toward a 1000 Hours Outdoors (https://www.1000hoursoutside.com). The following are a few family photos that highlight the delight, learning, relaxation, joy, and memories created for her family by boating, catching frogs, skiing, building igloos, and examining a worm. There are family activities for all seasons.

Figure 9.6 Boating.

Source: Permission Timiny Bergstrom.

Figure 9.7 Skiing.

Source: Permission Timiny Berstrom.

Figure 9.8 Frogs.
Source: Permission Timiny Berstrom.

Figure 9.9 Igloo.
Source: Permission Timiny Berstrom.

Figure 9.10 A Salamander.
Source: Permission Timiny Berstrom.

Grandparents as Role Models

Participation in Action

Violet is a first grader that shares a keen love and concern for nature and the planet with her grandmother Joyce. Joyce is an environmentalist that has shared the joys of nature and the interconnectedness of the environment and all people.

Figure 9.11 Oyster Recovery Zone.
Source: Permission Joyce Baker.

Together they have begun a project to purify water around their home and their state by growing oysters. This long-term commitment takes several years and is supported by the Maryland Grow Oysters Program (www.mdgrowoysters.org).

The pier at Violet's house has been authorized as an Oyster Recovery Zone and Grandma Joyce and Violet will continue to nurture the oysters until they are fully ready to be harvested. The sign posted on the dock that Violet is holding certifies it is an Oyster Recovery Zone. It explains the purpose of harvesting oysters in the following way.

"Oysters are critical to the Chesapeake Bay Recovery. One oyster filters up to fifty gallons of water a day and oyster reefs provide critical habitat for many marine species. The cages on the dock are miniature living oyster reefs hosting an abundance of aquatic life such as mud crabs, grass shrimp, worms, baby eels, and minnows." (https://oysterrecovery.org/marylanders-grow-oysters/)

In time, these oysters will be placed in local sanctuary reefs, where they will continue to grow and flourish. Violet explained why she wanted to harvest oysters and commit to this industrious project. "I know the oysters help clean water. I want to help clean the water with them."

Elders Climate Action

We call on all of our generation to rise and join us in support of the global youth climate movement.
–Elders Climate Action

Elders Climate Action (ECA) is a nonprofit project that seeks to educate and engage the older generation in fighting climate change and supporting the youth movement. They took part in the 2017 Peoples Climate March in Washington DC. The following is adapted from the Elders Climate Action website www.eldersclimateaction.org. It speaks to their goals and commitment to join youth in educating and promoting change.

When *Elders Climate Action* was formed in 2014, the youth were in our hearts. For our children, our grandchildren, and all future generations, we have worked to mobilize the wisdom, the voices, the votes and the collective power of our older generations to end the climate emergency that threatens life on our planet. ECA salutes the powerful rising of youth climate activists seizing this moment to lead the struggle for the just and sustainable way of life that they deserve. ECA and its members stand in solidarity with our youth climate activists. We are proud to strike with them (virtually or in person), to march behind their banners and sing their songs (Elders Climate Action, 2021)

Parents as Role Models

We are a community of moms and dads united against air pollution – including the urgent crisis of our changing climate – to protect our children's health.

–Moms Clean Air Force (Tenenbaum, 2020)

Moms Clean Air Force

Moms Clean Air Force is a group of women and men determined to create a global conversation on climate change. Its field director, Heather McTeer Toney, testified at a two-day hearing on the impact of the Trump administration to abandon life-saving standards in the House of Representative's inquiry into the Threat to America's Children.

Figure 9.12 Moms for Climate Change.

Source: Photo by Mauricio Artieda on Unsplash.

She explains, "Climate Action is the social justice movement of our time. African Americans should demand action from state, local, and federal leaders on climate action now" (Tenenbaum, 2020). Heather was the first African American, first female, and youngest mayor of Greenville, Mississippi, a position she feels enabled her to be a more effective climate activist for children. As a mother and woman of color, Heather is compelled to create change for her family and all families on the planet.

Climate Mamas

Climate Mamas and Papas are a group of parents that realize we have a unique opportunity right now to make significant change for the betterment of the planet. Harriet Shugarman is the executive director of Climate Mama. Harriet was chosen to be trained by Al Gore and has worked closely with the

Climate Reality Project. She has also become a professor teaching climate change and society at Ramapo College in New Jersey and author of *How to Talk to Children about Climate Change* (2020). Harriet is a mom with two children and maintains her life journey is to create a better, healthier life for her children and all the children on the planet.

Their mission as stated on their website is:

1. To educate and inform Climate Mamas and Papas of all ages from all around the world about the realities of the climate crisis.
2. To inspire and empower Climate Mamas and Papas to work together – creative, thoughtfully, and purposefully – to help create a better, stronger, and healthier world.
3. To offer hope and a collective path which we all follow, so that we can find the moral courage to fight for and demand a clean, renewable, and sustainable future for ourselves, our children, and for generations to come. Website: www.climatemama.com

One Climate Mama, Margie Muenzer, and her Sister Jane Reis authored a book for children with an accompanying coloring and activity book. It is titled, *Si'ahl and the Council of Animals 2020*. Margie is a climate reality leader and educator, and hopes this resource will help parents, teachers, and caring adults to listen and speak to kids about climate change. Her storybook serves as a model to effect change for families, inspired by children's concern for nature and animals. The workbook provides children a forum for coloring many pictures, some which include animal habitats and behaviors, the value of trees, and energy usage. Both children's resources can be used to begin a dialogue, supply information during a teachable moment, and offer activities to help the planet (see Chapter 5: Creating a Conversation).

Science Moms

A universal question of motherhood would probably be, "What kind of a world do I want my child to grow up in, and what can I do to create that world for all children? Mothers want a safe and healthy world for their children, and some fear that is not presently happening. Science Moms is a group of five mothers and scientist that have joined together to disseminate factual information and educate the public, especially parents, what they can do to help move forward the manifestation of a healthy planet. When one of these moms, atmospheric scientist Katherine Hayhoe was asked a similar question. She responded to the young mom to channel her fear into action and speak with friends and family and advocate in your community, state, and national forum (Kaplan, 2021a).

Katherine followed her own advice and took this advice to the national level. Joining with five fellow climate scientists, they formed a team with Potential Energy, a nonprofit marketing firm. Together they launched a ten-million-dollar campaign airing on National TV in March 2021 to educate and empower mothers to do something about climate change. These ads will then be extended to states.

Science Moms also has a website that share facts and resources, including books for kids that talk about climate change. Hayhoe hopes these ads will counter any misinformation with facts about the environment. Mothers are a group that trust other mothers and listen to motherly concerns. Hayhoe explains,

> What we want to do is empower other moms to become messengers. I really believe that using our voices is the way to make a difference. One of the most powerful ways for us to connect over climate change is ... this fundamental value that we share. We all want to ensure a better and safer future for our child. (Kaplan, 2021a)

On the website for Climate Moms, www.sciencemoms.com, this group of mother scientist advocates states their purpose the following way:

> We are a group of climate scientists and mothers who care deeply about the planet that our children will inherit. Together we aim to demystify climate change, talk honestly about how it will affect our children and give moms the facts they need to take action.

Climate Dads

Climate Dads is an organization that works to educate dads to help create a safe environment for their children to grow up in. They explain the following on their website www.climatedads.org. "We dads know that climate change is happening. It's time to get ready. Let's keep our families safe, educate the next generation, and build a more stable future" (2021).

Climate Dads have a threefold plan to accomplish their goals. The first is to teach, sharing resources, guides, and outdoor activities to join with their children. The second part of their advocacy includes resourcefulness, preparation, and action. They suggest energy-efficient options for home improvement work and updated products useful to conserve energy. The third segment of advocacy is connection with other dads in the hopes of creating a strong dad network to bring their concerns to the highest levels of government to create change.

Climate Dads accomplish their hopes by maintaining the need for a 100 percent transition to renewable energy. One manifestation of this hope is Electric School Bus Campaign, a drive to dismantle diesel-fueled buses that they feel fill children's lungs with smoke and replace them through needed contributions with electric school buses (see Chapter 10). This campaign was fueled by Climate Dads in Philadelphia that became aware of diesel-fueled buses that filled smoke into kid's lungs. Philly had a very high rate of asthma. The school district could not afford the transition, and so the dad's campaign was birthed. As they state on their website, "Too big a challenge? Definitely not. We're organizing a coalition of advocates. We're researching sources of funding to electrify our schools' bus fleets. We're finding the cash to make change happen."

Figure 9.13 Electric School Bus.

Source: Permission from Climate Dads.

Thomas the Train Goes Green

The United Nations and Mattel, Inc have joined together to produce an animated children's series, Thomas & Friends, that features the UN Sustainable Development Goals (SDGs) to preschool children. This project began on September 7, 2018, and continued with programs that speak to these goals throughout the year. Their concern for nature and climate is paramount, as they feature videos, downloadable materials, interactive activities, and parent information on varied goals that that include sustainable cities and communities, clean water and sanitation, responsible consumption and production, and life on land.

One of the goals of the program is to provide a short amount of content that allows parents to introduce meaningful conversations about global well-being with young children. The hope is to help youngsters realize they can take part in global initiatives and help keep planet Earth healthy. "Thomas' unique focus on empathy, collaboration, and friendship is more relevant than ever and such an effective way to introduce children to the most important global values of their lifetimes – as embodied by the Sustainable Development Goals" (United Nations, 2018), said Richard Dickson, president and COO of Mattel.

A Family Edutainment Interactive Activity

The aim of each family activity is to create an understanding and discussion of goals for the young child such as sustainably managing forests, combating desertification, reversing land degradation, and halting biodiversity loss. Each activity begins with a short video link about the goal from Thomas & Friends (https://www.allaboardforglobalgoals.com/en-ca).

Figure 9.14 All Aboard.

Source: *Permission Mattel and UN.* "The content of this publication has not been approved by the United Nations and does not reflect the views of the United Nations or its officials or Member States." Link to UN Sustainable Development Goals *https://www.un.org/sustainabledevelopment/.*

Life on Land SDG 15: An Interactive Family Activity

The following is one of the many lessons in child learning for families, Life on Land SDG 15, adapted from Parent Tips, All Aboard for Global Goals (2019)! https://www.allaboardforglobalgoals.com/en-ca.

Conversation starters: Parents are given different questions to motivate dialogue after a one-minute video.

Why are trees important to us?

How many animals can you name that live in trees?

What would happen if we didn't have trees?

What can we see on a tree?

Then each activity offers playful learning.
Playful learning: Suggested for three-year-olds and up.

The family activity for Life on Land begins with the suggestion for everyone to start with a seed. Supplies of dirt, pots, water, and seeds should be available. Everyone in the family joins together to decide where the seeds will be planted – indoors or outdoors. Parents can then initiate a conversation about what a seed needs to grow, such as water, food, and sunlight. Together children and parents care for the seed each week to help it grow, recording its growth with photos and measurements.

Follow-up Activities

As younger children pick seeds to plant, they can count how many they are planting. After planting, kids can also take a nature walk and look for animals that use trees and the different types of trees they see. There are useful links and downloadable information for each UN goal activity for parents and children. They also suggest useful resources on the topic of taking care of the environment such as *The Great Kapok Tree* by Lynne Cherry.

Explorers for the Global Goals

Another valuable resource for family activities to initiate, nurture, and support a love of nature and caring for the environment in young children is Explorers for the Global Goals. Working in collaboration with UNICEF, they have created the mission of developing global citizens who are creative, empathetic, global citizens that are curious about their world – and highlighting to parents that "one day your children could be the ones building a better world" (Explorers for the Global Goals, Worlds Largest Lesson, 2020, https://worldslargestlesson.globalgoals.org/wp-content/uploads/2020/10/Parents-Guide-Explorers-for-the-Global-Goals.pd).

They offer the "World's Largest Lesson Plan" (see Chapter 11) for four- to eight-year-olds with a starter pack to be read with children before they begin their first of five activities. This pack provides a guide for parents to help them introduce young kids to the Global Goals and provides a certificate for the children when they have completed the activity. Printable stickers and badges are included as a reward for participation as well as Global Goals poster (https://worldslargestlesson. globalgoals.org/).

Over 193 countries of the United Nations came together in 2015 to create Sustainable Development Goals for the planet with a wide range of categories that include education, health, justice, and peace for all people and the environment. They maintain there are five attributes children can grow to broaden their ability to become an explorer for the Global Goals, which include empathy, curiosity, problem solving, creativity, and effective communication. These attributes can be supported and enhanced through the family activities provided to begin learning.

Edible Education at Home: Know, Sow, and Grow

Alice Waters (see Chapter 11) has inspired the Edible Schoolyards curriculum, lessons for Edible Education at home. One example is the six experientially garden-based activities designed to teach the basics of plant parts and basic gardening skills in a non-threatening easy and fun way that families can enjoy together. These lessons build vocabulary and concepts, provide interactive learning, promote communication, and are free and downloadable from the website resource library, https://edibleschoolyard.org/resource-search.

The following is an outline of the six lessons establishing garden-based, problem solving activities, vocabulary building, and interaction with plants and nature authored by Raquel Vigil and Nick Lee (www.edibleschoolyard.org) for Edible Education at Home. Families are supported to explore these lessons together and begin to create an experiential love of nature and growing food, cooking food, and sharing food together. The following is an overview adapted from the website of what these downloadable lessons involve, and ways families can work together for the planet.

Know, Sow, and Grow Lessen Set for Edible Education at Home

Lesson 1 (Seed Parts and Sprouting Starts): Student outcomes include understanding the difference between dicots and monocots, identifying four seed. parts: the seed coat, endosperm, and embryo, beginning to understand the function of the various seed parts, and successfully germinating seeds.

Lesson 2 (Root Investigations): Student outcomes are to understand the difference between primary roots and secondary roots and identify key functions of roots.

Lesson 3 (Discovering Flowers): Student outcomes include identifying four flower parts: the peduncle, receptacle, sepal, and petal, using their senses to make observations, and understanding how function informs structure in flowers.

Lesson 4 (Create Your Own: Planter Box): Student outcomes are to understand why both drainage and irrigation are important for plant health, identify various sources of organic plant fertilizers, build their self-efficacy in gardening, and practice following a multistep procedure.

Lesson 5 is based on how to read a seed packet, and Lesson 6 involves how to direct seed. Both involve building self-efficacy with gardening, as well as learning about life cycles and developing key vocabulary.

There is also a group of extension lessons that include exploring nature at home, learning how to make seed balls, creating, and growing organic, and growing from food scraps. All these extension activities provide opportunities for families to come together, learn together, and fall in love with nature together.

A Model of Family Commitment: The Rubenstein's

Together we will build a movement that must – and will – become irresistible.

–Monbiet, 2020

The Mother Earth Project (MEP) is a nonprofit organization founded in 2015 by internationally renowned sculptor and scientist Barton Rubenstein, cofounder and son Ari, and his family. Barton Rubenstein is also the chairperson of the Environment Committee in his Town of Somerset, Chevy Chase, Maryland. Originally, the Rubenstein family was actively recycling at home, including metal, plastic, and paper, installing LED lights, composting, becoming vegetarians, and using solar energy to heat water and assist in heating the home. Seeing that there were a few other neighbors composting, a small group encouraged the neighborhood leadership to offer a composting program for everyone, which they did. The neighborhood is also a leader in sustainability and has introduced LED street lighting, which can reduce up to 90 percent of energy.

Feeling the momentum, the family began to promote sustainability by engaging schools and universities with the Mother Earth Project Inflatable Booth. Compelled to make a global impact, cofounder Ari Rubenstein reached out in 2017 to 15-year-old Kallan Benson, who had decorated a 24′ diameter parachute with a large, beautiful butterfly. She had also collected 1,600 signatures on the parachute from other students in the Washington DC region, who were also concerned about the environment.

The butterfly parachute and other decorated parachutes were displayed during the 2017 Climate Strike in Washington, DC. Inspired by the successful public awareness campaign of the HIV/AID Quilts in the 1990s, Mother Earth Project cofounders and Kallan's family considered distributing parachutes worldwide, culminating in the creation of Parachutes for the Planet, described in detail in Chapter 8 as a project that encourages communities worldwide to decorate parachutes with artwork and their next sustainable actions, march with their parachutes, and take them to their local politicians to demand better climate laws.

The Mother Earth Sculpture

The final piece to this important puzzle is engaging countries and cities directly. Toward that goal, Barton Rubenstein designed and created "Mother Earth," a five-meter-high profile sculpture, which now acts as

Figure 9.15 Mother Earth Sculpture in DC.
Source: Permission Mother Earth Project.

the Symbol of Sustainability, given to countries participating in the Paris Climate Conference of 2015. This sculpture, to be placed in major cities around the world acts to recognize countries who have submitted their environment-saving actions and timelines to the United Nations Climate Change Conference and incentivize other countries to join this world partnership.

This photograph is of the Mother Earth sculpture. It was taken on the Potomac River in Washington DC with the Key Bridge in the distance.

The sculpture has been placed in many cities throughout the world. Guilin, a city in China, is an example of site chosen for a Mother Earth sculpture, celebrating China's focus on saving the environment. The banner reads, "To Protect the Environment, we are in Action."

Specifically, the Boya Academy, a K-12 international school with 31 like-academies around China, is excited to have Mother Earth at its Guilin campus. It is in the school's art corner, a place where students discuss art projects. MEP is excited to begin this collaboration with the Boya Academies. The dedication was September 2020.

Figure 9.16 China.

Source: Permission Mother Earth Project.

The Family Team: An Inspired Model

The cofounding MEP team in 2016: Sabrina Rubenstein CMO, Shereen Rubenstein, Benjamin Rubenstein, Ari Rubenstein School Liaison and FFF Climate Strike Organizer, and Barton Rubenstein. This is truly a family commitment, with each member doing their individual part and then joining together for global goals attainment.

During the pandemic period the Rubenstein family posted different parachutes in front of their house and distributed 100 parachutes to neighbors and pedestrians that walked by. Many took a free parachute from a box next to the displayed parachute. The family decorated them, and neighbors then displayed them in their front yards and on their houses during Earth Day.

The first displayed parachute was visually the Mother Earth Project and the UN Sustainable Development Goals (see chapter 10). The second parachute exemplifies the plea to demand environmental justice now, proclaiming racism is toxic.

In April 2020, Mother Earth Project family cofounders created a Bat Parachute, inspired by a *Washington Post* article by Karen Bruilliard that connects COVID-19 to the climate emergency. It emphasized the connection between disturbing natural habitat and disease.

The family also placed a box of free parachutes for neighbors to take, decorate with art, express environmental concerns, and join in sustainable actions. All of this was offered during the COVID-19 to stay at home in lockdown.

Figure 9.17 Family Team.
Source: Permission Mother Earth Project.

Figure 9.18 UN Goal Parachute.
Source: Permission Mother Earth Project.

Figure 9.19 Racism Is Toxic.

Source: Permission Mother Earth Project.

Figure 9.20 Bat Habitat.

Source: Permission Mother Earth Project.

"The Talk" about Climate Change

In the past, talking to children about the birds and the bees was a tricky topic. Today discussing birds and bees is an important component of the climate change discussion.

Linda Goldman

Parenting involves talking to kids about challenging topics. Climate change has risen to a topic comparable to talking with youngsters about sex, drugs, and violence. As with all difficult topics, the conversations need to be age appropriate and developmentally sound (see Chapter 4). Throughout this resource, adults have been given simple facts about climate change (see Chapters 4 and 5) for clear definitions to enhance dialogue.

Children's questions are usually a window allowing others to explore what they have heard or what they are thinking. Kids can glean information from other kids, observing their environment, or using their innate expertise on social media. Jonny lived in a poverty-stricken area in California. The only nature he and his family experienced was visiting a California National Park. With the horrendous disaster caused by the wildfires, all the National Forests in California are closed to visitors as a precautionary measure of safety (Yee, 2021). Jonny saw the closing on the news. "Oh no!" he shouted and began to cry. "We can't go to the park. It's not fair!!!"

Five-year-old Isabella asked mom, "Why are the fires burning so much in California?" She had consistently seen the fires on television. Wisely, mom knew the fires must be on Isabella's mind and asked, "What have you heard about the fires? Is there anything you are worrying about? This expanded the conversation as mom found out what facts Isabella know, and her concerns about breathing smoke. She had images of the raging fires and the commentary that the fires were overtaking everywhere, and fireman could not put them out. Isabella became frightened they would be at her house next. Mom explained the fires were far away. Isabella still was distraught. "I heard on the news, even if we are far away, the smoke can make us sick." This interchange led to a talk about pollution, air quality, temperature rises, and extreme heat. Parents adjusted scientific information and language corresponding to her age (see Chapter 2: Children's Understandings at Developmental Stages), and were able to help her discriminate between fact and misinformation.

Fear inspired by the media can enhance anxiety about an experienced disaster. Alexander and his family survived Hurricane Ida 2021 but lost their home and their dog Max. Everyday Alexander watched the news. When he got to school, he constantly asked his teacher, "What's the weather today? What's the weather today?," fearing the hurricane would return. And it did return two weeks later as Hurricane Nicholas, devasting their area again. The constancy of climate disaster and the anticipatory grief Alexander felt is discussed in Chapter 2.

It is important to keep responses with children simple, optimistic, stressing they are safe, and adults are working to keep them safe. In the same vein, adults can model and share feelings, normalizing concerns surrounding climate change without bias. Kids in the concrete stage of development "strive to strengthen his or her relationship with the environment so that when the time comes, he/she, they them will have already developed a passion and appreciation for nature." "Taking your children to camping, allowing them to garden, and (perhaps particularly) reading books about our oceans, forests, plants, and animals will instill values to 'help your child become a protector of the planet and a better learner'" (Scholastic Parents Staff, 2021).

As youngsters mature, they seek more accurate information and are more astute at distinguishing fact from fiction. They may want to become active in family projects or peer projects that represent how they feel about climate change such as the Global Strike and Fridays for Future (see Chapter 7). Discussions can extend to future ways they can help the planet politically, professionally, and socially.

Family Activity Suggestions: Nature and Environmental Health

1. *Join in environmental family meetings* whereby children and parents participate and agree on all actions. Begin with a resource to read as a family. *10 Things I Can Do to Help My World* by Melanie Walsh is a resource that opens discussions about family activities (like those in number 2) and how everyone feels about climate change.
2. *Build a checklist of environmental activities* to be done individually and as a family collectively developed as a family. This checklist may include suggestions, nature involvement, and environmental actions like:

   - Plant seeds and care for a family garden.
   - Turn water off when brushing teeth.
   - Throw trash away.
   - Use both sides of paper.
   - Feed the birds.
   - Make toys from things around the house.
   - Sort recycling.
   - Compost.
   - Turning off lights.
   - Bike instead of driving.
   - Walk to school.
   - Family hikes.

3. *Make a checklist of healthy hygiene habits* (see Chapter 3):

   - Brushing teeth
   - Washing hands before and after eating
   - Sneezing into a sleeve or Kleenex
   - Wearing a mask
   - Social distancing if needed

4. *Create an emergency kit* for unexpected events. Here is a list of items one family felt they needed. This could be the basis of discussion and adding to meet individual family needs.

   - Water
   - Energy bars

- A whistle
- Phone numbers to get help
- Batteries and chargers
- Powdered milk

5. *Look for signs of burnout* (especially after experiencing a firsthand disaster)

   - Fatigue and/or apathy
   - Climate depression "What's the use?"
   - Climate anxiety "I can't sleep. I am worried about my future."
   - Hyperfocused on disaster "Will the tornado come back today?"
   - Drop in grades

6. *Monitor media exposure* and inspire teachable moments. The news and even commercials on TV can become a teachable moment for kids, or vice versa if children have information to share about the environment.

7. *Read Beginning the Climate Conversation:* A Family's Guide (https:// www.climaterealityproject.org/family). This downloadable free e-book by The Climate Reality Project gives insights and ideas for conversation about climate change with children of all ages. It suggests parents learn the basic facts given in this booklet about climate change to be prepared for the time kids begin to ask questions and seek discussion.

8. *Participate as a family for action:* Many of the families in this resource have joined forces to protest together for climate change and climate justice. Aria (Chapter 8) with her family, Lauren, and brother Skyler was part of a global strength for climate change. Ari and his dad Barton were a family team to create and share Parachutes for The Planet and Mother Earth Project globally. Jesse carried a sign she made while marching with her family for Earth Day. It said, "Because you litter, we are bitter!"

9. *Promote your children's interest* and concern about the environment by helping them discover National Geographic Kids (https://kids. nationalgeographic.com). This website inspires girls and boy to see if they are habitat heroes, biodiversity champions, climate change warriors, or pollutions preventers by participation in a simple quiz, and then provides ways to promote their specific interests.

10. *Make a commitment:* George Monbiot wrote an honest and heartfelt article as a parent who felt his generation had let the young people down, by living in a world of denial and discounting. Monbiot urges parents to join with their children and let them lead the way. His following quote speaks for an older generation to a younger one, promising commitment, collaboration, and a pledge to join these young environmentally conscious counterparts in reversing the tide of disinterest into a greener and healthier world.

In Summary

You have issued a challenge to which we must rise, and we will stand in solidarity with you.

Though we are old, and you are young, we will be led by you. We owe you that, at least. By combining your determination and our experience ... together we must demand a different way, a life-giving system that defends the natural world on which we all depend. A system that honors you, our children, and values equally the lives of those who are not born.
–George Monbiot, 2020

In summary, this chapter speaks to the heart of this book. We know kids watch what we do, not what we say. What could be more striking and profound for our children, than becoming role models for a healthy planet. When a mom suggests to her kids, "Let's go outside and pick up some litter and beautify our neighborhood," she opens a door for participation by example.

In the same vein, the idea that a child can lead the way, may inspire youngsters to give information to their parents and suggest family activities. One first grader begged his father: "Dad, please, please, can we compost as a family? I'll explain everything to you and take charge of what we do. It will be a family project!"

Figure 9.21 Fun in Nature with Dad.
Source: *Photo by Joice Kelly on Unsplash.*

Part IV

Change

Environmental Justice, Nature Deprivation, Climate Action, Resources

10 Environmental Justice and Young People

The Climate crisis is also a justice crisis.

–Newsletter Climate Justice 2020

Figure 10.1 A Justice Crisis.

Source: Photo by Nandhu Kumar on Unsplash.

DOI: 10.4324/9781003051770-14

> *Green spaces make people healthier and happier, but decades of systemic racism have left many people of color living in areas without access to nature.*
> –Alejandra Borunda, July 29, 2020

Introduction

Nature is not just a luxury for children and families, it is an integral piece of creating healthy mental and physical environments for our young people. Borunda (2020) maintains that "the opportunity to take a moment in nature is something many researchers have increasingly identified as valuable for people's mental and physical health." There is a stark reality in the United States that black and brown Americans have less immediate access to nature than white Americans. The Hispanic Access Foundation and The Center for American Progress authored a report (Hananel, July 21, 2020) that highlights this disparity. The report states that people of color, low-income communities, and families with children are most likely to be deprived of the benefits that nature provides. Key findings from this report include (Hananel, 2020):

1. Communities of color are three times more likely than white communities to live in a place that is nature deprived.
2. Seventy percent of low-income communities across the country live in nature-deprived areas – 20 percent higher than communities with moderate or high incomes.

Figure 10.2 Climate Justice Now.

Source: Photo by Markus Spiske on Unsplash.

3. Nature destruction has had the largest impact on low-income communities of color: More than 76 percent of low-income communities of color live in nature-deprived places.

Their research found that communities of color live with little to no access to parks, paths, and green spaces as compared to their white

Figure 10.3 Climate Justice.
Source: Photo by Siddhant Soni on Unsplash.

counterparts. During the COVID pandemic this has become extremely prohibitive with restriction to outdoor recreation making greenery even more difficult for this group to access.

Aalayna Green is a 22-year-old co-environmental education director for Black Girl Environmentalist. She explains this is a "supportive community of Black girls, women, and nonbinary environmentalists… Understanding those dimensions ensures that any climate change activism isn't going to be automatically catered to one type of person in society" (Greenfield, 2021). Green continues that the only way many diverse youth activists understand and fight for climate-justice issues is through an intersectional lens. This intersectional lens means one is "taking into account the dimension of gender, socio-economic class, and race that all ultimately influence how one is related to and experiences the effects of climate change" (Greenfield, 2021).

The fourth annual New Horizons in Conservation 2021 included a diverse array of youth activists discussing equity and inclusion within the conservation field virtually hosted by the Yale School of the Environment. Dorceta Taylor, a Yale Environmentalist, attended the conference and stated, "The media tends to focus attention on climate activism on young white activists in the United States, and Europe" (Greenfield, 2021). The conference

> demonstrates that young students of color are engaged in climate activism and are interested in being a part of the solution… Many speakers drove home the point that the climate movement, conversation, and the broader environmental movement cannot be successful

if white leaders, policymakers, practitioners do not collaborate with communities and activists of color. (Greenfield, 2021)

Eighteen-year-old Mexican-Indigenous climate advocate and cofounder of Re-Earth Initiative, Xiya Batista, strongly felt that Gen Z's approach to climate justice activism was the most inclusive and diverse youth movement for today. The organization focuses on the intersection of social justice and climate justice www.reearthin.org. She cited the example of the Re-Earth Initiative having activists in over 15 different time zones. Information from the group is translated into six different languages, underscoring diversity and universality. "Re-Earth board includes people from almost every continent, and we operate in a non-hierarchical way that actually listens to the whole body when it comes to what we are going to do... In our own youth organizations, we are modeling the world we want to see" (Greenfield, 2021).

Xiya explains she was raised through the lens of caring for Mother Earth in a cultural way. When her hometown in Mexico experienced severe flooding, she realized that climate disaster could happen anywhere at any time. She understood her community and many others did not have the resources to remedy the damage caused by the floods. This motivated Xiya to create an environmental school club in the flooded community. She began her activism for change by lobbying for the Climate and Leadership Community Protection Act, testifying on climate emergency, and organizing Clean Water Act Strikes.

The following facts illustrate the overriding injustice surrounding climate crisis (Justich, 2021): (1) 55 percent of people who live less than two miles from hazardous waste sites are people of color. (2) 47 percent of people who live close to hazardous waste sites are Black or Latinx. (3) 50 percent of black people are exposed to 50 percent more air pollution than white people. (4) 40 percent of black and brown communities are 40 percent more likely to have unsafe drinking water. These statistics indicate how plastic, air, and water pollution have become a part of environmental racism.

> The fight for climate justice is a fight against the many systems that affect vulnerable communities which are primarily Black, Brown, and Indigenous... I see my role as really a climate communicator... talking about the climate justice aspect and intergenerational injustice aspect that comes from the (climate) crisis. (Justich, 2021)

Impact of Climate Change on Human Welfare

While the eyes of the world have been riveted on polar bears, Antarctic penguins, and other endangered inhabitants of the Earth's shrinking ice caps, relatively few researchers have turned serious attention – until recent years – to quantify the prospective long-term effects of climate change on human welfare. (Skoufias, 2012, p. 2)

The impact of climate change on children and families must be highlighted through the eyes of social justice – not only underscoring poverty but, inequality as well. Disadvantaged and marginalized children and families are socially and economically disproportionally affected by climate change. Skoufias notes that "climate change impacts tend to be regressive, falling more heavily on the poor than the rich" (p. 6), with significant variation with already poor regions being more affected than prosperous regions (p. 5).

Three Effects of Inequality on Disadvantaged Groups

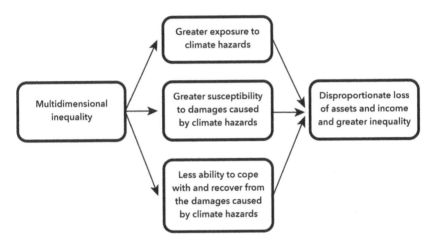

Figure 10.4 Effects of Inequality.

Source: S. Nazrul Islam & John Winkel. (2017). Climate Change and Social Inequality. DESA Working Paper No. 152. New York: United Nations (ST/ESA/2017/DWP/152) (pp. 5 and 6, for the first and second figures, respectively – Figure 10.4 and Figure 10.5).

Inequality hinders the disadvantaged population in the following ways:

1. Increase in the exposure to climate hazards.
2. Increase in the susceptibility to damage caused by climate hazards.
3. Decrease in the ability to cope with and recover from damage. P. 5

As a result of these three findings about climate change, disadvantaged children and families bear the burden of disproportionate loss of income and assets. This makes inequality unjust and continuing the cycle.

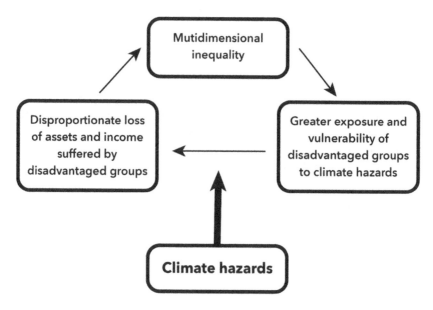

Figure 10.5 Inequality and Climate Change Vicious Cycle.

Source: S. Nazrul Islam & John Winkel. (2017). Climate Change and Social Inequality. DESA Working Paper No. 152. New York: United Nations (ST/ESA/2017/DWP/152) (pp. 5 and 6, for the first and second figures, respectively – Figure 10.4 and Figure 10.5).

Nature Deprivation Has Consequences

Communities that carry the burden of the impact and cost of nature destruction receive less of the benefits of nature's benefits in terms of air and water purification, disease control, health, relaxation, and opportunities for recreation and parks. "Studies have found that, because they are more likely to live in polluted areas without sufficient tree cover and space to get outdoors, people of color and low-income families are more vulnerable to "developing immunocompromising illnesses such as asthma – a high risk COVID factor. Other studies have established a direct link between exposure to air pollution and COVID-19 mortality."

Knowlton et al., (2016) in conjunction with the American Public Health Association, Climate for Health, and ecoAmerica presented a webinar series program Climate Changes Children's Health. These researchers maintain climate change is "the burning of fossil fuels causing the release of carbon dioxide. This buildup in the atmosphere causes the earth's temperature to rise." In the last century, the Earth's atmosphere temperature has increased by nearly 1.5°F. Knowlton et al. assert that not only does climate change produces changes in the weather, but weather patterns such as wildfires, heat waves, super storms, and rising sea levels as well.

Climate Change and Children's Health

Climate change impacts children and families economically, socially, and health wise. A few of the many facts about children's health and climate change are as follows (Climate Changes Children's Health 2016):

- Children under five years old carry the burden of around 88 percent of the global diseases.
- Over two million children who suffer from asthma live in area with unhealthy ozone levels.
- Health-related deaths of infants under one-year-old are four times as high as persons one to 42-year-olds.

Figure 10.6 Young Child Exposure.
Source: Photo by Nina Hill on Unsplash.

- Children living in homes with damage from Super Storm Sandy were five times more likely to become depressed and anxious and eight times more likely to have difficulty sleeping.

These researchers give various reasons why children are more vulnerable than other populations. The first is that they are lower to the ground and weigh less. They are more prone to picking up pollutants on the ground, as they are more apt to crawl on the ground and put things in their mouth. Kids' immature immune systems make them more sensitive to exposure to environmental hazard. Children spend more time outside, and therefore have more exposure to pollutants and to extreme heat and cold.

In an article written by Claire McCarthy, MD, she states the policy of The American Academy of Pediatrics (AAP) on climate change and its impact on children. "When pediatricians take care of children, we aren't just thinking about their health and safety now—we are thinking about their health and safety in the future, too" (McCarthy, 2021). Maintaining climate change is a reality, McCarthy explains its impact on children in the following ways. Underserved kids are more vulnerable to heat waves, and extreme weather events such as wildfires, floods, hurricanes, and so on, not only directly threaten children's safety and put them at risk of mental health problems but also can create an enduring impact for the future. They also maintain poor air quality from climate change that can create respiratory issues such as asthma and allergies, and an increase in infections. In certain places on the planet climate change can lead to less food and less healthy food (McCarthy, 2021).

Exposure to Nature Helps

Nature provides positive gains for children and families, as well as cities and communities. Yet green spaces and urban nature play are often neglected in city planning and their value underappreciated. Borunda explains that

> natural spaces sop up stormwater, trees shade pavement in concrete cooling neighborhoods, plants suck up heavy metal from the soil, and so on... Less flooding means a reduction in mold and the stresses of flooding. Trees and plants clean the air and keeps lungs healthy. (Borunda, 2020)

Jenny Shea, co-author of the Center for America progress reports, explains "just a tiny rise in the amount of pollution increased the likelihood of dying from COVID-19 by 8 percent." Natural environments are assets to the brain as well as the body. Many reports indicate mental health improves when vacant lots are beautified by plants and cleaned up.

Walking in nature reduced heart rates and stress, and left people happier than a walk on concrete. For children this information is crucial. Luis Villa, executive director of Latino Outdoors, maintains, "Early exposure to the natural world can have profound effects on children... The nature gap is directly correlated to the wealth gap" (Borunda, 2020).

The Nature Gap

Across the country, 75 percent of all non-white families with children live in a census tract-essentially, a neighborhood with less natural land than the state average. Residents of black communities across the country breathe about 20 percent more harmful particles than residents of white communities do, though they bear less responsibility for causing the problem by driving, consuming goods, or other actions that contribute to air pollution.

Figure 10.7 We Need Trees.
Source: Photo by Kiana Bosman on Unsplash.

The lungs absorb a "pollution burden" far disproportionate to their impact on the planet (Borunda, 2020).

Amenities that include natural spaces to walk and sit surrounded by trees and plants are often only in white neighborhoods. Villa asserts, "As human beings, we are hardwired to be connected to natural spaces. The greatest evidence of that has come from the pandemic is the longing to be outdoors" (Borunda, 2020).

Rowland-Shea et al. present the following findings from studies that underscore the benefits of nature in communities for children and adults.

> Access to urban nature—and specifically the addition of green spaces to the poorest neighborhoods—can provide mental health benefits. In fact, scientists estimate that every dollar spent on creating and maintaining park trails can save almost three dollars in health care alone—a benefit that is being denied to the most economically distressed communities. Natural spaces also act as climate regulators that mitigate urban heat islands—metropolitan areas that are warmer than their surrounding rural areas due to their surfaces and the human activities taking place—cooling the surrounding area by as much as 10 degrees Fahrenheit. These are even more important given that climate change is already poised to disproportionately affect those with the fewest economic resources for adaptation. (July 21, 2020)

Shanna Edberg, director of conservation programs for the Hispanic Access Foundation, states a platform for all children and families to have access to nature in their environment.

At a time when Latinos and other communities of color are disproportionately suffering from COVID-19 and the myriad impacts of racism the report highlights that they are also missing out on the health, economic, and resilience benefit of having nature nearby. We must take the finding of the report as a call to action to protect and restore natural areas in an inclusive and equitable way, ensuring that they are close, accessible, and welcome to all. (Hananel, 2020)

Benefits of Green Schoolyards

Green schoolyards can provide mental health benefits. Studies from Luis et al. show empirical evidence on the benefits of designing green schools. Their study indicates green schoolyards can contribute to "mitigate the *nature deficit disorder* – greener schoolyards promoted a stronger restorative experience in elementary school. The perceived restorative effect was stronger for children who had lesser contact with nature" (Luis et al., 2020). It is essential to realize and institute the concept that mental health plays a critical role in the cognitive, emotional, and social development of young people. Essential to all areas of developmental mental health is the understanding that green schoolyards can enhance mental, well-being, and promote social-emotional skill development.

Kids feel calmer and less stressed when they can view nature through green landscapes from their classroom windows (Chawla et al., 2014). They seem to recover faster from stressful events and become more able to restore a more positive attitude and diminish negative emotions (kelz et al., 2015). Resilient behaviors are increased by natural green schoolyards, promoting feelings of competence and increased support and helpful social relationships (Chawla et al., 2014).

Nedovic and Morrissey (2013) also maintain that practice of relationship skills in green schoolyards allow children to increase cooperative play, behavior, and social relationships. Girls and boys develop greater self-awareness and self-management in this environment, tending to reduce aggression and discipline problems. Interacting with nature through gardening helps students feel proud of their planting, more responsible for taking care of the environment, and confident in their ability to preserver with a project and succeed.

Kuo et al. (2018) presented a research study examining the link between "greenness-academic achievement" in urban, high-poverty schools. Their findings indicated that "greening" has the potential to mitigate academic underachievement in high-poverty urban schools, focusing on the fact that "school trees might boost academic achievement, the paucity of tree cover in low-income areas is not merely an aesthetic issue but an important environmental justice issue."

The following is an analysis of the research data by Kuo et al., (2018):

- The more disadvantaged schools had less green in and immediately around their schoolyards than schools facing less disadvantage.
- Schools serving more white, well-off students had more tree cover than other schools.
- Extremely disadvantaged schools had only about half the amount of tree cover as the less disadvantaged schools.
- Measurements of green cover predicted statistically significant better school performance on standardized tests of math and marginally statistically significant results for reading.
- Tree cover was a stronger predictor of academic achievement than other types of greenness.
- School trees were more strongly linked to both reading and math scores.

In conclusion, the study contributed by Luis et al. leads to the conclusion that green schoolyards play a significant role in promoting restorative experiences, enhancing attitudes, and creating a connection to nature. They suggest these finding could be vital in securing a greener future for so many kids that live in underserved areas deprived of nature, and strongly suggest "city planners and policy makers need to focus more attention and effort on planning how best to (re)connect children with nature, which should contribute greatly both to achieving healthy societies and overcoming a wide range of environmental issues" (Luis et al., 2020).

The following Children and Nature Network image infographic supports the greenness-academic achievement findings and encourages green schoolyards. Green schoolyards provide mental health benefits of calm, positive emotion, resilience, relationship skills, and self-awareness.

Bringing Nature into Underserved Communities

Many doctors want to prescribe nature for communities of color. The Spanish-language nature walk in Santa Rosa resource center is one of the activities promoting diversity in state parks for parents. Many professionals feel this is essential to improving health among families that are not exposed to nature. Barriers to the outdoors for children and families include fees, transportation, language, and fixed work schedules.

Sammy Caioli (2018) presents the most recent statistics on demographics, a visitor National Park survey 2009, that indicates "one-third of Hispanic and African-American respondents had visited a park in the last two years, compared to more than half of white respondents." Health implications are a by-product, as children who get outside the least have the greatest rates of chronic diseases such as diabetes, asthma, and obesity.

Figure 10.8 Green Schoolyard Infographic https://www.childrenandnature.org/.
Source: Permission Children and Nature Network.

Dr. Nooshin Razani is a researcher who believes kids from underserved communities with greater exposure to green spaces could reverse these health trends. "We see two crises happening at the same time: We see an environmental crisis, and we see a crisis in pediatric health… We need to create environments that sustain flourishing lives. It's the same battle" (Cailoi, 2018).

Figure 10.9 Environment Makes a Difference.
Source: Photo by Michael Mimms on Unsplash.

One new program in Oakland California is Outdoor Afro. The motto on their website is "where black people and nature meet." California State Parks have been working to bring black history into state parks. Grants to bring low-income students, foster youths and students with limited language skills seek innovative transportation project to give low-income youth access to nature. Being outside is a stress reducer. Outdoor activities can include exercise, gardening, and picnicking can have a positive impact from birth weight to life expectancy. Having a plant inside the home or on the porch can make a difference for kids.

In conclusion, the research study done by Mendelson et al. in *Abnormal Child Psychology Journal* 2010, Feasibility and Preliminary Outcomes of a School-Based Mindfulness Intervention for Urban Youth, indicates mindfulness intervention is potentially a valuable tool to use in a school setting with limited nature, particularly with urban youth. The premise of these researchers is that underserved urban youth are at a disadvantage and often manifest challenging behaviors, poor school performance, anxiety and stress, and social and emotional issues. Approaches within the school using mindfulness practices indicate student's accommodation to these problems using self-regulatory practices increased positive attitudes and diminished intrusive thoughts and heightened emotions. Focusing less on symptoms and more on optimistic youth development created better results.

This study supports previous research suggesting that

> mindfulness-based approaches may be beneficial for enhancing responses to stress among youth … a school-based intervention involving mindfulness and yoga may be feasible and acceptable to youth, teachers, and school administrators in urban public schools serving chronically stressed and disadvantaged youth – Enhancing regulatory capacities and responses to stress among at-risk youth has the potential to facilitate development of core competencies that will promote a range of positive emotional, behavioral, and academic outcomes. (Mendelson et al., 2010, p. 8) See Chapter 6.

The Positive Impacts of a Nature Experience for Third Graders

Timiny Bergstrom completed a research project, The Positive Impacts of a Nature Experience for Third Graders, at Southern New Hampshire University, December 18, 2020. Her findings concluded what she felt instinctively and much of the research validated, nature provides stress reduction and attention restoration. Within her work she examines two theories related to nature. The first is the Stress Reduction Theory (SRT) by Ulrich which underscores that when stress is reduced, the mind is more available for other functions which includes learning. The second is Kaplan and Kaplan (1989) Attention Restoration Theory (ART), which states directed attention creates fatigue, and involuntary attention found in a restorative experience in nature is restorative. Ms. Bergstrom explains,

> As it becomes more apparent that time spent in nature is good for humans and children in particular, it is time to consider whether nature experiences have a role in and should be consistently implemented in public education by further investigating the value and the positive impacts of nature experiences for elementary age students. (2020, p. 6)

Timiny investigated a group of third graders to expand her research question, "what are some of the positive impacts of a nature experience for third graders in a Vermont public school?" The study focused on the benefits for these third graders on attention and stress after a 20- to 30-minute nature experience. Students were asked to report their increased feeling of happiness, attention, and calm.

The participants responded to a survey taken pre-nature and post-nature experience. The students reported an increase in post nature ability to pay attention in school, an increase in self-regulation, and a heightening of calm. Here are the reported student's levels of happiness (with permission, 2020, p. 10). Ten students reported a change in happiness level.

Happiness Rating (5= Very happy, 1 = Very unhappy)	Pre-nature experience total # of students:	Post-nature experience total # of students:	Changes in Happiness
5	6	10	• Five students reported an increase (four + 1, one + 2).
4	8	5	• Two students reported a decrease (one - 1, one - 2).
3	3	1	• Ten students reported no change.
2	0	0	
1	0	1	

Figure 10.10 Happiness.

Source: Permission Timiny Bergstrom.

These third-grade students also were invited to respond through dialogue. Here is some of the student's feedback and observations from researchers.

Happiness (p. 15, Observation data) November 6, 2020

It was really fun, and I was feeling good before, now I'm feeling better because I'm still feeling good, and I got to go outside and be in nature.

I had fun walking with some of my friends, talking.
Some kids were dancing and jumping up and down in the thicker piles of leaves.

I like the crunching sound of leaves. I liked how it was kind of loud. At the nature experience, Whenever I saw something that was on the list I could check it off so I wouldn't have to do it at the end when I would forget.

I feel the exact same but a little calmer after the nature experience. Students waiting patiently in class post nature experience and the room was quiet and described as calm.

I was going along, and I felt something weird on the ground. I checked and it was a daddy longlegs and I felt good that I didn't kill it.

One child found a plastic bag and held it up to me, "I picked it up!" he proudly showed me. (Observation data, November 6, 2020).

My drawing that I'm showing you is what my checklist looks like and I checked all the things off for sight, sound, touch, smell and taste. (Five Senses Nature Scavenger Hunt List)

Observations (November 6, 2020) includes, "Kids calling out to one another, 'I found it'" (from their scavenger hunt list).

Attention (p. 16, Observation data) November 6, 2020

Calm (p. 17, Observation data)

Connection to Nature and Caring (p. 17)

Engagement in Learning (p. 18)

Don't Worry Be Happy: Spend Time with Nature

The outcomes of the research were apparent. Findings indicated that 20–30 minutes experienced in nature do positively impact happiness levels of the third graders. Nature is innately restorative and directs attention from the fatigue of the digital world to a simpler involuntary attention amplified by being present in the moment. It allows kids to reduce their stress response to living conditions and tumult from the outside world. Nature holds a plethora of ways to play and have fun, and allows our children to relax, be present, and enjoy a beautiful moment.

"Don't worry be happy" is a popular phrase that has become a well-known song. It could very well be a natural tune Mother Earth sings to her children as they enjoy the wonders of nature.

Our Children's Trust

Exercising my 'reasoned judgement,' I have no doubt that the right to a climate system capable of sustaining human life is fundamental to a free and ordered society.

–U.S. District Judge Ann Aiken

https://www.ourchildrenstrust.org/juliana-v-us

Our Children's Trust is an organization with a goal to secure the legal right to a safe climate and a healthy atmosphere for all present and future generations. It is the world's only nonprofit public interest law firm dedicated exclusively to securing the legal right for youth to a healthy atmosphere and safe climate, based on the best available science. It provides strategic, campaign-based legal service to youth from diverse backgrounds to secure their legal rights to a safe climate.

Our Children's Trust is composed of lawyers dedicated to protecting the Earths' climate system. Young people are represented in global legal efforts to secure binding and enforceable legal right to a healthy and stable climate focus on constitutional claims. This is fundamental and enduring right for everyone to have life liberty and the pursuit of happiness, especially in their environment. The voices of our youth are amplified through a legal campaign that targets media, education, and public engagement work to support the youths' legal actions. There has been a shift of cases from individual projects to a system that furthered overdependency on fossil fuels despite is effect on the environment (https://www.ourchildrenstrust.org/).

The work of Our Children's Trust is guided by constitutional, public trust, and human rights law and the laws of nature to endure systemic and science-based climate recovery planning and remedies at the federal, state, and global levels.

Working with Youth Traumatized by Climate Change

The process of working with young people who have been traumatized by some aspect of climate change has left this organization very concerned and educationally aware of using a trauma informed approach to working with youth. Their view is concentrated on recognizing long-term chronic trauma, and acute trauma.

Figure 10.11 Youth Plaintiff.
Source: OCT.

Mat dos Santos, managing attorney, had explained in an interview on December 9, 2020, what the trust felt was their role when representing youth plaintiff, being acutely mindful of their present experiences, sensitivity to retraumatizing these young people, and awareness if any secondary and/or vicarious trauma. Mat and his collogues are developing a program to support youth going through these trials. They are presently engaged in action through a Trauma Informed Plan to support the mental health of these youth. This Trauma Informed Plan includes (1) timeline, (2) training for staff, (3) toolbox for youth and lawyers, and (4) boundaries that are safe and honored.

Earth Guardians

Earth Guardians is the organizational plaintiff in the landmark climate lawsuit Juliana v. United States. Twenty-one young plaintiffs from across the United States assert that the government's affirmative actions on climate change have violated their constitutional rights to life, liberty, and property, as well as failed to protect essential public trust resources.

Figure 10.12 Earth Guardians.
Source: OCT.

These young people have become leaders and spokespeople for global climate, environment, and social justice actions. They present a platform, resources, and collaborative opportunities to impact change through the arts, engagement, and legal action. Earth Guardians also assists in mobilizing communities in support of Juliana v. United States and other youth-led climate litigation involved with Our Children's Trust. The following is their statement on Global Legal Actions adapted from their website.

Global Legal Actions

The website for Our Children's Trust shares the following concise picture of the work they have done and are doing to protect young people and planet. Through pro-bono litigation in many countries, challenging governments take responsibility for climate issues within their region.

> *Our Children's Trust* represents, supports, and inspires youth and attorneys around the world who develop and advance legal actions to compel science-based government action on climate change in their own countries. The staff at *Our Children's Trust* support these locally led partner efforts by providing legal, outreach, and communications assistance and expertise.
>
> The success of our partners includes Norway's successful adoption of a public trust –based constitutional climate amendment, which is now pending in the Norwegian Supreme Court; Urgenda's big court win in the Netherlands mandating specific nation emission reductions; and the Supreme Court of Pakistan allowing young Rahab Ali's constitutional climate case to proceed on behalf of the public and future generations.
>
> *Our Children's Trust* also assisted with the youth plaintiffs' victory in Colombia, where their Supreme Court affirmed their constitutional rights to a healthy environment, life, health, food, and water; recognized legal personhood for the Colombian Amazon forest as well as a duty of the Columbian government to protect it; and ordered the Colombia government to create and implement plans to halt deforestation, update and orient existing land management plans towards climate change mitigation and adaptation, and develop an "intergenerational pact for the life of the Colombian Amazon" with the plaintiffs, affected communities, and scientific organization.
>
> –Our Children's Trust Website, 2021

Figure 10.13 Our Mission.

Source: Photo by Markus Spiske on Unsplash.

> *Our mission is to build an equitable and inclusive climate movement is only possible if we continue to fight for the health, safety, opportunity, and basic human rights of all people.*
> –The Climate Reality Project, June 1, 2020
> https://www.climaterealityproject.org/press/statement-racial-justice

11 Someone Is Listening and Acting…

Joining our voices with all generations, for our grandchildren, future generation, and all life.

–Elders Climate Action

Figure 11.1 Elders Act Now.
Source: Permission Elders Climate Action.

DOI: 10.4324/9781003051770-15

Introduction

How can we use government policy as a teachable moment and confirmation of commitment to reinforce to our young people that someone is listening? This resource has sought to create a framework of accountability and attentiveness to and for young people to hear, accept, and act on their pleas for securing the health of the planet. Each chapter advocates for confirmation that today's youth are being heard and their suggestions implemented. Techniques to create conversations on climate change, provide vocabulary, legitimize environmental concerns, and establish meaningful activities and advocacies have been solidified. Information throughout the book verifies support from peers, environmental groups, parents, teachers, and caring adults. As we conclude progress made by the efforts of our young people, we must underscore the impact of these efforts on governments both on a community, national, and global scale.

The increase in climate depression and eco-anxiety may have a correlation to policies that did not support environmental change. Through media exposure, protests, education, and environmental sound activities, the tide is turning toward the progression from apathetic inaction to the perspective of bold new action, especially in government and global policies.

The goal of this chapter is to present action, hope, and affirmation to our young people that the urgency of their climate change movement has been and is being heard, and that people and institutions are joining the youth movement to transform the planet, its inhabitants, and the environment into a healthy and safe home for all. Providing teachable moments, dialogues, and factual input on notable progress and support, our young people can begin to realize that someone and many at all levels of society are listening.

> *We will bring back in the business to leading the world in climate change. We will bring a path on achieving a carbon pollution free electric sector by the year 1935 that no future President can turn back. I believe that every American has a fundamental right to breathe clean air and drink clean water. We are going to build 1.5 million new energy efficient homes in public housing units, alleviating the affordable housing crisis and reducing the wealth gap linked to home ownership.*
>
> –President Biden, CNN, January 19, 2021

Political Progress on Climate Change Action

Former President Trump announced in June 2017 he would abandon the climate agreement signed by 200 countries. On the first day of President Biden's administration, he signed an executive order to reenter the pact. On Friday, February 19, 2021, the United States rejoined the Paris climate accord aimed at reducing harmful greenhouse gas emission globally to diminish the impact of climate change (Guzman, 2021). President Biden appointed a special presidential envoy for climate, John Kerry.

Kerry stressed there is more work to be done. "We know that just doing Paris is not enough. If every country delivered, we'd still see a warming planet Earth" (Frazin, 2021). Kerry's role is to foster climate diplomacy throughout the world, including attendance at the United Nations conference on Climate Change November 2021 in Scotland to join other countries in formally pledging to stronger climate commitments.

Secretary of State, Antony Blinken (2021), confirmed the importance of addressing climate change as an immediate and substantial piece of the government's agenda. Blinken explains, "Climate change and science diplomacy can never be 'add-ons' in our foreign policy discussions. Addressing the real threats from climate change and listening to our scientists is at the center of our domestic and foreign policy priorities." Gina McCarthy is the White House domestic climate adviser stressed to the public that following through with the country's climate goals

> needs to be done in a way that gives people (especially young people) hope. If we work together, we can make sure that we don't just protect the planet, but we grow jobs with clean energy, that we do it in a way that's going to rebuild our economy. (Frazin, 2021)

Countries throughout the globe agreed under the Paris accord to strive to limit the planet's global warming to less than two degrees Celsius below pre-industrial levels. The accord is committed to another goal of limiting warming to 1.5 degrees. President Biden stated while campaigning that a United States goal to achieve net-zero emissions could be achieved by 2050 (Wright & Duster, 2021), which sends a powerful message the United States is prepared to cooperate in the fight against climate change and reclaim its leadership role. This sentiment was echoed by John Holden, a professor teaching environmental science and policy at Harvard University. "It sends a very important signal to the rest of the world on one of the biggest problems we have. I think it is very important the US demonstrates once again that it will take the global climate change challenge seriously" (Kann & Atwood, January 20, 2021).

Electric School Bus Coalition

On February 25, 2021, officials from the national Electric School Bus (ESB) Coalition reintroduced the Clean School Bus Act in the US Senate and the House of Representatives. This coalition includes a diverse partnership of organizations that represent equity, labor public health, clean energy, and environmental organizations. The following statements were issued by a few of its members (Pita Juarez, 2021):

> Electrifying our nation's school bus fleet is an important step towards reaching our goal of zero emissions and 100% clean energy. *The*

Clean School Bus Act puts us on the path to eliminating the diesel emissions too many children breathe and protects our local air and climate. We are thankful for Senator Cortez Masto, Senator Murray, and Representative Hayes' and Representative Cárdenas' leadership on this important effort and look forward to working with them to ensure a zero-emissions future for future generations.

–Athena Motavvef, Associate Legislative
Representative with Earthjustice

We look forward to kids getting back to school. The twenty-five million U.S. children who ride on school buses every day deserve a clean, healthy ride instead of breathing asthma-inducing fumes from dirty diesel buses. We need to replace the dirty diesel fleet with zero-emission electric buses that protect students' health, their communities and the climate. We welcome the Clean School Bus Act, which will help support the transition to pollution-free electric buses across the Midwest and the country.

–Susan Mudd, Senior Policy Advocate,
Environmental Law & Policy Center (ELPC)

We thank Senators Cortez Masto and Murray and Representatives Hayes and Cárdenas for leading this effort to help school districts upgrade from diesel-fueled school buses to zero-emission school buses. This is a strong down payment on our way to reaching full electrification of the nation's school bus fleet. We know that we need so much more to ensure that 25 million children, especially in communities of color and low-income communities, are breathing healthy air on their way to school and in their neighborhoods. We look forward to working together to boost funding to accelerate the transition of the U.S. polluting school bus fleet to zero emissions.

–Johana Vicente, National Director of Chispa, a community
organizing program of the League of Conservation Voters

This project was instituted by Climate Dads (see Chapter 9). The Electric School Bus Coalition is moving it forward. Its momentum is an example of a non-partisan diverse community that is listening, speaking out, and acting upon what they have heard. Political action is a by-product of paying attention to young people, and these legislatures and organizers serve to underscore to our youth that the adults around them are indeed joining them with pleas to make our planet a safe and healthy environment.

The Environmental Protection Agency (EPA) Is Helping

The Magic School Bus, a long-standing institution and educational resource presenting climate change issues to kids for 30 years, has now partnered with the EPA with a new book for children, *The Magic School Bus Gets Cleaned Up*. Now this pioneering series partnering with the EPA

Figure 11.2 Magic School Bus Clean.

Source: Scholastic/Original publisher with permission.

is in the forefront for our Gen Alpha's (see Chapter 1) to absorb early in life nature and care for the environment.

In collaboration with Scholastic, the original publisher of the Magic School Bus, this new book in the magical school bus series once again presents Ms. Frizzle taking her class on a field trip. This time she explores the pollution coming from their own diesel engine school bus. The kids realize they can help promote idle reduction to reduce health issues that can arise from diesel exhaust. The book ends with the "Magic School Bus" getting a diesel particulate matter filter. It is a pollution control device that reduces particulate matter/pollution by 90 percent (Epa.gov/dera/magic-school-bus, 2021). The EPA regulates inhalable particles. They explain that "particulate matter contains microscopic solids or liquid droplets that are so small they can be inhaled and cause serious health problems" (EPA, 2021).

The EPA reports that school buses carry 25 million children a year, with many being impacted by diesel exhaust creating health challenges. The EPA's Clean School Bus is a national program created to reduce emissions from older school buses still in use. EPA offers funding for these existing diesel engines and provides strategies for emission reduction – the most useful method is to replace older buses and reduce idling. The Diesel Emission Reduction Act of 2010 states the EPA offers rebates as well as grant to reduce harmful emissions from older diesel vehicles.

The EPA also offers IDLE, Free Schools Toolkit for a Healthy School Environment. This toolkit includes information about idling reduction for a school-based campaign to reduce toxic vehicle exhaust and provides resources to create a student run science involvement project. They offer a free downloadable Clean School Bus USA Idle-Reduction Teacher's Guide epa.gov/clean school bus 2021? https://www.epa.gov/sites/default/files/2019-11/documents/5_clean_school_bus_teachers_guide.pdf).

Captain Planet Foundation

The Captain Planet Foundation is an outgrowth of the TV Environmentalist Superhero program so many of our young people grew up with and were influenced by (see Chapter 1). As they state on their website, they have been "empowering next generation change makers. For 30 years, we've been committed to working collaboratively to engage and empower young people to be problem solvers for the planet" (2020).

Their mission has evolved into three dynamic programs. The first is Project Learning Garden (see Chapter 10). This program provides schools with basic strategies to establish and cultivate garden-based learning programs. The second initiative is Project Hero (see Chapter 5), challenging and supporting students to educate themselves and others and become involved in activities that can make a difference for local endangered species. The third program is Ocean Heroes Bootcamp (see Chapter 9, Violet). This environmental bootcamp helps young people learn to become carriers of the environmental torch on social and community issues that impact the planet.

In 2020, with the advent of COVID-19, the Captain Planet Foundation rose to the occasion to help underserved communities by transforming more than 100 of their Atlanta Project Learning Garden Schools into an amazing foundation of fresh, organic, home grown produce to share with local food pantries. It provided 80,000 pounds of food and over 300,000 healthy meals. Gardening for good, as Project Giving Gardens has been explained, is a child and community-based project rising from challenges we face on the planet by reaching out and helping others through the healing use of Mother Earth.

Pope Francis

Pope Francis sent a video message to the UN Virtual Climate Summit 2020. In it the Pope emphasized that now is the time to change direction and highlighted his efforts to promote a "culture of care" to combat climate change. He explains his goals in the following way:

"The effects of the ongoing pandemic and climate change—which are relevant not only for the environment but also for the spheres of ethics, society, economics, and politics—weigh most heavily upon the lives of the poor and vulnerable" (Watkins, 2020). This Pope is raising the priority of climate change on a global scale.

In the video he outlines the actions the Vatican City State is taking and emphasized it is dedicated to achieving net-zero emissions by 2050. The Vatican is also promoting an improved environment by reducing water and electricity use, and encouraging new procedures for energy efficiency, sustainable transportation, reforestation, and waste recycling. Pope Francis ended his message with a plea to all world leaders to realize the urgency and immediacy of climate change, "The time has come to change direction. Let us not rob younger generation of their hope in a better future" (Watkins, 2020).

President Biden and his administration are comrades with the Pope in addressing climate change. As Joe Biden points out, "Pope Francis is right in 'Laudato Si' – 'Never have we so hurt and mistreated our common home as we have in the last two hundred years,'" Mr. Biden wrote in an op-ed for Religion News Service in December 2019. "My faith teaches me that we should be a nation that not only accepts the truth of the climate crisis but leads the world in addressing it" (da Silva, 2021).

The Laudato Si (2015) is Pope Francis' encyclical on the environment. From the beginning of this document, he writes he wants to create a conversation with all people about our common home. The Pope references the Bible in urging all to us to "til and keep" the garden of the world, underscoring a mutual relationship between nature and human beings. He maintains that every community can take what they need from the Earth's bounty for subsistence, but it is our responsibility to protect the Earth and guaranty its fruitfulness for future generations (Cotter, 2021).

Global Pledge

Scientists tell us that this is the decisive decade, this is the decade we must make decisions that will avoid the worst consequences of a climate crisis.

–President Biden (Shesgreen, 2021)

In April 2021, President Biden called for a 50 percent reduction in US greenhouse pollution by 2030. He pledged at a virtual climate summit that week held with, "These steps will set America on a path of net-zero emissions economy by no later than 2050... forty world leaders, that there will be overarching changes to American energy" (Shesgreen, 2021). Biden in his speech explained that the United States only represents half of the world's emissions and explained, "No nation can solve this crisis our own. All of us, and particularly those of us who represent the world's largest economies, we have to step up."

The summit displayed to the world the gathering of the highest officials on the globe for the simple purpose of creating a future plan for climate change. India's Prime Minister Modi and President Biden launched an Indo-US climate and clean energy agenda for 2030 partnership that promises to mobilize investments, launch clean technology, and promote green collaboration. China's President Xi Jinping also pledged at the summit to peak carbon emission by 2030 and achieve carbon neutrality before 2060. Xi Jinping agreed with Biden and Modi that "We must be committed to green development. To improve the environment is to boost productivity." Vladimir Putin stated at the summit that "Russia is genuinely interested in galvanizing international cooperation so as to look further for effective solutions to climate change" (Knickmeyer et al., 2021).

In this virtual summit the United States reclaimed its leadership on climate change and urged global leader to commit to the same pledge. Biden informed listeners that there will be economic benefits from the reduction of fossil fuels and carbon emissions. "When we invest in climate resilience and infrastructure, we create opportunities for everyone. That is the heart of my jobs plan," Biden said. "Every country will need to invest in new clean energy technologies" (Frazin & Chalfant, 2021). He explains that directing financial resources into climate change can create fresh advances in construction and manufacturing, and that the creation of new careers to meet the challenge of climate change will be unfolding.

Alice Waters: Founder of Edible Schoolyards

In an inspiring interview on March 23, 2021 with trailblazer Alice Waters, recipient of the Global Environmental Citizens Award, Alice presented her beautifully transformative view of change in terms of food and reducing carbon footprints. Alice founded the Edible Schoolyard Project in 1995 and maintains over 25 years later that this "delicious revolution" can transform our relationship with nature. She explains to her food is love, and by producing food through growing it, cooking it, and feeding ourselves and others, we create a natural bond that allows a direct experience of community, diversity, and health for our bodies and the environment.

Alice envisions a world where all public schools provide organic foods and recreates the model begun at Martin Luther King Middle School in Berkeley, California. The concept of Edible Schoolyards has served as a reproducible model for all school systems globally. This school lunch initiative exists today in North Carolina, California, and other states whereby varied climates and population regions have all met with equal success in education and exposure for children on nature and food through this experiential project. Alice emphasized values of sharing, diversity, communication, and health can be imprinted at early ages through this firsthand learning and commitment to organic foods. "Nature is our teacher," she adds, and transformation happens effortlessly.

Alice maintains not only is food about love, but it is also about universality. Her goal is to see every country feed and educate students in the way the Edible Schoolyard project has achieved over the past 25 years. Stewardship, community, and equality have been promoted in over 6,000 schools. When young people grow food organically, cook the food, and then eat the food, they internalize the process that becomes a living understanding of their relationship with nature. A by-product that evolves is their visceral knowledge that they are the "stewards of the land." Alice feels if we can take kids and these activities into the kitchen, we will inspire the next generations.

Diversity comes when children gain "a deep falling in love with nature" and at the same time, educate the senses by eating with values of diversity and sharing with all cultures. Alice explains on the Edible Schoolyard website that her vision is grounded in the following key principle: Children deserve to be nurtured in body and mind, treated with dignity, and shown that they are valued.

> *The Edible Schoolyard Project takes literature, politics, biology, history, and science out the classroom and lets young people cultivate their disciplines in a garden, stew them in a kitchen, and discuss them over a table, together and with love. The result: some of the most joyful, committed, and thoughtful young people I've ever met.*
>
> –RAJ Patel (website, 2021)

Edible Schoolyards as a Model

The schoolyard's far-reaching model originated with Alice Waters in 1995. It incorporates the idea of learning across the curriculum using edible education. Academics are integrated with growing, cooking, and sharing wholesome, great tasting food. Alice has inspired a visionary model for sustainable farming and nutrition for students, with a mandate to school systems to incorporate Edible Education for all. The Edible Schoolyard Network connects 5,681 programs from 53 US states and territories as well as countries around the world (https://edibleschoolyard.org/).

The Edible Schoolyard at Martin Luther King, Jr. Middle School Berkeley, California, serves as the Edible Schoolyard Project's demonstration site and innovation hub. It has been gardening and cooking with sixth, seventh, and eighth graders – and working closely with the school community – since 1995. The following is an explanation adapted from the website https://edibleschoolyard.org/berkeley about the overview of the program and its goals.

The Innovative Model

In the Edible Schoolyard, students are farmers, cooks, learners, and teachers. In the kitchen classroom, chef teachers are guides to the exploration of how culture and identity shape personal relationship and access to food. Students, teachers, and community volunteers gather around the table to share meals and conversation.

Figure 11.3 The Table.
Source: Permission Edible Schoolyard.

In the garden classroom, students are the keepers of the soil and shepherds of the harvest.

Figure 11.4 The Garden.
Source: Permission Edible Schoolyard 11.4.

They sow seeds and tend to the produce that fills bellies and fuels creativity, imagination, and learning at school and home (see Chapter 9). The Edible Schoolyard program is fully integrated into the fabric of the school and the academic experience of every student. Over their three years at Martin Luther King, Jr. Middle School, a student has 60 classes in the program. Students come to the garden with their science teacher and to the kitchen with their humanities teacher.

The Edible Schoolyard curriculum

The teaching staff designs lessons in close collaboration with King Middle School's science and humanities teachers. This helps create intentional academic connections that allow a student's full learning experience at school to become more relevant and engaging. Free and downloadable material and lessons are available on the website. The image is an example of a lesson from the Edible Schoolyard curriculum included in academic learning.

Figure 11.5 Classroom Lesson.
Source: Permission Edible Schoolyard.

The Edible Schoolyard Berkeley's curriculum as stated on their website,

> Aims to develop curious, engaged learners who demonstrate a sense of curiosity and dignity, the ability to work as a team to complete a job well, respect for oneself and others, an appreciation for diversity and an ability to learn from difference. Students also gain an understanding of how engaging with the food we can teach us, crystallize connections between anyone and anything, and cultivate relationships that make our families and communities resilient.

Family Nights Out

Family Nights Out at the Edible Schoolyard Berkeley is open to all King Middle School families. The classes provide an opportunity for parents, trusted adults, and siblings to experience what students are learning in the kitchen classroom. During a Family Nights Out class, students, family members, and trusted adults cook and eat a meal together while sharing and learning recipes and techniques for preparing meals at home.

> *To spend time in an Edible Schoolyard is to realize how much more is going on here than teaching kids how to garden or cook. Kids begin to learn about food in all its dimensions – as an edible medium of culture, science, ecology, and even social justice. The Edible Schoolyard is an eloquent and practical answer to some of the most pressing questions facing us as a society.*
>
> –Michael Pollan, Edible Schoolyard Berkley Website

Research: Carbon Footprint Reduction through Food

Alice Waters maintains that eating with a climate friendly diet can have a more profoundly impact on climate change than not driving cars or using solar panels. Many researchers agree with Alice and develop the dialogue that our carbon footprint can be reduced by the foods we eat. A carbon footprint is defined by the Nature Conservancy as "the total amount of greenhouse gases (including carbon dioxide and methane) that are generated by our actions." Pirnia states that "greenhouse gases that include water vapor carbon dioxide, methane, ozone, nitrous oxide, and chlorofluorocarbons are causing the Earth to get warmer" (2021).

Garin Pirnia's (2021) article maintains this can be a factor in more climate disaster, health issues and disruption in food supply. In the United States, the average human's carbon footprint is 16 tons a year, compared to four tons per person for the global average. The core understanding highlighted in Pirnia's article suggests if people and institutions could adopt a climate friendly diet or a low-carbon diet, the carbon footprint would be greatly reduced.

Dana Hunnes in UCLA Sustainability 2021 suggests a way to create this process. "If each and every person in the United States gave up meat and dairy products on one or more days of the week, ideally, all days of the week, we would save the environment from thousands of tons of carbon emissions." Joseph Poore (2018) co-authored a University of Oxford study that discovered a person's carbon footprint can be reduced by seventy three percent through incorporating a vegan diet.

> A vegan diet is probably the single biggest way to reduce your impact on planet Earth, not just greenhouse gases, but global acidification, eutrophication, land use and water use. It is far bigger than cutting down on your flights or buying an electric car. Avoiding consumption of animal products delivers far better environmental benefits than trying to purchase sustainable meat and dairy. (Petter, 2020)

Meatless Mondays

Meatless Monday is a global movement that originated in 2007 encourages people and institutions to reimagine their eating in terms of meat by cutting out meat one day a week for their health and the planet. Their hope is to educate and inform others to reduce consumption of animal products and enlarge consumption of plant-based alternatives. Chris Taylor (2020) states the following information in her article, "Yes, alternative meat can help stop climate change." Taylor cites the 2014 US Land Use Study that found

> livestock is the cause of one-fifth of all climate change causing greenhouse gas emissions, with cattle taking the greatest toll on the health of the planet. Each cow needs twenty-eight times more land and eleven times more water than the average agricultural animal... One pound of beef is worse for the planet than a gallon of gasoline. (Taylor, 2020)

As a young activist explained, there are over one and a half billion cows on the planet, taking up enormous farmland to feed and also dispose of their manure. This can reduce trees and produce water pollution. I am only eating meat once a month!!!"

Meatless Mondays offers on its website delicious kid-friendly recipes, guidance in implementing program at school and home that promotes global food sustainability. Meatless Monday expanded to all New York city schools beginning 2019–2020. Over one million students will be a part of the program every week, eating a healthy all vegetarian lunch every Monday.

A Viable Solution

Alice Waters is listening and acting. In her book, *We Are What We Eat* 2021, she explains the key is public school systems that provide a slow food, climate friendly lunch for every student. Universal values are a natural outgrowth of the Edible Schoolyard project because the program is intertwined within the distinct characteristics of each school relating to environment, climate, culture, and tradition. A diverse network evolves that can learn from each other's ideas and successes. She maintains the food system must play a prominent role if we are to genuinely tackle climate change issues. Alice presents an urgent plea and an option of choice attainable through education and experiential learning. Her simple solution is to create direct and pleasurable change by changing the way we eat.

> When enough of us change the way we eat in our everyday lives, the effects, as in any movement, will be monumental (p. 184).

School-supported agriculture—with its centerpiece of a free regenerative school lunch for every child—is the alternative economic engine every community can embrace that would cultivate self-sustaining agricultural support networks everywhere and nourish all our students.(Waters, 2021, p. 185)

The Rodale Institute

"The climate crisis is here, but regenerative agriculture can help fight it," explains Jeff Moyer et al., Rodale Institute 2020. In the white paper article, "Regenerative Organic Agriculture and the Soil Carbon Solution," these authors maintain the climate crisis is an enormous opportunity to change course and create a future that honors life, health, clean air, and clean water, while cultivating progressive ways to cooperate with nature. Ultimate change can occur when healthy soils sequester carbon so that a slowdown will occur when we choice healthy soil over chemically laden soil. This choice can be actualized in gardens, farms, parks public lands, and school yards.

The Rodale Institute proposes that

> soil carbon sequestration through regenerative agriculture is a human-scale remedy to global warming that is ready for implementation now... The specter of the climate crisis has provided an unparalleled opportunity to harness cutting-edge technological understanding, human ingenuity, and the rich history of farmers working in tandem with the wisdom of natural ecosystems to arrive at a stable climate. It's time now to heal our land and ourselves. (p. 30)

NOW: Action for Reforesting

Xiuhtezcatl Martinez has been a climate activist since he was six-year-old. He is now 19. He contributed to the landmark lawsuit against the federal government, Juliana et al. v. United States (see Chapter 10). The constitutional right of children to have a safe environment challenged the government for not taking meaningful action on climate change, knowing greenhouse gas emission warm the atmosphere with disastrous repercussions. Martinez has watched temperatures rise, wildfires burn uncontrollably, flooding waters, and extreme storms and drought.

Martinez has begun a nonprofit, NOW, seeking to transform the climate change movement into real action. He proposes a platform that reconceptualizes climate change and empowers everyday people to join movement. "The climate crisis is about all of us. It's about all that we care about. It's not a partisan conversation, it's about the humanity that's being threatened every day" (McCarthy, 2019). The mission of Now as stated on their website https://www.generation-now.com/why is to accelerate a cultural shift to stop the climate crisis and build a radically different future. The nonprofit aspires to plant one trillion trees with people donating ten dollars a month to reforest the planet, in the hopes of removing 200 billion tons of carbon from the environment (McCarthy, 2019).

World's Largest Lesson

The following is an email interview with the World's Largest Lesson completed on March 29, 2021, that indicates how much this team is listening to our young people worldwide, and what they are doing about it.

Each question that is given is followed by a response from the team working on the World's Greatest Lesson as completed on March 29, 2021.

The Interview: Questions and Answers

World's Largest Lesson works in partnership with UNICEF to promote use of the Sustainable Development Goals (SDGs) – or Global Goals in learning, so that children can contribute to a better future for all. We produce creative tools for educators and action-focused learning experiences for children and young people.

Our aim is that these resources build skills and motivation, inspiring the next generation to take positive action for the SDGs, people, and the planet. Each year we create campaigns and challenges to keep learning engaging and relevant. We support these with local activations around the world, to make sure no one is left behind.

Figure 11.6 World's Largest Lesson.

Source: With permission World's Largest Lesson.

We believe that education is key to delivering the promise of the Goals, so our resources are free, open source, and translated into over 30 languages. Since 2015, we have brought the Global Goals to children all over the world. In 2019, we reached 17.9 million children located in over 160 countries. We work with a diverse, global network that ranges from United Nations agencies to local youth networks so that everyone can take part. We stand alongside partners, including UNICEF and UNESCO to advocate for formal Education for Sustainable Development and encourage the widespread use of the Goals through education systems.

What are some practical examples of the World's Largest Lesson?

In 2016, we made three films with Oscar winning Aardman animations and educationalist Sir Ken Robinson, to set a context for the Goals and encourage student engagement and action. These animations are introduced by a range of high-profile figures in native languages such as Malala Yousafzai, Serena Williams, Neymar Jr., Kolo Touré, Emma Watson, Hrithik Roshan, Nancy Ajram, and Queen Rania of Jordan.

To engage young people and educators deeply in the Goals they are then invited to take part in real world projects, challenges, and social action that establish the Goals as the purpose for developing twenty-first-century skills. From using our Design Thinking Project to generate ideas and practical solutions, which support the circular economy and positive climate action, to participating in data collection for #FromWhereIStand, a Gender Equality Project for the Global Goals supported by Emma Watson. These resources and campaigns are designed to motivate all to act, inspiring the next generation of changemakers.

All images and information given with permission from World's Largest Lesson, website https://worldslargestlesson.globalgoals.org/.

As one youth made poster reveals, our young people want to "be a part of the solution, not the pollution."

Figure 11.7 The Solution.
Source: Permission World's Largest Lesson.

World's Largest Lesson in Nigeria, 2019

Figure 11.8 Nigeria Largest Lesson.
Source: Permission World's Largest Lesson.

In 2019, the World's Largest Lesson helped to bring the SDGs to over 1.2 million Nigerians. We ran a weeklong, countrywide youth activation led by over 4,000 youth volunteers where children took part in a lesson that invited them to think about the future that they want for Nigeria and resulted in them making an "ask" to the Ministry of Education for the inclusion of the SDGs in the national curriculum.

World's Largest Lesson Live, June 2020

On June 16, 2020, we launched *World's Largest Lesson Live*, an educational show for teens. The show premiered on YouTube and brought together experts and young people in conversation to reflect on the past few months and discuss how reimagining the future post COVID-19. Hosted by NBC News and MSNBC Correspondent Savannah Sellers, it explored the themes of education, health, and the future – addressing some of the key issues at the forefront of young people's minds during the COVID-19 pandemic. The show has now been viewed more than 370,000 times! Parents and teachers can also use the free downloadable activities and discussion guides that go along with the show, to help spark conversations in the classroom or around the kitchen table.

Figure 11.9 World's Largest Lesson Live

Source: Permission World's Largest Lesson.

Conclusion

The quest for immediacy of action by the youth movement cannot be ignored. This chapter illustrates the depression and anxiety plaguing many young people about climate change is being heard and indeed acted upon. The examples given ranging from individuals to institutions and government policies serve as models of hope and resilience for a generation of youngsters all too often feeling isolated and disenfranchised.

Through recognizing and highlighting the advances being made today and those innovations envisioned for the future, our planet and its children can feel safer and more protected. The youth movement foreseeably can embrace the perspective that they are not alone but joined by a multigenerational support system working effectively to create change.

Together young and old alike can re-envision and transform an old pattern of seeing, of apathy, and of complacency into a fortress of energy needed to restructure ideas and systems no longer functional in today's world. Through technology, compassion, education, and perseverance we can all truly unite to move forward.

Health, happiness, and prosperity can be achieved on planet Earth and gifted to all who live there.

Figure 11.10 Together.

Source: Photo by Juan Pablo Rodrigus on Unsplash.

12 Resources for Professionals, Parents, and Children on Climate Change, Global Warming, Nature, and Expressing Feelings

Young people today are our hope for the future. Everywhere, once they know the problems and are empowered to take action, they become excited, passionate and determined to change the world.
–Dr. Jane Goodall, DBE, Founder of the Jane Goodall Institute & UN Messenger of Peace

Figure 12.1 Resources.
Source: Photo by Sarah Delaware on Unsplash.

DOI: 10.4324/9781003051770-16

The following is an annotated bibliography for professionals, parents, and children's issues associated with climate change by topic and age. These resources offer age appropriate insights, activities, and information on climate challenges, climate vocabulary, climate information, and climate action.

Books for Children

About Feelings

Alber, Diane. (2019). *A little spot of anxiety*. This is a resource to help young children calm their worries. Diane Alber Art LLC Publisher. Ages 4–8.

Berry, Joy. (2010).*Let's talk about feeling jealous*. This book helps children understand being jealous is normal. New York: Joy Berry Books. Ages 3–7.

Berry, Joy. (2010). *Let's talk about needing attention*. This book helps children understand their need for attention. New York: Joy Berry Books. Ages 3–7.

Burns, Ellen. (2009). *Nobody's perfect*. This is a storybook for children about perfectionism. Washington, DC: Magination Press. Ages 7–12.

Buron, Karl. (2006). *When my worries get too big*. This is a book for children, which present ways for them to recognize and work with anxiety and worry. Shawnee Mission, Kansas: Autism Asperger Publisher. Ages 5–9.

Cook, Julia. (2006). *My mouth is a volcano*. This book discusses the social nuance of polite conversation, not interrupting, and when to stop talking. Chattanooga, TN: National Center for Youth Issues. Ages 4–8.

Cook, Julia. (2012). *Wilma Jean the worry machine*. This story is about childhood anxiety. Chattanooga, TN: National Center for Youth Issues. Ages 7–11.

Doleski, Teddi. (1983). *The hurt*. The wonderful story about a little boy who keeps all of his hurt inside, until the hurt grows so big it fills his room. When he shares his feelings, the hurt begins to go away. Mahwah, NJ: Paulest Press. All ages.

Goldblatt, Rob. (2004). *The boy who didn't want to be sad*. This is a story about a boy who doesn't want to be sad and tries to run away from his sadness. Washington, DC: Magination Press. Ages 5–9.

Huebner, Dawn. (2006). *What to do when you worry too much*. This is a kid's guide to overcoming anxiety. Washington, DC: Magination Press. Ages 6–12.

Johnson, Lindan. (2005). *The dream jar*. This is a story about a girl that turns a bad dream into a good one. Boston, MA: Houghton Mifflin. Ages 5–9.

Lichtenheld. Tom. (2007). *What are you so grumpy about?* This book helps children to change a grumpy mood. New York: Little Brown Books. Ages 5–9.

Mayer, Mercer. (2005). *There are monsters everywhere.* This is a story about childhood concerns. New York: Dial Press. Ages 4–9.

Meiners, Cheri. (2010). *Cool down and work through anger.* This book presents constructive ways for children to deal with anger. Minneapolis, MN: Free Spirit Publisher. Ages 4–8.

Parr, Todd. (2005). *The feelings book.* This is a board book for young children about feelings. New York: LB Kids. Ages 4–8.

Steig, William. (2011). *Spinky sulks.* Spinky is angry and begins to sulk. No one can make him stop. New York: Square Fish. Ages 4–8.

Voirst, Judith & Ray Cruz. (2009). *Alexander and the terrible horrible no good very bad day.* Alexander has a day where everything goes wrong. Everyone can relate to this. New York: Atheneum Books. Ages 4–8.

Weaver, Susan. (2011). *Worry busters.* This is an activity book for kids who worry too much. Herndon, VA: Rainbow Reach Series. Ages 5–11

Wolff, Ferida & Harriet Savitz. (2005). *Is a worry worrying you?* This is a helpful book for children that worry. Indiana: Tanglewood Press. Ages 5–10.

About Grief

Goldman, Linda. (2014). *Lucy let's go.* The story of Lucy's journey through grief when her big sister Tasha dies and ways that she felt and remembered her. Omaha, Nebraska: Centering Corporation. Ages 4–8.

Goldman, Linda. (2020). *Children also grieve.* A storybook about Henry and Tashi and their journey after grandfather dies. All ages. Independent Publisher. Free downloadable copy at www.greivingchildren.net.

About Magical Thinking

Monte, Marrielle. (2018). *Magic Thinking for Kids.* This book helps change negative thoughts into positive ones. Seize the Day Publishing. Ages 4–8.

Percival, Tom. (2021). *Ruby Finds a Worry.* A little girl has a worry that keeps getting bigger. NY: Bloomsbury Children's Books. Ages 3–6.

Rappaport, Doreen. (1995). *The new king.* A wonderful book about a boy who becomes king after his father dies. He uses magical thinking to try and bring him back to life. New York: Dial Books. Ages 6–12.

About Technology

Collins, Suzanne & Mike Lester. (2005). *When Charlie McButton lost power.* This is a story about Charlie, a little boy who loves his computer so much and has to deal with no power. New York: Puffin Books. Ages 4–8.

Jacobs, Thomas. (2010). *Teen cyberbullying investigated.* This book covers over 50 actual court cases involving young people and cyberbullying and the real dangers and legal consequences. Minneapolis, MN: Free Spirit Publishing. Teens.

Leavitt, Jacalyn & Sally Linford. (2006). *Faux Paws: Adventures in the Internet.* This is a storybook and CD Rom for young children to help teach them to protect themselves on the Internet. Produced by iKeepSafe.org. Indianapolis, Indiana: Wiley Publishing. Ages 5–9.

Ostow, Micol. (2011). *What would my cell phone do?* Sixteen-year-old Aggie losses her cell phone, her lifeline after a move, and begins an online search for it. New York: Penguin. Teens.

About Life Cycles

Adams, John. (2007). *The dragonfly door.* This is a story for young children about the life cycle. Maple Plain, MN: Feather Rock Books. Ages 5–10.

Buscaglia, Leo. (1982). *The fall of Freddie the leaf.* The story of the changing seasons as a metaphor for life and death. Thorofare, NJ: Charles B. Slack. Ages 4–8.

Gerstein, Mordica. (1987). *The mountains of Tibet.* This is a story of a woodcutter's journey from the mountains of Tibet through the universe of endless choices and back to his home again. New York: Harper and Row. Ages 7 and up.

Goble, Paul. (1993). *Beyond the ridge.* This book captures the essence of the Native American belief system on dying and death and the great circle of life. New York: Aladdin Books. Ages 5–10.

Hoban, Tana. (1971). *Look again.* This book of photographs illustrates to children that we may not always know the larger picture when we see only one small part. New York: Macmillan. Ages 4–7.

Mellonie, Bryan & Robert Ingpen. (1983). *Lifetimes: The beautiful way to explain death to children.* This book explains the ongoing life cycle of plants, animals, and people. New York: Bantam Books. Ages 3–10.

Munsch, Robert. (1995). *Love you forever.* This is a beautiful book for adults and children alike about the continuance of love throughout life. Willowdale, Canada: A Firefly Book. All ages.

About Natural Disaster

Bromley, Anne. (2010). *The Lunch Thief.* This is the story of a little boy who has lost everything in a fire and is stealing lunches from hunger. Gardiner, Maine: Tilbury House Publishers. Ages 8–12.

Burgan, Michael. (2011). *Surviving earthquakes*. This is a book of children's true stories on surviving earthquakes. North Mankato, MN: Heinemann-Raintree. Age 8 and up.

Grimes, Nikki. (2010). *Almost Zero: A Dyamonde Daniel Book*. This is a story of a young girl that creates a clothing drive for a child who has lost everything in a fire. NY, NY: Putnam Juvenile. Ages 7–11.

Raum, Elizabeth. (2011). *Surviving floods*. This is a book of children's true stories on surviving floods. North Mankato, MN: Heinemann-Raintree. Ages 8 and up.

Williams, Vera. (1984). *A chair for my mother*. After a fire destroys their home, Rosa, mom, and grandmother save their money for a big chair to share. New York: Mulberry Books. Ages 5–10.

About Trauma

Chara, Kathleen. (2005). *A safe place for Caleb*. This is an interactive book for kids and teens on early trauma. London: Jessica Kingsley. Ages 8 and up.

Holmes, Margaret. (2000). *A terrible thing happened*. This is a book for children who have witnessed violence or trauma. Washington, DC: Magination Press. Ages 4–9.

Palmer, Libbi. (2012). *The PTSD workbook for teens*. This book presents effective skills for healing trauma. Oakland, CA: Instant Help. Ages 13 and up.

Shuman, Carol. (2003). *Jenny is scared*. This is a story about a child afraid of scary events. Washington, DC: Magination Press. Ages 4–8.

About Homelessness

Carmi, Glora. (2006). *A Circle of Friends*. This is a story about a boy who shares his snack with a homeless man and inspires good will. NY: Star Bright Books. Ages 4–8.

Gunning, Monica. (2004). *A Shelter in Our Car*. This is the story of a young girl and her mom who are forced to live in their car because mom can't find a job. San Francisco, CA: Children's Book Press. Ages 6–11.

Landowne, Youome. (2005). *Selavi, That is Life*. This is a story of hope about a boy who finds himself homeless in Haiti. El Paso, TX: Cinco Puntos Press. Ages 6–12.

McDonald, Janet. (2010). *Chill Wind*. This story tells of a teenage mom and what happens when welfare payments run out. NY: Farrar, Straus and Giroux. Ages 12 & up.

About Depression

Andrews, Beth. (2002). *Why are you so sad?* This is a child's book about parental depression. Washington DC: Magination Press. Ages 5–9.

Chan, Paul. (2006). *Why is mommy sad?* This is a child's guide to parental depression. Mission Viejo, CA: Current Clinical Strategies Publishing. Ages 5–9.

Schab, Lisa. (2008). *Beyond the blues.* This is a workbook to help teens overcome depression. Instant Help. Ages 13 and up.

About Autism and Asperger's

Bishop, Beverly. (2011). *My friend with autism.* This is a book for children about autism with a CD of coloring pages. Arlington, TX: Future Horizons. Ages 7–11.

Grossberg, Blythe. (2012). *Asperger's rules.* This book explains how children make sense of Asperger's at school and with friends. Washington, DC: Magination Press. Ages 9–13.

Peete, Holly, Ryan Peete, & Shane Evans. (2010). *My brother Charlie.* This is the story of a boy with autism. New York: Scholastic Press. Ages 7–12.

Robbins, Lynette. (2009). *How to deal with autism.* This is a book to help children deal with autism. Logan, IA: PowerKids. Ages 7–11.

Tourville, Amanda. (2010). *My friend has autism.* This is a book about a child that has a friend with autism. Mankato, MN: Picture Window Books. Ages 5–9.

Wine, Angela. (2005). *What it is to be me! This is a children's book about Asperger's.* Fairdale, KY: Fairdale Publishing. Ages 5–10.

About Inspiration and Resilience

Aslan, Chrisopher. (2008). *Wenda the wacky wiggler.* This is the story of a girl that has the courage to dance to her own music. Vancouver, BC: Benjamin Brown Books. Ages 5–11.

De La Pena, Matt. (2015). *Last stop on market street.* A little girl and her grandmother discover the beauty and special qualities in their neighborhood. New York: G.P. Putnam's Sons. Ages 4–8.

De La Penta, Matt. (2018). *Camela: Full of Wishes.* This is a storybook for families and underserved children to find hope in the most unexpected places. NY: G.P. Putnam. Ages 4–8.

Hallinan, P.K. (2006). *A rainbow of friends.* This is an easy to read book about celebrating differences and the uniqueness of others. Nashville, TN: Ideals Children's Books. Ages 3–8.

Leaf, Munro. (2011). *The story of Ferdinand.* This is a classic story of a peaceful bull named Ferdinand. New York: Viking Juvenile. Ages 3 and up.

Muth, Jon. (2005). *Zen Shorts.* Three classic Zen stories are presented with inspiration through beautiful watercolor and ink illustrations. New York: Scholastic Press. Ages 5–12.

Robinson, Anthony & A. Young. (2010). *Gervelie's journey: A refugee diary*. This is the true story of a young child fleeing militia attacks and civil war in West Africa. London: Francis Lincoln Children's Books. Ages 8 and up.

Sabin, Ellen. (2004). *Hero*. This is a book that helps children learn lesson from the people they admire. New York: Watering Can Press. Ages 6–11.

Stepanek, Mattie. (2001). *Heartsongs*. Mattie was a poet and peacemaker that inspired many. Virginia: VSP Books. Children of all ages.

Wyeth, Sharon. *Something beautiful*. This beautifully illustrated book helps kids to see the beauty in everything, people, and places. Decorah, Iowa:Dragonfly Books. Ages 5–10.

About Courage

Dismondy, Maria. (2008). *Spaghetti in a hot dog bun*. This storybook is about kids having the courage to be who they are. Michigan: Making Spirits Right Publisher. Ages 5–10.

Gorman, Amanda. (2021). *Change Sings*. This book gives hope for the future and motivation to achieve change. NY, NY: Viking Books. Ages 4–8.

Greive, Bradley. (2007). *Teaspoon of courage for kids: A little book of encouragement for whenever you need it*. This book offers children encouragement through life. Kansas City, Missouri: Andrews McMeel Publishers. Ages 10 and up.

Levine, Ellen. (2007). *Henry's Freedom Box*. This is a true story about the underground railroad. NY: Scholastic Press. Ages 4–8.

Pearson. (2017), Emily. *Ordinary Mary's extraordinary deed*. The story of a little girl that picks blueberries and make muffins that is given to stranger. It shows actions can help others. Kaysville, Utah: Gibbs Smith Publisher. Ages 4–8.

Waber, Bernard. (2002). *Courage*. This is a wonderful book sharing different moments of courage for children. Boston: Houghton Mifflin Co. Ages 5–10.

About Kindness

Barton, Patrice. (2013). *The invisible boy*. This is a heartfelt book about a quiet boy befriended at school. It helps kids see everyone is different, and all are welcome to participate in activities. NY, NY: Knoph Books. Ages 6–9.

Bussolari, Cori. (2021). *Empathy is your superpower*. This is a book about understanding the feelings of others. Plano, Texas: Rockridge Press. Ages 4–10.

Luyken, Corinna. (2019). *My heart*. This book speaks to young people about love and acceptance. New York: Dial Press. Ages 4–8.

Miller, Pat Zietlew. (2018). *Be kind*. This story is about a little girl who continually tries to be kind and realizes how hard it is, but feels it is worth it. NY, NY: Roaring Book Press. Ages 3–6 years.

Muth, Jon. (2002). *The three questions: Based on a story by Leo Tolstoy*. This book asks three questions: When is the best time to do things? Who is the most important one? What is the right thing to do? It becomes a tool to dialogue on helping others. New York: Scholastic Books. All ages.

About Happiness

Barnes, Derrick & Gordon James. (2020). *I Am Every Good Thing*. This is a powerful story of Black boyhood. NY, NY: Nancy Paulsen Books. Ages 3–7.

McCloud, Carol. (2015). *Have you filled a bucket today? A guide to daily happiness for kids*. If kids have an invisible bucket, they can use it to hole good thoughts and be kind to others. Chicago, IL: Bucket Fillers Publisher. Ages 4–9.

Lawson, Arno. (2015). *Sidewalk flowers*. This book speaks to the everyday beauty a child can find in life to create inner happiness. Toronto: Groundwood Books. Ages 4–8.

Tallie, Mariahadessa Ekere. (2019). *Layla's happiness*. Layla is a seven-year-old who shares lots of things that make her happy. New York: Enchanted Lion Books. Ages 5–9.

About Mindfulness

Garcia, Gabi. (2018). *I can do hard things: Mindful affirmations for kids*. Texas: Skinned Knee Publishing. Ages 4–8.

Hanh, Thich Nhat. (2008). *Mindful moments: Ten exercises for well-being*. This resource explains mindfulness and offers exercises for kids and adults. Berkeley, CA: Parallax Press. All ages.

Hanh, Thich Nhat. (2012). *A handful of quiet*. A pebble meditation is a unique way of introducing kids to meditation. Berkeley, California: Plum Blossom Books. All ages.

McGhee, Holly. (2019). *Listen*. A young girl listens with her ears and her heart to nature and the world around her. New York: Roaring Brook Press. All ages.

Meiners, Cheri. (2013). *Be confident!* This book inspires worth and self-confidence for kids. Minneapolis, MN: Free Spirit Press. Ages 4–8.

Meiners, Cheri. (2013). *Be positive.* This book provides ideas and language to help kids create a positive attitude. Minneapolis, MN: Free Spirit Press. Ages 4–8.

Meiners, Cheri. (2014). *Bounce back.* This book explores resilience and promotes a child's ability to bound back from challenges. Minneapolis, MN: Free Spirit Press. Ages 4–8.

Meyer, William. (2021). *Healing Breath.* This is a guided meditation through nature for kids. Novato, CA: New World Library. Ages 5–9.

Muth, Jon. (2002). *The three questions (based on a story by Leo Tolstoy).* This story of a little boy searching for the meaning of life brings the reader into the present moment with three questions. New York, NY: Scholastic Press. For children of all ages.

About Empathy

Bussolari, Cori, PsyD. (2021). *Empathy is your super power.* This book helps kids understand the feelings of others. Emeryville, CA: Rockridge Press. Ages 5–10.

Cohen, Barbara. (2015). *How Jake learned to see with his heart.* Jake learns what it feels like to see with your heart. Walnut Creek, California: Sufism Reoriented. Ages 5–10.

Sanders, Jayneen. (2017). *You, me and empathy.* This book teaches children about empathy, feelings, and kindness. Victoria, Australia: Educate2Empower Publisher. Ages 5–10.

Verde, Susan. (2018). *I am human: A book of empathy.* This book is a celebration of our human family and how we can choose to be empathetic. New York: Abrams Books. Ages 4–8.

About Unity

Curtis, Jamie Lee & Laura Cornell. (2006). *Is there really a human race?* A little boy questions how we can make this world a better place. New York: HarperCollins. Ages 5–10.

Miller, Philip & Sheppard Greene. *We all sing with the same voice.* This is a song book that joins kids globally. It encourages global awareness for young children, and that everyone can come together to sing a song.

Obama, Barack. (2011). *Of thee I sing.* This is a letter from Barack Obama to his daughters about his heritage and their multicultural world. New York: Knopf. Ages 5–11.

About Perseverance

Piper, Watty & Reimaged by Dan Santat. (2020). *The little engine that could.* This timeless storybook institutionalized the chant "I think I can!"

that inspires kids to move forward with confidence. New York: Grosset & Dunlop. All ages.

About Nature

Cherry, Lynne. (2020). *The great Kapok tree: A tale of the Amazon rain forest*. Special Edition. This is a story about a community of animals that live in a special tree in the rain forest. New York: Houghton Mifflin. Ages 5–10.

Greig, Louise. (2018). *A walk through the woods*. Nature is calling children to step into a woodland wonder, that unfolds with a delightful papercut world on every page. New York: Sterling Children's Books. Ages 4–10.

Harajili, Huda. (2020). *All about weather*. This is a first weather book for young children. Emeryville, CA: Rockridge Press. Ages 4–8.

Luyken, Corinna. (2021). *The tree in me*. This book is a celebration of the gifts of nature that surround us. New York: Dial Books. Ages 4 and up.

Paterson, Katherine. (2011). *Brother sun, sister moon*. This book demonstrates respect, love, and wonder for the world we inhabit through the words St. Francis used to celebrate life. San Francisco: Handprint Books. All ages.

Sayre, April. (2018). *Thank you, earth: A love letter to our planet*. This book is a thank you note to the earth, the water we drink, and the air we breathe. New York, NY: Greenwillow BooksGreenwillow Books. All ages.

Silverstein, Shel. (2004). *The giving tree* (40th Anniversary Ed. with CD). This is a beautiful story about a boy and a tree, and their love for each other. The book speaks to generosity and kindness, and our inter-relationship with nature. New York: HarperCollins. Ages preschool and up.

Underwood, Deborah. (2020). *Outside in*. This book beautifully illustrates how we are all a part of nature and the universe. New York: Houghton Mifflin Harcourt. Ages 4–10.

Wohlleben, Peter. (2019). *Can you hear the trees talking?* This interactive resource beautifully illustrates the wonder of the forest. Vancouver, Canada: Greystone Publisher. Ages 8–11 years old.

Wood, Douglas & Chang-Khee Chee. (2007). *Old turtle*. This fable captures the message of peace on earth and oneness with nature. New York: Scholastic Press. Ages 6 and up.

About Endangered Species

Bergen, Lara. *The polar bears home: A story about global warming*. A young girl learns about polar bears and the effects of global warming. Little Simon. Ages 5–10.

Clinton, Chelsea. (2019). *Don't let them disappear: 12 endangered species across the globe.* This book introduces readers to a selection of endangered animals and provides helpful tips that everyone can do. New York: Philomel Books. Ages 5–11.

Jenkins, Steve. (2006). *Almost gone: The world's rarest animals.* New York: HarperCollins Publishers. Ages 5–10.

Sayre, April Pulley. (2010). *Turtle, turtle, watch out!* This resource shares the challenges turtles face as the grow, travel, and breed. Watertown, MA: Charlesbridge Publishers. Ages 5–10.

About Climate Action

Bergen, Lara. (2009). *Don't throw that away.* Kids learn with a lift the flap book about recycling, reusing, and making things out of trash. New York: Little Green Books, Simon and Shuster. Ages 3–6.

Clinton, Chelsea. (2015). *It's your world.* A best seller for young people become informed about climate change and be inspired to create change. New York: Puffin Books. Teens and up.

Clinton, Chelsea. (2018). *Start now! You can make a difference.* This book encourages teens to action and to understand they can truly make a difference. New York: Puffin Books. Teens.

Earhart, Kristin & EPA. (2007). *The magic school bus gets cleaned up.* The Magic School Bus gets cleaned up with up-to-date emission control technologies. New York: Scholastic, Inc. Ages 5–10.

Godsey, Maria. (2018). *Not for me, please! I choose to act green.* This book conveys the simple message about waste and how children can make a difference. Middleton, Delaware: CreateSpace.

Green, Jen. (2020). *Why should I recycle?* This is a book for young children explaining reasons why recycling is important. Hauppauge, NY: B.E.S. Press. Ages 5–9.

Green, Jen. (2020). *Why should I protect nature?* This is a book for young children explaining reasons why it is important to protect nature. Hauppauge, NY: B.E.S. Press. Ages 5–9.

Holasova, Anita. (2021). *Bruno the beekeeper: A honey primer.* Bruno the beekeeper helps kids help bees and make honey too. Massachusetts: Candlewick Press. Ages 7–12.

Kriesberg, Daniel. (2010). *Think green, take action: Books and activities for kids.* This book shares many techniques to help kids understand the environment and how to take action. California: Libraries Unlimited. Ages 10 and up.

Lindstrom, Carole. (2020). *We are water protectors.* A beautiful book inspires by the many indigenous-led movements across North America, presents a pleat to safeguard the Earth's water from harm. New York, NY: Roaring Book Press. Ages 3–8.

Margolin, Jamie. (2020). *Youth to power*. This is a book for teens and young adults inspiring them to act for climate change. England: Hatchette Go. Ages 13 and up.

McGhee, Holly. (2017). *Come with me*. A little girl explores what she can do to make the world a better place and realizes what we do matters. New York: G.P. Putnam's Sons. Ages 4–9.

Muenzer, Margie. (2020). *Si'ahl and the council of animals: A story of our changing climate for children and their parents.* Muenzer, Margie and Jane Lister Reis. Ages 6–10.

Parr, Todd. (2010). *The earth book*. Todd Parr helps young children with ideas to protect the Earth. New York: Little Brown and Company. Ages 3–6.

Siddals, Mary McKenna. (2010). *Compost stew: An A to Z recipe for the Earth*. This resource educates kids on composting, and the do's and don'ts about what to use. New York: Dragonfly Books. Ages 5–10.

Stahl, Bethanie. (2020). *Save the bees*. This book explains pollination and how people can join together to save the bees. Bethany Stahl Publisher. Ages 5–10.

Walsh, Melanie. (2012). *10 things I can do to help my world*. This book suggests to simple activities that kids can do that make a difference. Somerville, MA: Candlewick Press. Ages 3–7.

Winter, Jeanette. (2019). *Our house is on fire*. Greta Thunberg's call to save the planet. This is Greta's story about activism and her perseverance to action for the planet. New York: Beach Lane Books. Ages 5–10.

About Climate Change

Cherry, Lynne & Gary Braasch. (2008). *How we know what we know about our changing planet*. Scientist and kids explore climate change and global warming. Nevada City, California: Dawn City Publications. Ages 10 and up.

Harding, Trent. (2017). *Global warming and climate change with Theodore*. Theodore explains the causes of climate change and what kids can do to help. CreateSpace Independent Publishing Platform. Ages 5–10.

Herman, Gail. (2018). *What is climate change?* A comprehensive book for kids to learn the facts about climate change. New York: Penguin Books. Ages 11 and up.

Reis, Jane & Margie Muenzer. *Si'ahl and the council of animals*. This is a story of our changing climate for children and parents. Washington: Jujapa Press. Age 5–10.

Rockwell, Anne. (2006). *Why are the ice caps melting? The dangers of global warming*. New York, NY: HarperCollins. Ages 8–12.

Romm, Joseph. (2016). *Climate change: What everyone needs to know*. New York: Oxford University Press.

About COVID-19

Black, Heather. (2020). *Why did the whole world stop? Talking with kids about COVID-19.* This book is meant to be read by parents and kids together to create clarity and reassurance about the virus. Mindful Moments Publisher. Ages 5–10.

Baker, Peter. (March 31, 2020). *We can't go back to normal: How will the coronavirus change the world.* The Guardian. https://www.theguardian.com/world/2020/mar/31/how-will-the-world-emerge-from-the-coronavirus-crisis

Cheung, Catherine. (2020). *COVID-19 for kids: Understand the coronavirus disease and how to stay healthy.* Singapore: Small Space Sprouts Publisher. Ages 2–6.

Chevalier, Dr. Tiffanny. (2020). *Baby put your mask on!* Independently Published. Ages 5–10.

Luckey, Lindsey. (2020). *What is social distancing? A children's guide & activity book.* Logan explains the pandemic and why kids cannot go to school. Independently Published. Ages 5–10.

Morgan, Rob. (2020). *Madi goes to virtual school.* Independent Publisher. Ages 5–10

O'Meara, Kitty. (2020). *And the people stayed home.* Miami, FL: Tra Publisher. Ages 4–8.

Quillen, Marylou. (2020). *Perry and Steve's new normal: Life during COVID-19* (Penguin Adventure).

Ross, Nicole. (2020). *Virtual first day.* Lily is nervous about virtual learning on first school day. She learns it will be OK. Independent Publisher. Ages 5–10.

Roumanis, Alexis. (2020). *What is COVID-19? (Engaging Readers, Level 1).* Children learn about the spread of COVID-19 and how to stop it. British Columbia, Canada: Engage Books. Ages 3–6.

Saunders, Rachel. (2020). *Going back to school during coronavirus.* A young girl goes back to school and navigates staying healthy. Independently Published. Ages 4–8.

Thompson, Lisa. (2020). *Lucy's mask.* Lucy is quarantined during the virus and has fun with her mask. Independently Published. Ages 4–8.

About Climate Justice and Diversity

Alexander, Kate. (2020). *Generation brave.* This book feature the Gen Z kids and highlights those that are changing the world. Kansas City, Missouri: Andrews McMeel Publisher. Ages 11 and up.

Bryant, Kadeesha. (2020). *Anti-racism starts with ME!* This is a coloring book for kids about racism. Devela Publishing. Ages 3–12.

Byers, Grace. (2018). *I am enough.* An inspiring book to help kids love who they are, respect each other, and be kind. New York: Balzer & Bray. Ages 5–10.

Celano, Marianne. (2019). *Something Happened in Our Town*. This is a child's story about racial injustice. Washington, DC: Magination Press. Ages 4–8.

Charles, Tami. (2020). *All because you matter*. This beautifully illustrated resource is a tribute to all children being important and the recognition they matter. New York: Orchard Books. Ages 5–10.

Cherry, Mathew. (2019). *Hair love*. This resource honors and validates everyone is unique and free to be who they are. New York: Penguin Books. Ages 4–8.

DinoKids Press. (2020). *All Colors Are Beautiful*. This is an anti-racism coloring book for kids with quotes to promote inclusion and diversity. Independently Published. Baby to 12 years old.

Madison, Megan. (2021). *Our Skin*. This is a first conversation about race and racism. NY, NY: Rise + Penguin Workshop. Ages 2–5.

Merberg, Julie. (2020). *No!: My First Book of Protest*. This book is a simple compilation of actions that change the course of history. NY, NY: Downtown Bookworks. Baby – 3 years old.

Paul, Miranda. (2020). *Speak Up*. This is a book about speaking up against racism. NY, NY: Clarion. Ages 4–7.

About United Nations Sustainable Goals

Sjonger, R. (2020). *Taking action to end poverty: UN Sustainable Development Goals*. This book gives valuable insights and ideas in joining the conversation and action on UN Global Goals. Ages ten through teens. New York: Crabtree Publishing Company.

United Nations. (2017). *The Sustainable Development Goals*. This tiny book presents the UN Sustainable Goals in simple form for young children. New York: United Nations. Ages 5–10.

United Nations. (2019). *Frieda makes a difference: The Sustainable Development Goals and how you too can change the world*. Frieda guides children to understand the UN Global Goals and what they can do to help. New York: United Nations. Ages 5–10.

Books for Parents and Educators

Arnold, Carrie. (2018). *Understanding child and adolescent grief: Supporting loss and facilitating growth*. New York: Routledge.

Bruce, Nefertiti & Karen Cairone. (2011). *Socially strong, emotionally secure: 50 activities to promote resilience in young children*. Devon, PA: The Devereux Foundation.

Craig, Susan. (2008). *Reaching and teaching children who hurt: Strategies for your classroom*. Baltimore: Paul Brookes Publishing.

DeMocker, Mary. (2018). *The parents' guide to climate revolution*. San Francisco, CA: New World Library.

Fonda, Jane. (2021). *What can I do? The path from climate despair to action.* Penguin.

Gold, Lorna. (2018). *Climate generation: Awakening to our children's future.* New Lancaster, Pennsylvania: Veritas Publisher.

Goldman, Linda. (2022). *Life and loss: A guide to help grieving children* New York: Routledge.

Holland, John. (2016). *Responding to loss and bereavement in schools.* London: Jessica Kingsley.

Kellogg, Kathryn. (2019). *101 ways to go zero waste.* New York: The Countryman Press.

Macy, Joanna & Chris Johnstone. (2012). *Active hope.* San Francisco, CA: New World Library.

Payne, Ruby. (2013). *A framework for understanding poverty: A cognitive approach.* Texas. Aha! Process, Inc.

Reimers, Fernando. (2017). *Empowering students to improve the world in sixty lessons.* ASIN: B0722ZVXG5. Create Space Independent Publishing Platform.

Shugarman, Harriet. (2020). *How to talk to your kids about climate change.* Jackson, Tennessee: New Society Publishers.

Truebridge, Sara. (2014). *Resilience begins with beliefs.* New York: Teachers College Press.

Waters, Alice. (2021). *We are what we eat: A slow food manifesto.* New York: Penguin Press.

Community, National, and Global Resources on Climate Change

Websites

Emphasizing to children and teens that "we are all in it together" takes on a deeper meaning and a deeper understanding regarding climate change. We live in a global family whereby the actions taken in China, Africa, or Puerta Rico have an impact on the health and well-being of people and nature in Alaska and Tahiti. There is no escaping climate change is a global topic, and by joining together with others we create a common ground to grow healthy lives and a healthy planet. This chapter presents useful community, national, and international resources related to climate change. The following are a few highlighted examples of youth and parent-based initiatives.

Global Climate Strike is a worldwide youth movement calling on people across the world to take part in "ClimateStrikeOnline" actions (https://globalclimatestrike.net).

The Child Movement for climate justice, child rights and to provide education to arm conflict victim children founded by Licypriya Kangujam in July 2018 (http://www.thechildmovement.org/).

Fridays for Future is a youth social movement by students to create awareness of the climate change emergency by participating in global Friday strikes as well as global digital strikes (https://fridaysforfuture.org/).

Turn It Off Campaign is a student-based campaign to decrease emissions produced by idling drivers (https://www.nrdc.org/stories/green-your-school).

Meatless Mondays is an initiative sweeping school cafeterias to lessen the climate impact of weekday lunches (https://www.nrdc.org/stories/new-york-city-students-are-taking-climate-change-starting-lunchroom).

Moms Clean Air Force is a community of over 1,000,000 moms and dads united against air pollution and committed to fighting for climate safety to protect our children's health (https://www.momscleanairforce.org).

Science Moms is a campaign by science moms to engage mothers about climate change (https://sciencemoms.com).

Climate Kids is a website with teacher activities on climate change from K-12 and a downloadable kid coloring book on climate change (https://climatekids.nasa.gov/).

City Schoolyard Garden partners with Charlottesville City Schools (CCS) to connect youth with how their food is grown (http://charlottesvilleschools.org/city-schoolyard-garden/).

Our Children's Trust (OCT) is an American nonprofit organization based in Oregon that has filed several lawsuits on behalf of youth plaintiffs against governments, arguing that they are infringing on the youths' rights to a stable climate system (https://vimeo.com/ourchildrenstrust).

Global Citizen is an organization that works with issues of the environment and poverty (http://www.globalcitizen.org).

Websites

For Young People

A Student's Guide to Global Climate Change: www.archive.epa.gov/climatechange/kids

Climate Kids: *NASA's Eyes on the Earth:* www.climatekids.nasa.gov

Mother Earth Project: https://motherearthproject.org/

Millennium Kids Inc: https://www.millenniumkids.com.au/

Fridays for Future: www.fridaysforfuture.org

Youth Climate Movement: www.youthclimate.org

Global Climate Strike: https://globalclimatestrike.net/

Climate Action Network: https://www.usclimatenetwork.org/

Children and Nature Network: https://www.childrenandnature.org/contact-us/

One Million of US: https://www.onemillionof.us/

Captain Planet Foundation: Empowering Next Generation Changemakers: https://captainplanetfoundation.org/

The Magic School Bus Gets Cleaned Up: https://www.epa.gov/dera/magic-school-bus

Parachutes for the Planet: https://motherearthproject.org/parachutes/

Outdoor Afro: https://outdoorafro.com/

Black Girl Environmentalist: https://linktr.ee/BlackGirlEnvironmentalist

The Child Movement: http://www.thechildmovement.org/

Earth Guardians: https://www.earthguardians.org/

National Geographic Kids: https://kids.nationalgeographic.com

Zero Hour: http://thisiszerohour.org/who-we-are/

Hispanic Access Foundation: www.hispanicaccess.org

Live Climate: Music with a Mission: www.liveclimate.com

NOW: https://www.generation-now.com

Roots and Shoots: https://www.rootsandshoots.org

For Climate Justice

Thomas & Friends and UN Development Program. *All Aboard for Global Goals* explorers for the Global Goals: https://worldslargestlesson.globalgoals.org/wp-content/uploads/2020/10/Parents-Guide-Explorers-for-the-Global-Goals.pdf

Earth Justice: www.earthjustice.org

Dream Corps: Green for all: https://www.thedreamcorps.org/our-programs/green-for-all/

Elders Climate Action: www.eldersclimateaction.org

Our Children's Trust: https://vimeo.com/ourchildrenstrust

Global Citizen: http://www.globalcitizen.org

Re-Earth Initiative: https://reearthin.org/

Latino Outdoors: https://latinooutdoors.org/

Climate Reality Project: https://climaterealityproject.org

For Teachers, Parents, and Caring Adults

Maryland Pesticide Network: https://mdpestnet.org/about/

Mauna Loa Observatory: Trends in Atmospheric Carbon Dioxide: https://mdpestnet.org/about/www.esrl.noaa.gov/gmd/ccgg/trends/monthly.html

National Oceanic and Atmospheric Administration Climate Site: www.oceanservice.nosa.gov

Ocean and Climate Change Institute, Woods Hole Oceanographic Institution: https://www.whoi.edu/main/occi

Rodale Institute: file:///Users/lindagoldman/Desktop/Regenerative%20Organic%20Agriculture%20and%20the%20Soil%20Carbon%20Solution%20-%20Rodale%20Institute.html

Sea Level Rise Viewer: www.coast.noaa.gov/sir

Sesame Street: https://autism.sesamestreet.org/coping-with-covid/

Edible Schoolyard Project: www.edibleschoolyard.org

Holistic Life Foundation: https://hlfinc.org/

Mom's Clean Air Force: https://www.momscleanairforce.org/

Science Moms: https://sciencemoms.com/

Climate Dads: www.climatedads.org

1000 Hours Outdoors: https://www.1000hoursoutside.com/blog/why-1000-hours

Climate Mama: www.Climatemama.com

World's Largest Lesson Plan: Activities for young children on UN Goals: https://worldslargestlesson.globalgoals.org/

Climate Psychology Alliance North America: https://climatepsychology.us

Figure 12.2 Nature for All.

Source: Photo by Caroline Hernandez on Unsplash.

In Summary

The subtitle of this book is *turning grief and anxiety into activism* the ending and the beginning of this ongoing journey to release young people from the burden they feel they are carrying alone about climate change concerns and solutions. The UN Intergovernmental Panel on Climate Change (2021) released its most comprehensive assessment on climate change asserting in the first sentence of their summary,

> It is unequivocal that human influence has warmed the atmosphere, ocean, and land. There is no uncertainty that global warming is caused by human activity and the burning of fossil fuels. The report maintains temperatures will continue to rise, weather will get more extreme, Artic summers will vanish, and sea levels will rise. (Friederike Otto, IPCC co-author, in Januta, 2021)

We need to make a paradigm shift as a collective human consciousness. Actions that produce hopefulness can include donation of materials and finances, volunteering time and information, and making practical life choices in actions throughout the day for the health and well-being of the planet and its inhabitants.

It only seems appropriate to conclude with the following words of Greta Thunberg, the relentless global youth advocate who not only sparked a planetary fire around climate crisis issues but also ignited a strength of understanding and research on the climate solution. "The climate crisis has already been solved. We already have all the facts and solutions. All we have to do is to wake up and change" (TEDxStockholm, 12/18, eco-age).

After striking against the dismissiveness and neglect of organizations and people in power unwilling to see a problem, her reaction to this UN Climate Change Report was one of action, hope, and commitment to change by acceptance of scientific facts, dissemination of education, and providing solutions based on those findings.

Upon hearing the report, Greta tweeted that "the alarming report contained no real surprises, and simple confirms what we already know from thousands previous studies and reports. It's a solid (but cautious) summary of the current best available science." Greta continues to emphasize to world leaders, politicians, and government agencies to respond to this climate emergency because people are suffering, getting sick, and dying. A second tweet confirms her hopeful attitude.

It doesn't tell us what to do. It is up to us to be brave and take decisions based on the scientific evidence provided in these reports. We can still avoid the worst consequences, but not if we continue like today, and not without treating the crisis like a crisis.

–Greta Thunberg, 2/2, August 9, 2021

Figure 12.3 Protect the Future.

Source: Photo by Taksh on Unsplash.

Epilogue

*Nothing in nature lives for itself. Rivers do not drink their own water;
trees do not eat their own fruit; the sun does not shine on itself, and
flowers do not spread their fragrance for themselves. Living for others is
a rule of nature. And therein lies the secret of life.*

–Amit Gupta, 2016

Figure 12.4 Someone Is Listening.
Source: Photo by Nurpalah Dee on Unsplash.

Climate change may be the greatest challenge our young people face
today, and our young people may be the greatest solution to solve this
challenge. Their passion, intensity, and caring for themselves, others, and
planet Earth is astounding from minds and hearts that are so young, yet
so aware of the world around them. These children are forever vigilant to
be heard and recognized as a true force for transformation.

From toddler to adulthood, these youth activists carry the torch capable of
extinguishing the existing global excess, denial, and ignorance, and reshaping
ideas it into a new normal that respects mankind, dignifies all its inhabitants,
and nurtures the environment. Through acceptance of what presently exists
and actions to implement change, this new normal can emerge with youth
leading the way to transform education, politics, injustice, and pollution into
a cleaner and healthier world. They realize this essential principle – every
word we speak, every action we take, every thought we think is interrelated to
other people, the environment, and planet Earth.

Resilience is a concept tossed around for quite a few decades. It sometimes connotes immediate healing and instantaneous achievable outcomes. Thus, the urgency our youth cry out for and their deep feelings of not being heard, can sometimes increase perceptions that the call for action is falling on deaf ears.

There is a popular notion that kids must be resilient, rise to the immediacy of the occasion, and obtain lightning speed results with a cheerful attitude. The reality is that resilience is a process, a life-long process. Our planet must have time to heal, governments must evolve to create that healing, and cultures must mature to maintain the solutions.

Our children and elders cannot solve the problems of climate change in a week, a month, or a year. It is ongoing and eternal, and the expectation of immediate gratification for success can only breed disappointment. We must take an honest look at the challenges in our environment. The goals for now and moving forward are ones that inspire the development of a resilient planet with resilient human beings willing to accommodate the ever-present struggles and subsequent successes associated with climate change.

–Linda Goldman

A New Beginning…

We are on the threshold of a new age. Our youth are pushing us forward and challenging us to pay attention.

This younger generation not only carries layers of loss and societal challenges but it also begs the question to the elder generation… When will you do something about it?

Young people consistently remind us we are not evolving together *on* planet Earth; we are evolving together inwardly and outwardly *with* planet Earth.

Figure 12.5 Evolving Together.

Source: Photo by Madalin Olariu License on Istock.

References

AFP. (2020, March 24). Greta Thunberg says she "likely" had new coronavirus. Gretathunberg Instagram. www.Instagram.com.

Ahdoot, S. (Lead author). (2015). Global climate change and children's health. Policy statement. *Pediatrics*, 136 (5), 992–997. 10.1542/peds.2015-3232

Akpan, N. (2019, September 30). How to talk to your kids about climate change. *PBS*. https://www.pbs.org/newshour/science/how-to-talk-to-your-kids-about-climate-change

Alexander, K. (2020). *Generation brave: The Gen Z kids*. Kansas City, Missouri: Andrews McMeel Publishing.

Amatulli, J. (2021, August 9). Greta Thunberg speaks on UN's Climate 'Crisis' Report: We can still avoid the worst. *HuffPost*. https://www.huffpost.com/entry/greta-thunberg-climate-crisis-united-nations_n_6111498de4b00142855689c5

Anglin, J.P. (2002). *Pain, normality, and the struggle for congruence: Reinterpreting residential care for children and youth*. New York: Haworth Press.

Anglin, J.P. (2014). Pain-based behavior with children and adolescents in conflict. *Reclaiming Children and Youth*, 22(4), 53–55.

Baker, C. (2021, September 5). Climate disasters will strain our mental health system. It is time to adapt. *The Washington Post*. https://news.yahoo.com/climate-disasters-strain-mental-health-175548782.html

Baker, P. (2020, March 31). We can't go back to normal: How will the coronavirus change the world. *The Guardian*. https://www.theguardian.com/world/2020/mar/31/how-will-the-world-emerge-from-the-coronavirus-crisis

Barone, V. (2020, April 8). Pope Francis says coronavirus could be 'nature's response' to climate change. *New York Post*. https://nypost.com/2020/04/08/pope-says-coronavirus-could-be-a-reaction-to-climate-change/

Bath, H. (2008a). The three pillars of trauma-informed care. *Reclaiming Children and Youth*, 17(3), 17–21.

Bath, H. (2008b). Calming together: The pathway to self-control. *Reclaiming Children and Youth*, 16(4), 44–46.

BBC News. (2020, January 23). Derby staff and students given climate change anxiety therapy. *BBC*. https://www.bbc.com/news/uk-england-derbyshire-51222924

Berardelli, J. (2021, July 8). Northwest heat wave "virtually impossible" without climate change, study says. *CBS News*. https://www.cbsnews.com/news/climate-change-heat-wave-pacific-northwest/

Bergstrom, T.E. (2020, December 18). *The positive impacts of a nature experience for third graders* (pp. 1–44). Manchester, New Hampshire: Southern New Hampshire University.

Berinato, S. (2020, March 23). That discomfort you're feeling is grief. *Harvard Business Review*. https://hbr.org/2020/03/that-discomfort-youre-feeling-is-grief

Berrigan, F. (2019, March 17). Our kids know we're failing them on climate change. *Truthdig*. https://www.truthdig.com/articles/its-time-to-face-were-failing-our-children/

Bilow, R. (2018, September 27). Third grader inspires Williston business to ditch plastic straws. *The Observer*. https://www.willistonobserver.com/third-grader-inspires-williston-business-to-ditch-plastic-straws/

Borunda, A. (2020, July 29). How 'nature deprived' neighborhoods impact the health of people of color. *National Geographic*. http://www.nationalgeographic.com/science/2020/07/how-nature-deprived-neighborhoods-impact-health-people-of-color/

Brulliard, K. (2020, April 3). The next pandemic is already coming, unless humans change how we interact with wildlife, scientists say. *The Washington Post*. https://www.washingtonpost.com/science/2020/04/03/coronavirus-wildlife-environment/

Caiola, S. (2018, October 31). Doctors want to prescribe nature to communities of color. Here's how California might help. *Capradio*. https://www.capradio.org/articles/2018/10/31/doctors-want-to-prescribe-nature-to-communities-of-color-heres-how-california-might-help/

Calix, L. (2015). My favorite Dr. Seuss quotes. *New York Public Library*. https://www.nypl.org/blog/2015/07/20/favorite-dr-seuss-quotes

Captain Planet Foundation. (2020). Empowering next generation changemakers. https://captainplanetfoundation.org/

Career Guide. (2020, December 8). 10 common characteristics of millennial generation employees. *Indeed*. https://www.indeed.com/career-advice/interviewing/10-millennial-generation-characteristics

Carrington, Damion Environmental Editor. (2019, March 1). Youth climate strikers: We are going to change the fate of humanity. *The Guardian*. https://www.theguardian.com/environment/2019/mar/01/youth-climate-strikers-we-are-going-to-change-the-fate-of-humanity

Carter, C. (2012, September 10). Greater happiness in 5 minutes a day: How to teach kids loving-kindness meditation. *Greater Good Magazine Mind and Body Articles*. https://greatergood.berkeley.edu/article/item/better_than_sex_and_appropriate_for_kids

Caruso, C. (2020, April 30). Meet the 8-year-old climate activist cleaning up India. *Global Citizen*. https://www.globalcitizen.org/en/content/youth-climate-activist-cleaning-up-india/?utm_source=Iterable&utm_medium=email&utm_campaign=US_May_8_2020_Content_Digest

Caspani, M., & Harte, J. (2021, September 3). NY, NJ officials vow to improve extreme weather resilience as Ida death toll rises to 46. *Reuters*. https://news.yahoo.com/ny-nj-governors-aid-coming-150454366.html?guccounter=1&guce_

referrer=aHR0cHM6Ly9teS55YWhvby5jb20vP2d1Y2NvdW50ZXI9MQ&
guce_referrer_sig=AQAAAJsaxQufkEIPJAKeZqf8lHxocfPaDiZ1JDkpSHAb
RUgolYrGnHkH8KwVFgEaYMj87lUXf2t5h_JRW_A17zzHxkPGiL-ZsHgp
4B6tbIoN_BeKyYyiV4oWfKnEa5fcnzBWRN3_mBfCnv1oD1tQfz0uSrQLbx
5TnwV32PnIc2yDsiKW

Cereijido, A. (2019, August 12). Dora the explorer's lasing impact. NPR: CODE SWITCH. https://www.npr.org/sections/codeswitch/2019/08/12/750495544/dora-the-explorers-lasting-impact

Chawla, L., Keena, K., Pevec, I., & Stanley, E. (2014). Green schoolyards as havens from stress and resources for resilience in childhood and adolescence. *Health & Place*, 28, 1–13. 10.1016/j.healthplace.2014.03.001

Clayton, S., Manning, C.M., Krygsman, K., & Speiser, M. (March 2017). Mental health and our changing climate: Impacts, implications, and guidance. *APA. Climate for Health. EcoAmerica*. https://www.apa.org/images/mental-health-climate_tcm7-215704.pdf

Climate Psychiatry Alliance. (2020). https://www.climatepsychiatry.org/

Clinton, C. (2019). *Don't let them disappear: 12 endangered species across the globe*. New York: Philomel Books.

Coelho, S. (2020, August 18). What are the benefits of meditation for kids? *Medical News Today*. https://www.medicalnewstoday.com/articles/meditation-for-kids#benefits

Comely, M. (2020, June 4). Environmentalists for black lives matter: Why climate change and racial justice go hand in hand. *Curious Earth*. https://www.curious.earth/blog/climate-change-black-lives-matter

Conlan, G. (2017, March 25). It is the law of nature, that creation does not live for itself, but for other creatures. OMI Lacombe, Canada. https://omilacombe.ca/law-nature-creation-not-live-creatures/

Cotter, K. (2021, January). Summary of Laudato Si, Pope Francis' encyclical on the environment. *Diocesan Priest*. https://diocesanpriest.com/summary-of-laudato-si-pope-francis-encyclical-on-the-environment/

Craig, K. (2020, May 1). How to look for the helpers (and be one!) during the coronavirus. *PBS for Parents*. https://www.pbs.org/parents/thrive/how-to-look-for-the-helpers-and-be-one-during-coronavirus

Cunsolo, A., & Ellis, N. (2018, April 4). Hope and mourning in the Anthropocene: Understanding ecological grief. *The Conversation*. Retrieved September 25, 2019, from https://theconversation.com/hope-and-mourning-in-the-anthropocene-understanding-ecological-grief-88630

Dalai Lama. (2015, April 25). His holiness the 14th Dalai Lama of Tibet. *The Natural World*. https://www.dalailama.com/messages/environment/the-natural-world

Dalia Lama. (2021, January 10). A conversation on the crisis of climate feedback loops. *Office of His Holiness the Dalai Lama*. https://www.dalailama.com/news/2021/a-conversation-on-the-crisis-of-climate-feedback-loops

Da Silva, R. (2021, January 28). Explainer: What are Pope Francis and the Vatican doing to fight climate change? *America: The Jesuit Review*. https://www.americamagazine.org/politics-society/2021/01/28/explainer-pope-francis-climate-change-vatican-239845

Davies, P. (2019, June 2). 29 of Greta Thunberg's best quotes. *Curious Earth.* https://www.curious.earth/blog/greta-thunberg-quotes-best-21

Dunleavy, B. (2020, April 24). 20% of children on lockdown in China suffer depression, anxiety, study finds. *UPI.* https://wwwupi.com/Health_News/2020/04/24/20-of-children-on-lockdown-in-China-suffer-depression-anxiety-study-finds/5291587741928/

Ebrahimji, A. (2021, February 26). A middle schooler was insecure about his haircut. So his principal fixed it himself instead of disciplining the boy for wearing a hat. *CNN.* https://www.cnn.com/2021/02/26/us/principal-student-haircut-trnd/index.html

Ecological grief. (2020, January 23). https://en.wikipedia.org/wiki/Ecological_grief, https://motherearthproject.org/parachute-details/?parachute_id=MzI4

Egan-Elliott, R. (2019, September 27). 'Eco-anxiety' energizes young activists in climate strikes. *Times Colonist.* https://www.timescolonist.com/news/local/eco-anxiety-energizes-young-activists-in-climate-strikes-1.23959411

Elders Climate Action. (2021). A project of elders action network. https://www.eldersclimateaction.org/supporttheyouth/

EPA. (2021, March 13). Magic school bus gets cleaned up. *Magic School Bus.* https://www.epa.gov/dera/magic-school-bus

Explorers for the Global Goals. (2020). Parent Guide. https://worldslargestlesson.globalgoals.org/wp-content/uploads/2020/10/Parents-Guide-Explorers-for-the-Global-Goals.pdf

Fallon, S. (2020, June 3). New Jersey becomes first state to incorporate climate change in K-12 curriculum. *NorthJersey.com.* https://www.northjersey.com/story/news/environment/2020/06/03/nj-becomes-first-state-require-climate-change-k-12-curriculum/3136671001/

Felsenthal, E. (2019). Person of the year: The choice. *Time.* Vol. 194, NOS, pp. 48–50.

First-Arai, L. (2019, May 24). This 16-year-old is taking the school climate strike to the U.S. Capitol. *Yes Magazine.* https://www.yesmagazine.org/environment/2019/05/24/climate-strike-american-capitol-student/

Firth-Bernard, B. (2020, April 8). The most inspiring Greta Thunberg quotes. *Good Housekeeping.* https://www.goodhousekeeping.com/uk/lifestyle/a33602835/greta-thunberg-quotes/

Flowers, G. (2021, July 27). West Coast facing uptick in wildfires thanks to climate change, experts say. *Yahoo news.* https://news.yahoo.com/experts-west-coast-facing-uptick-183346480.html

Following Francis. (2021). All are one. *Francis on the Hill.* https://www.followingfrancis.org/

Francis, T., & Hoefel, F. (2018, November 18). The influence of Gen Z – the first generation of true digital natives – is expanding. *McKinsey & Company.* https://www.mckinsey.com/industries/consumer-packaged-goods/our-insights/true-gen-generation-z-and-its-implications-for-companies

Frazin, R. (2021, February 19). US officially rejoins Paris climate agreement. *The Hill.* https://thehill.com/policy/energy-environment/539554-us-officially-rejoins-paris-agreement

Frazin, R., & Chalfant, M. (2021, April 23). Biden says US will work with other countries on climate innovation. *The Hill.* https://thehill.com/policy/energy-environment/549929-biden-says-us-will-work-with-other-countries-on-climate-innovation

Galvin, G. (2020, April 24). With schools closed, Chinese primary school students show signs of depression, anxiety. *U.S. News.* https://www.usnews.com/news/healthiest-communities/articles/2020-04-24/study-1-in-5-chinese-children-showed-depression-symptoms-during-coronavirus-lockdowns

Gerszberg, C. (2021, April 29). Best practice for bringing mindfulness into schools. *Mind.* https://www.mindful.org/mindfulness-in-education/

Golberstein, E., Wen, H., & Miller, B. (2020, April 14). Coronavirus disease 2019 (COVID-19) and mental health for children and adolescents. *JAMA.* https://pubmed.ncbi.nlm.nih.gov/32286618/

Goldman, L. (2002). *Breaking the silence: A guide to help children with complicated grief* (2nd ed.). New York: Taylor and Francis.

Goldman, L. (2006). *Raising our children to be resilient.* NY: Taylor and Francis.

Goldman, L. (2011, January). *Valuing expressive therapy in grief work.* ADEC Forum. Vol. 37, Issue 1, pp. 20–21.

Goldman, L. (2012). Helping the grieving child in the schools. *Healing Magazine*, Spring/Summer, 26–29.

Goldman, L. (2014). *Life and loss: A guide to help grieving children* (3rd ed.). New York: Taylor and Francis Publisher.

Goldman, L. (2017). *Creating inclusion and well-being for marginalized students: A whole school approaches to supporting children's grief, loss, and trauma.* England: Jessica Kingsley.

Goldman, L. (2022). *Life and loss: A guide to help grieving children. Classic Edition.* New York: Routledge.

Green, E.J., & Drewes, A.A. (2013). *Integrating expressive arts and play therapy with children and adolescents.* Hoboken, NJ: Wiley.

Greenfield, B. (2021, April 21). Why young people of color are leading the fight to save planet Earth. *Yahoo/life.* https://currently.att.yahoo.com/att/why-young-people-color-leading-fight-save-planet-earth-215303349.html?guccounter=1&guce_referrer=aHR0cHM6Ly93d3cuZ29vZ2xlLmNvbS8&guce_referrer_sig=AQAAAHE_CDimXwnU1QVGzy_OqxyQZRNcNPBP6CEmfPHQVqRSA7N28sRaayvv-gAoT-IwfJwjGFwxN60rL2_HfduPngLceskjULhAHxZw9IXwvdZnN26ZvGgekxqqAGkz26iVGQaIZ0lc50DEzREOq_k5D-o_bsTc80rnkl7t09Sa-ts4

Greenwald, R. (2005). *Child trauma handbook: A guide for helping trauma-exposed children and adolescents.* New York: The Haworth Maltreatment and Trauma Press.

Gupta, A. (2016, May 21). Living for others is the rule of nature. And therein lies the secret of life. Linkedin. Retrieved August 25, 2021, from https://www.linkedin.com/pulse/living-others-rule-nature-therein-lies-secret-life-amit-gupta/

Guzman, J. (2021, February 19). Us officially returns to the Paris climate accord. *The Hill.* https://thehill.com/changing-america/sustainability/climate-change/539561-us-officially-returns-to-the-paris-climate

Hammel, L., Lopes L., Munana C., & Brodie, M. (2019, November 27). *Kaiser family foundation/Washington Post climate change survey. KFF.* https://www.kff.org/report-section/the-kaiser-family-foundation-washington-post-climate-change-survey-main-findings/

Hananel, S. (2020, July 21). Release: New report shows racial and economic disparities in access to nature. *Center for American Progress.* http://www.americanprogress.org/press/release/2020/07/21/487873/release-new-report-shoes-racial-economic-disparities-access-nature/

Handel, S. (2018, April 20). Seven metaphors for cognitive defusion: How to accept and detach from any thought. *The Emotion Machine.* https://www.theemotionmachine.com/7-metaphors-for-cognitive-defusion-how-to-accept-and-detach-from-your-thoughts/

Hanh, T.N. (2008). *Mindful moments: Ten exercises for well-being.* Berkeley, CA: Parallax Press.

Hanh T.N. (2013). *Moments of mindfulness: Daily inspiration.* California: Parallax Press.

Hartley, E. (2021, August 10). Wildfires rage across the world as U.N. releases damning climate changed report. *Yahoo News.* https://news.yahoo.com/wildfires-rage-across-the-world-as-un-releases-damning-climate-change-report-171925952.html

Haspel, E. (2021, July 23). Climate change is forcing us indoors – and childhood will never be the same. *The Washington Post.* https://www.washingtonpost.com/outlook/2021/07/23/climate-change-childhood/

Haupt, A. (2016, December). Mindfulness in schools: When meditation replaces detention. *U.S, News and World Report.* https://health.usnews.com/wellness/mind/articles/2016-12-08/mindfulness-in-schools-when-meditation-replaces-detention

Hickman, C., Marks E., Pihkala, P., Clayton, S., Lewandowski, E., Mayall, E., Wray, B., Mellor, C., & van Susteren, L. (2021, September 7). Young people's voices on climate anxiety, government betrayal and moral injury: A global phenomenon. *SSRN.* https://papers.ssrn.com/sol3/papers.cfm?abstract_id=3918955

Hertsgaard, M. (2011, May 25). Meet Generation Hot.Huffpost. https://www.huffpost.com/entry/meet-generation-hot_b_737163

Ho, S. (2019, October 16). 67% of 6–9 years old's want to make saving the planet their career mission. *Green Queen.* Https://www.greenqueen.com.hk/generation-alpha-67-of-6-9-year-olds-want-to-make-saving-the-planet-their-career-mission/

Holcombe, M., & Hanna, J. (2021, September 3). Ida flooding: After dozens die in the East, NYC mayor urges cities prepare differently. *CNN.* https://www.cnn.com/2021/09/03/weather/ida-eastern-us-flooding-friday/index.html

Huizen, J. (2019, December 19). What to know about eco-anxiety. *Medical News Today.* https://www.medicalnewstoday.com/articles/327354

Hunnes, D. (2021). The case for plant based. *UCLA Sustainability.* https://www.sustain.ucla.edu/food-systems/the-case-for-plant-based/

Isai, V., Bilefsky, D., & Hubler, S. (2021, June 30). Death spike as heat broils Canada and the Pacific Northwest. *The New York Times.* https://www.nytimes.com/2021/06/30/world/canada/bc-canada-heat-wave.html

Islam, N., & Winkel, J. (2017, October). Climate change and social inequality. DESA Working Paper No. 152, ST/ESA/2017/DWP/152. *Department of Economic and Social Affairs.* https://www.un.org/esa/desa/papers/2017/wp152_2017.pdf

Ivie, D. (2019, June 24). Big Little Lies TV Series, Season 2 Episode Laura Dern's Climate Change Scene. Do you still wanna be a teacher? *Vulture.* https://www.vulture.com/2019/06/big-little-lies-season-2-laura-derns-climate-change-scene.html

Jackson, Michael (Recorded) Man in the Mirror". (1988). Lyrics and music by Glen Ballard and Siedah Garrett. Produced by Jackson and Quincy Jones.

Januta, A. (2021, August 9). Key takeaways from the U.N. climate panel's report. *Reuters.* https://www.reuters.com/business/environment/key-takeaways-un-climate-panels-report-2021-08-09/

Jones, S. (2019, May 23). Ditching detention for yoga: Schools embrace mindfulness to curb discipline problems. *EDW.* https://www.edweek.org/leadership/ditching-detention-for-yoga-schools-embrace-mindfulness-to-curb-discipline-problems/2019/05

Justich, K. (2021, April 21). How an indigenous climate-justice advocate, 18, got her start: 'I was raised with that lens of taking care of Mother Earth'. *Yahoo Life.* https://www.yahoo.com/lifestyle/indigenous-climate-justice-advocate-xiye-bastida-214130870.html?guccounter=1

Kamenetz, A. (2019, April 22). Most teachers don't teach climate change; 4 in 5 parents wish they did. (Heard on Morning Edition). *NPR.* https://www.npr.org/2019/04/22/714262267/most-teachers-dont-teach-climate-change-4-in-5-parents-wish-they-did

Kann, A., & Atwood, K. (2020, December 19). Biden's promise on the climate crisis. *CNN.* https://www.cnn.com/2021/01/20/politics/paris-climate-biden/index.html

Kann, A., & Atwood, K. (2021, January 20). Paris Climate Accord: Biden announces US will rejoin landmark agreement. *CNN.* https://www.cnn.com/2021/01/20/politics/paris-climate-biden/index.html

Kaplan, S. (2021a, January 12). Female scientists focus on a secret weapon to fight climate change: Moms. *The Washington Post.* https://www.washingtonpost.com/climate-solutions/2021/01/12/climate-science-moms/

Kaplan, S. (2021b, September 26). Today's kids will live through three times as many climate disasters as their grandparents, study says. *The Washington Post.* https://www.washingtonpost.com/climate-environment/2021/09/26/change-disasters-kids-science-study/

Kelz, C., Evans, G. W., & Röderer, K. (2015). The restorative effects of redesigning the schoolyard. *Environment and Behavior,* 47, 119–139. 10.1177/0013916513510528

Kirzinger, A., Kearney, A., Hamel, L., & Brodies, M. (2020, April 2). KFF Health Tacking Pol 1 – Early April 2020: The impact of coronavirus on life in America. *KFF.* http://www.kff.org

Klein, R., & Caroline, P. (2020, May 23). Are we read? How we are teaching and not teaching - kids about climate change. The Hechinger Report. 2019. Protesting Change. https://hechingerreport.org/are-we-ready-how-we-are-teaching-and-not-teaching-kids-about-climate-change/

Knickmeyer, E., Daly, M., & Larson, C. (2021, April 22). World leaders pledge climate cooperation despite other rifts. *AP.* https://apnews.com/article/joe-biden-climate-summit-2021-d27b869add251860acc82f58e2750fd7

Knowles, D. (2021a, April 12). Citing grave threat, scientific American replaces'climate change' with 'climate emergency.' *Yahoo News.* https://news.yahoo.com/citing-grave-threat-scientific-american-replacing-climate-change-with-climate-emergency-181629578.html?fr=sycsrp_catchall

Knowles, D. (2021b, June 23). Climate change tipping points are upon us, draft U.N. report warns 'The worst is yet to come.' *Yahoo News.* https://news.yahoo.com/climate-change-tipping-points-upon-202555727.html?fr=sycsrp_catchall

Knowles, D. (2021c, June 28). Thanks to climate change, heat waves and record temperatures in the Pacific Northwest may become commonplace. *Yahoo News.* https://news.yahoo.com/thanks-to-climate-change-heat-waves-and-record-temperatures-in-the-pacific-northwest-may-become-commonplace-193838495.html

Knowlton, K., Ahdoot, S.M.E., & Meyers, S.M.D. (2016, May 9). Making the connection: Climate changes children's health. Part II webinar series. *American Public Health Association (APHO).* https://apha.org/climate-changes-health

Kuo, M., Browning, M.H.E.M., Sachdeva, S., Lee, K., & Westphal, L. (2018). Might school performance grow on trees? Examining the link between "greenness" and academic achievement in urban, high-poverty schools. *Frontiers in Psychology*, 9, 1–14.

Landreth, G. (2012). *Play therapy* (3rd ed.). London, England: Routledge.

Landreth, G.L., Baggerly, J.N., & Tyndall-Lind, A.M. (1999). Beyond adapting adult counseling skills to counsel children: The paradigm shift to child centered play therapy. *Journal of Individual Psychology*, 55(3), 272–287.

Lawrence, E., & Aspegren, E. (2019, August 15). From not having kids to battling anxiety: Climate change is shaping life choices and affecting mental health. *USA Today.* https://www.usatoday.com/in-depth/news/nation/2019/08/14/climate-change-global-warming-shaping-life-choices/1887870001/

Luís, S., Dias, R., & Lima, M.L. (2020, November 3). Greener schoolyards, greener futures? Greener schoolyards buffer decreased contact with nature and are linked to connectedness to nature. *Frontiers in Psychology*, 11, 567882. PMID: 33281670; PMCID: PMC7691232, 10.3389/fpsyg.2020.567882

Malchiodi, C.A., Kim, D.Y., & Choi, W.S. (2003). Developmental art therapy. In C.A. Malchiodi (Ed.), *Handbook of art therapy.* New York: Guilford Press.

Margolin, S. (2020, May 18). Why kids love building forts – and why experts say they might need them more than ever. *The Washington Post.* Retrieved December 24, 2020, from https://www.washingtonpost.com/lifestyle/2020/05/18/why-kids-love-building-forts-why-experts-say-they-might-need-them-more-than-ever/

Marshall, R.D., Bryant, R.A., Amsel, L., Suh, E.J., Cook, J.M., & Neria, Y. (2007). The psychology of ongoing threat: Relative risk appraisal, the September 11 attacks, and terrorism-related fears. *American Psychologist, 62,* 304–316. 10.1037/0003-066X.62.4.304

Martinko, K. (2020, June 17). New Jersey adds climate change to curriculum for all K-12 students. *Treehugger.* https://www.treehugger.com/updated-k-12-school-curriculum-will-include-climate-change-5025081

McCarthy, C. (2021, February 9). How climate change affects children: AAP policy explained. *healthy children.org.* https://www.healthychildren.org/English/safety-prevention/all-around/Pages/Climate-Change-Policy-Explained.aspx

McCarthy, J. (2019, October 2). This youth activist wants people to pay $10 a month to fight climate change. *Global Citizen*. file:///Users/lindagoldman/Desktop/This%20Youth%20Activist%20Wants%20People%20to%20Pay%20$10%20a%20Month%20to%20Fight%20Climate%20Change.html

McCrindle. (2021). Understanding Generation Alpha. *McCrindle Insights*. https://mccrindle.com.au/insights/blog/gen-alpha-defined/

McDonald, B., & Mary. (2019, August 8). Climate change depression, climate grief and climate despair. *Boston Evening Therapy*. https://www.bostoneveningtherapy.com/2019/08/climate-change-depression-climate-grief-climate-despair/

McGough, A. (2019, July 1). "Big little lies'" climate change episode: What can we learn. *Salon*. https://www.salon.com/2019/06/30/big-little-lies-climate-change-episode-what-we-can-learn_partner/

Meatless Monday. (2020, September 20). Her is why meatless Monday is food for you and the planet. *Meatless Monday*. https://www.mondaycampaigns.org/meatless-monday/news/heres-why-meatless-monday-is-good-for-you-and-the-planet

Meichenbaum, D.H., & Goodman, J. (1971). Training impulsive children to talk to themselves: A means of developing self-control. *Journal of Abnormal Psychology*, *77*, 115–126.

Mendelson, T., Greenberg, M.T., Dariotis, J.K., Gould, L.F., & Leaf, P.J. (2010, May). Feasibility and preliminary outcomes of a school-based mindfulness intervention for urban youth. *Journal of Child Psychology*. 10.1007/s10802-010-9418-x

Mikkelson, D. (2013, April). Fred Rogers – 'Look for the helpers.' *Snopes*. https://www.snopes.com/fact-check/look-for-the-helpers/

Miller, B. (2021, August 9). Key takeaways from the UN report on climate change. *CNN*. https://www.cnn.com/2021/08/09/world/ipcc-climate-key-takeaways/index.html

Miller, R. (2019, September 20). '90s kids were asked to do 'simple things' to save the Earth. Gen Z is thinking bigger. *USA Today*. https://www.usatoday.com/story/news/nation/2019/09/20/climate-change-school-children-strike-can-they-save-earth/2372456001/

Minkiewicz, K., Staff writer, Katherine@sonomawest.com. (2018, December 5). The Healdsburg School sends cards and kindness to Camp Fire victims. *The Healdsburg Tribune*. http://www.sonomawest.com/the_healdsburg_tribune/news/the-healdsburg-school-sends-cards-and-kindness-to-camp-fire/article_e139846a-f8c7-11e8-b581-17fafcc75bd1.html

Monbiot, G. (2020, February 15). My generation trashed the planet. So I salute the children striking back. *The Guardian*. https://www.theguardian.com/commentisfree/2019/feb/15/planet-children-protest-climate-change-speech

Moyer, J., Smith, A., Rui, Y., & Hayden, J. (2020, September). Regenerative agriculture and the soil carbon solution. *Rodale Institute*. file:///Users/lindagoldman/Desktop/Regenerative%20Organic%20Agriculture%20and%20the%20Soil%20Carbon%20Solution%20-%20Rodale%20Institute.html

National Institute of Mental Health (NIMH). (2017). Any anxiety disorder. *NIH*. https://www.nimh.nih.gov/health/statistics/any-anxiety-disorder

Naumburg, M. (1987). *Dynamically oriented art therapy: Its principles and practice*. Spartanburg, South Carolina: Magnolia Street Publishers.

Nedovic, S., & Morrissey, A.-M. (2013). Calm active and focused: Children's responses to an organic outdoor learning environment. *Learning Environments Research*, 16, 281–295. 10.1007/s10984-013-9127-9

NPR. (2019, August 14). Dora's Lasting Magic. WAMU 88.5. Retrieved at https://www.npr.org/2019/08/14/750878177/doras-lasting-magic

Obama, B. (2020, May 17). READ: Former President Barack Obama's "Graduate Together' speech. *CNN*. https://www.cnn.com/2020/05/16/politics/obama-graduate-together-speech/index.html

Ogawa, Y. (2004). Childhood trauma and play therapy intervention for traumatized children. *Journal of Professional Counseling, Practice, Theory, and Research*, *32*, (1 Education Module), 19–29.

O'Meara, K. (2020). *And the people stayed home*. Miami, Florida: Tra Publishing.

Palmer, D. (2021, April). Climate activism and COVID-19. 2020. *Childrenvironment*. www.childrenvironment.org

Panache. (2019, December 12). Meet Licyriya Kangujam, the 8-year-old Indian 'Greta' who is urging leaders at COP25 to save the planet. *The Economic Times English Edition*. https://economictimes.indiatimes.com/magazines/panache/meet-licypriya-kangujam-the-8-yr-old-indian-greta-who-is-urging-leaders-at-cop25-to-save-the-planet/articleshow/72493089.cms

Parry, M.L., Canziani, O.F., Palutikof, J.P., van der Linden, P.J. & Hanson, C.E. (Eds.). (2007). Appendix I: Glossary. In *Climate Change 2007: Impacts, adaptation, and vulnerability. Contribution of Working Group II to the Fourth Assessment Report of the Intergovernmental Panel on Climate Change*. New York: Cambridge University Press. Retrieved from https://www.ipcc.ch/site/assets/uploads/2018/03/ar4_wg2_full_report.pdf

Pelly, J. (2020). Covid has invaded our kids' pretend play. Experts say it's a good thing. The Washington Post. https://www.spokesman.com/stories/2020/dec/02/covid-19-has-invaded-our-kids-pretend-play-and-exp/

Petter, O. (2020, September). Veganism is 'single biggest way' to reduce our environmental impact, study finds. *Independent*. https://www.independent.co.uk/life-style/health-and-families/veganism-environmental-impact-planet-reduced-plant-based-diet-humans-study-a8378631.html?utm_medium=Social&utm_source=Facebook&fbclid=IwAR37DkPMq3dBvXKUtZ2zxJOCBxhdQi1pOY68xOub8rHvGOJez9ZyL-NGnOs#Echobox=1559382669.

Pinsker, J. (2020, February 21). Oh no. They've come up with another generation label. *The Atlantic*. https://www.theatlantic.com/family/archive/2020/02/generation-after-gen-z-named-alpha/606862/

Pirnia, G. (2021, April 22). How to lower your carbon footprint with the foods you eat (and don't eat). *Huffpost*. https://www.huffpost.com/entry/foods-lower-carbon-footprint_1_606df9fcc5b6034a7083f6d8?ncid=APPLE NEWS00001

Pita Juarez, C. (2021, February 25). Coalition response to clean school bus act. *LCV*. https://lcv.org/article/coalition-response-to-clean-school-bus-act/

Plautz, J. (February 3, 2020). The environmental burden of Generation Z. *Washington Post Magazine*. https://www.washingtonpost.com/magazine/2020/02/03/eco-anxiety-is-overwhelming-kids-wheres-line-between-education-alarmism/?arc404=true

Pope Francis. (2017, June 12). Human rights corner. *TandagDiocese*. https://dezayasalfred.wordpress.com/2017/06/12/pope-francis/

Pope Francis in Conlan, Gerard. (2017, March 25). https://omilacombe.ca/law-nature-creation-not-live-creatures/

Postman, N. (1992). *The disappearance of childhood* (p. xi). NY, NY: Delacorte Press.

Ramaswamy, S. (2021, August 2). When turning on faucets is a source of stress: Climate change is starting to shape where American relocate. *USA Today*. https://usa24.org/when-turning-on-faucets-is-a-source-of-stress-climate-change-is-starting-to-shape-where-americans-relocate/

Re-Earth Initiative. (2021). Make a pledge for the planet. *Re-Earth*. https://reearthin.org/

Reimers, F. (2017). Empowering students to improve the world in sixty lessons. B0722ZVXG5. https://www.researchgate.net/publication/316890922_Empowering_Students_to_Improve_the_World_in_Sixty_Lessons/link/5a1ef8f10f7e9b9d5e021715/download

Reser, J., & Swim, J. (2011, May-June). Adapting to and coping with the threat and impacts of climate change. *American Psychologist, 66*(4), 277–289.

Resnick, B., & Scruggs, D. (2019, September 20). Photos: What the youth climate strike looks like around the world. *VOX*. https://www.vox.com/energy-and-environment/2019/9/20/20875523/youth-climate-strike-fridays-future-photos-global

Reuters Staff. (2020, March 24). Greta Thunberg says probably had COVID-19, urges #StayAtHome. *Reuters*. https://www.reuters.com/article/us-health-coronavirus-greta-thunberg-idUSKBN21B37C

Ries, J. (2021, August 9). How wildfire smoke exposure affects your health. *Huffington Post*. https://www.huffpost.com/entry/wildfire-smoke-exposure-health_l_610aa964e4b0552883e823f4

Robinson, S.K. (2021). The global goals for sustainable development. *World's Largest Lesson*. https://worldslargestlesson.globalgoals.org/resource/certificate-of-participation-2/

Rodriguez, L., & Gralki, P. (2020, June 5). New Jersey is now the 1st state to require schools to teach climate change. *Global Citizen*. https://www.globalcitizen.org/en/content/nj-introduces-climate-change-curriculum-schools/

Rogers, C. (1961). *On becoming a person: A therapist's view of psychotherapy*. Boston, MA: Houghton Mifflin.

Rogers, C. (1989). *On becoming a person: A therapist's view of psychotherapy*. New York, NY: Houghton Mifflin Publishing Company.

Rogers, C. (1995). *On becoming a person: A therapist's view of psychotherapy*. Boston, MA: Mariner Books Publisher.

Rogers, F. (2019). *Life's journeys according to Mr. Rogers: Revised edition*. England: Hachette Books.

Rogers, F. (n.d.). *AZQuotes.com*. Retrieved February 29, 2020, from https://www.azquotes.com/quote/384245

Root, R. (2020, February 1). How to deal with climate anxiety. *San Francisco Chronicle*. https://www.sfchronicle.com/opinion/article/How-to-deal-with-climate-anxiety-15021754.php

Rosenfield, J. (2016, July 21). Facing down "environmental grief." Quoting Kriss Kevorkian. *Scientific American*. Retrieved September 25, 2019, from www.scientificamerican.com

Rosenfield, J. (2016, July 21). Chasing down environmental grief. *Scientific American*. https://www.scientificamerican.com/article/facing-down-environmental-grief/

Rowland-Shea, J., Doshi, S., Edberg, S., & Fanger, R. (2020, July 21). The nature gap: Confronting racial and economic disparities in the destruction and protection of nature in America. *Center for American Progress*. https://www.americanprogress.org/issues/green/reports/2020/07/21/487787/the-nature-gap/

Rubenstein, A. (2020). *Interview with Linda Goldman*. Chevy Chase, Maryland.

Russ, S. (2007). Pretend Play: A resource for children who are coping with stress and managing anxiety. *NYS Psychologist*, XIX, 5, 13–17.

Sarwar, H. (2020, January 2). Meet Leah Namugerwa: The 15-year-old leading climate activism in Uganda. *The Rising*. https://therising.co/2020/01/02/leah-namugerwa-climate-activism/

Sengupta, S. (2019). Young people take to Streets in a Global Strike. *The New York Times*. https://www.nytimes.com/2019/09/20/climate/global-climate-strike.html

Schlanger, Z. (2017, April 3). We need to talk about "ecoanxiety." Climate change is causing PTSD, anxiety, and depression on a mass scale. https://qz.com/948909/ecoanxiety-the-american-psychological-association-says-climate-change-is-causing-ptsd-anxiety-and-depression-on-a-mass-scale/

Scholastic Parents and Staff. (2020, February 2). Communicate with your kids about climate change ages 5–13. *Scholastic Parents*. https://www.scholastic.com/parents/family-life/global-awareness/communicate-your-kids-about-climate-change.html.

Schugarman, H. (2020, July 7). Connecting the dots: The importance of climate education in schools. *The Climate Reality Project*. https://climaterealityproject.org/blog/connecting-dots-importance-climate-education-schools?utm_source=advocacy&utm_medium=email&utm_campaign=general&utm_content=reali-tynow-email-7-)

Sesame Street, Nature. https://cdn.sesamestreet.org/sites/default/files/media_folders/Images/NationalParks_Printable_GatewayNests.pdf?_ga=2.126091272.420985602.1583066958-888164168.1583066958

Shaw, A. (2018). Climate change. *National Geographic Kids*. https://kids.nationalgeographic.com/explore/science/climate-change/

Shen, Y. (2002). Short-term group play therapy with Chinese earthquake victims: Effects on anxiety, depression, and adjustment. *International Journal of Play Therapy*, *11*(1), 43–63.

Shesgreen, D. (2021, April 22). President Biden calls for 50% reduction in US greenhouse gas emissions at climate summit. *USA Today*. https://thehill.com/policy/energy-environment/549929-biden-says-us-will-work-with-other-countries-on-climate-innovation

Shinn, L. (2020, January 4). Your guide to talking with kids of all ages about climate change. *Natural Resources Defense Council. EcoWatch*. https://www.ecowatch.com/how-to-talk-to-kids-about-climate-change-2643952418.html?rebelltitem=1#rebelltitem1

Shugarman, H. (2020). How to talk to your kids about climate change. *Climate Mama*. https://www.climatemama.com/author-page

Sirola, M. (2019, June 11). The case for school-based mindfulness programs. *CMHN*. https://www.cmhnetwork.org/news/the-case-for-school-based-mindfulness-programs/

Skoufias, E. (Ed.). (2012). *The poverty and welfare impacts of climate change: Quantifying the effects, identifying the adaptation strategies.* Washington, DC: World Bank.

Smith, M. (2020, July 20). The boy wants to help save the earth: One park at a time. *People Magazine* p. 29.

Smith-Jannsen, K. (2020, January 30). He's leading D.C.'s movement for climate action – and he's a high school senior. *Natural Resources Defense Council NRDC*. https://www.nrdc.org/stories/hes-leading-dcs-movement-climate-action-and-hes-high-school-senior

Sobel, D. (2001). *Children's special places: Exploring the role of forts, dens, and bush houses in middle childhood.* Detroit, Michigan: Wayne State University Press.

Sreenivasan, H. (2017, February 21). Faced with outsized stresses, these Baltimore students learn to take a deep breath. *PBS*. https://www.pbs.org/newshour/show/faced-outsized-stresses-baltimore-students-learn-take-deep-breath

Stevenson, S.S. (2020, May 1). Socially distanced but spiritually connected. *Sisters of Mercy*. http://www.sistersofmercy.org/blog/2020/05/01/spiritually-connected-socially-distanced-covid/

Sullivan, A. (2019, October 17). Jane goodall quote. A new era of discovery in Gombe thanks to Disney Family Trust. *Jane Goodall's Good for All News*. https://news.janegoodall.org/2019/10/17/a-new-era-of-discovery-in-gombe-thanks-to-disney-family-trust/

Suttie, J. (2016, September 15). How to protect kids from nature-deficit disorder. *Greater Good Magazine*. https://greatergood.berkeley.edu/article/item/how_to_protect_kids_from_nature_deficit_disorder

Sutton, J., Guy, M., & Silverman, H. (2021, July 20). The Bootleg Fire in Oregon is so large, it's creating its own weather. https://www.cnn.com/2021/07/20/weather/us-western-wildfires-tuesday/index.html

Taylor, C. (2020, July 12). Yes, alternative meat can help stop climate change. Here's why. *Mashable*. https://mashable.com/article/environmental-impact-of-meat-substitutes/

Tenenbaurm, S. (2020, February 14). Moms make news. *Moms Clean Air Force*. Https://www.momscleanairforce.org/author/stenenbaum/

The Climate Reality Project. (2018a, June 7). Just for kids: What's climate change? And what can we do? (Reprint from April 2018 Save the Earth, National Geographic Kids). *The Climate Reality Project*. https://www.climaterealityproject.org/blog/just-kids-what-climate-change-and-what-can-i-do

The Climate Reality Project. (2018b, November 19). Beginning the climate conversation: A family's guide. *Climate Reality Project*. https://www.climaterealityproject.org/blog/beginning-climate-conversation-family-guide

The Guardian. (2020, January 12). How scientists are coping with "ecological grief." *The Guardian*. https://www.theguardian.com/science/2020/jan/12/how-scientists-are-coping-with-environmental-grief

The Guardian. (2019, March 1). Climate crisis and a betrayed generation. *Environmental Activism, Letters.* https://www.theguardian.com/environment/2019/mar/01/youth-climate-change-strikers-open-letter-to-world-leaders

The Nature Conservancy. (2021). Calculate your carbon footprint. https://www.nature.org/en-us/get-involved/how-to-help/carbon-footprint-calculator/#:~:text=A%20carbon%20footprint%20is%20the,highest%20rates%20in%20the%20world

Thompson, T. (2021, September 22). Young people's climate anxiety revealed in landmark survey. *Nature, 597,* 605. 10.1038/d41586-021-02582-8

Turner, C. (2016, February 19). Why science teachers are struggling with teaching climate change. *NPRED: How Learning Happens.* https://www.npr.org/sections/ed/2016/02/19/467206769/why-science-teachers-are-struggling-with-climate-change

United Nations. (2018, September 7). United Nations, Thomas & Friends Launch SDG Collaboration. *Sustainable Development Goals.* https://www.un.org/sustainabledevelopment/blog/2018/09/united-nations-thomas-friends-launch-sdg-collaboration/

United Nations. (2019). *Frieda makes a difference: The sustainable development goals and how you too can change the world.* New York: United Nations.

Vacar, T. (2020, January 22). East Bay women honored for service during deadly Camp Fire. *KTVU Fox 2.* https://www.ktvu.com/news/east-bay-woman-honored-for-service-during-deadly-camp-fire

Wadsworth, B. (2003). *Piaget's theory of cognitive and affective development* (5th ed). Pearson College.

Walsh, M. (2012). *10 things I can do to help my world.* Mass: Candlewick Press.

Waters, A. (2021). *We are what we eat: A slow food manifesto.* New York: Penguin Press.

Watkins, D. (2020, December 12). Pope to UN Climate Summit: 'Now is time to change direction.' *Vatican News.* https://www.vaticannews.va/en/pope/news/2020-12/pope-francis-videomessage-un-climate-summit-2020-vatican.html

Wedge, M. (2018, September 18). 7 ways mindfulness can help children's brains. *Psychology Today.* https://www.psychologytoday.com/us/blog/suffer-the-children/201809/7-ways-mindfulness-can-help-children-s-brains

White Pony Express. (2021). All of us taking care of all of us. *White Pony Express.* https://www.whiteponyexpress.org/

Whyte, A. (2017, March 13). IS TV really sheltering kids from climate change? *Kidscreen.* https://kidscreen.com/2017/03/13/is-tv-really-sheltering-kids-from-climate-change/

Wikipedia. (2018). Camp Fire. https://en.wikipedia.org/wiki/Camp_Fire_(2018)

Wikipedia. (2020, February). Climate grief. https://en.wikipedia.org/wiki/Ecological_grief#cite_note-7

Willard, C. (2016, August 25). Two simple mindfulness practices for back-to-school. *Mindful.* https://www.mindful.org/two-simple-mindfulness-back-to-school/

Williams, T.-A. (2020, Janurary 24). University of Derby offers climate change anxiety classes to staff and students worried about the future of the planet. *Mailonline Daily Mail.com.* https://www.dailymail.co.uk/news/article-7925467/University-Derby-offers-climate-change-anxiety-classes-staff-students.html

Winston, A. (2019, March 26). Young people are leading the way to climate change, and companies need to pay attention. *Social Responsibility – Harvard Business Review*. https://hbr.org/2019/03/young-people-are-leading-the-way-on-climate-change-and-companies-need-to-pay-attention

Winter, J. (2019). *Our house is on fire: Greta Thunberg's call to save the planet.* New York: Beach Lane Books.

Woods, B. (2016, November 6). Baltimore school turns to meditation as threat of violence loom over students. *The Guardian, In Baltimore*. https://www.theguardian.com/us-news/2016/nov/06/baltimore-school-students-meditation-patterson-high

World's Largest Lesson Plan. (2021). Welcome to the World's Largest Lesson Plan. https://worldslargestlesson.globalgoals.org/

Wright, H., & Duster,C. (2021, January 31). John Kerry says current goals under Paris climate agreement 'inadequate' to reduce Earth's temperature. *CNN*. https://www.cnn.com/2021/01/31/politics/john-kerry-paris-climate-accord-cnntv/index.html

Xiang, C. (2021, August 7). "We are shattered and lost": Largest wildfire in U.S. decimates a Northern California town. *Yahoo News*. https://www.aol.com/shattered-lost-largest-wildfire-u-133138727.html

Xinyan, X., & Zhou, Y. (2020, April 24). Mental health status among children in home confinement during the coronavirus disease 2019 outbreak in Hubei Provence, China. *JAMA Pediatrics*. http://www.jamanetwork.com

Yahoo News Photo Staff. (2019, September 20). Photos: Climate change protest around the world. *Yahoo News*. https://www.yahoo.com/news/photos-climate-change-protests-around-the-globe-142838005.html

Yale School of the Environment. (2021). New horizons in conservation conference. *Yale University Virtual Host*. https://jedsi.yale.edu/new-horizons-conservation/2021-conference

Yee, G. (2021, August 30). Forest service officials confirm all California national forests to temporarily close. file:///Users/lindagoldman/Desktop/Forest%20Service%20officials%20confirm%20all%20California%20national%20forests%20to%20temporarily%20close.html

Yurich, V. (2021). Why 1000 hours outdoors? *1000 Hours Outside*. https://www.1000hoursoutside.com/blog/why-1000-hours

ZERO HOUR. (2021). This is Zero Hour. http://thisiszerohour.org/

Image Permissions

Figure 10.9 Environment Makes a Difference, Michael Mimms, Figure 10.13 Our Mission Markus Spiske, Figure 11.10 Together, Juan Pablo Rodrigus, Figure 12.1 Resources Sarah Delaware, Figure 12.2 Nature For All, Caroline Hernandez, Figure 12.3 Protect Our Future, Taksh, Figure 12.4 Someone is Listening, Nurpalah Dee

-*StephBurt*, Figure 5.5 Melting Ice Caps, Cooper Bennett Burt

-*APA, Reser and Swim*, APA Figure 1.7 with permission from APA.

-*Following Francis, Terry Hogan, Chief Operating Officer and Executive Director of -Following Francis* Figure 2.9 Food, 2.10 Holiday Bags, 2.11 Coats, 2.19 Backpack Drive.

-*Linda Goldman* Figure 2.5 A Tornado (2002, p, 123_), Figure 2.6 Gracie, Figure 2.7 Life Before and After (2014, p.75), Figure 2.8 My Magical Place (Goldman, 2021 p.), Figure 2.12 Play Props, Figure 2.13 Emma's Angel, Figure 2.14 A Better Place/Planting, Figure 2.15 A Better Place/Trash, Figure 2.16 Wearing Masks, Figure 2.17 Children Also Grieve. Figure 2.18 Lucy Let's Go, Figure 3.8 Sneeze and Baby Bear, Figure 3.11 A Mask for Lion

-*Andres Gonzalez.HLF Figure 6.1 through 6.16*

-*Madeleine and Katherine Fugate* Figure 3.4 The COVID Memorial Quilt

-*Lulu Sullivan* Figure 3.5 Teen Grief

-*Sesame Street* Figure 3.6 Talking to Kids About COVID19, Figure 3.7 How to Wash Hands 3.8 H is For Handwashing, Figure 3.10 Healthy Habits, Figure 4.6 Nature Words, Figure 4.7 Nature Puzzles, Figure 4.8 Nature Journal

-*Parachutes for the Planet* Figure 4.9 Snails, Figure 4.10 Treat the Earth, Figure 5.17 Care for the Planet Figure 7.1 Bear, Figure 7.2 Parachutes, Figure 7.3 Building Dialogue, Figure 7.4 Recycle plastic, Figure 7.5 Trash, Figure 7.6 Youth for climate laws – Figure 7.7 Parachute Display, Figure 7.8 Salem High School. Figure 7.9 Save the Birds, Figure 7.10 Preserve Conserve Protect Figure 7.11 Prayer for Healing The Earth, Figure 7.12 Sunnydale, Figure 7.13 Save the Bees, Figure 7.14 Don't Throw Trash, Figure 7.15 What have you killed, Figure 7.16 Climate Camp, Figure 7.17 Chavez Elementary, Figure 7.18 Stop Building, Figure 7.19 China, Figure 7.19 Nigeria, Figure 7.20 Parachutes and the Pope, Figure 7.22: Nelson British Columbia, Figure 7.23 Abuja, Figure 8.3 Ari Calls for Action, Figure 9.15 Mother Earth Sculpture Washington DC, Figure 9.16; China, Figure 9.17 Family Team, Figure 9.18: UN Goal Parachute, Figure 9.19: Racism is toxic, Figure 9.20 Bat Habitat

-*John Hillegass* Figure 4.11 The Last Generation. Figure 7.26 Global Coordination

-*Aria and Lauren Redman* Figure 8.4 Aria, 8.5 Aria's Painting, Figure 8.6 The Bees,

-Riordan and Kelly Adams (Mom) Figure 5.4 The Letter

-Elena Peterson Figure 5.6 The Turtle and Figure 5.7 The Bird

-Mila and Anita Sanchez and Greta Hoffman and Pegg Hoffman Figure 5.8 Litter, Figure 5.9 Save the Bay

-Lynn Lewis Figure 5.11 Artic Melting, Figure 5.12 Helping Monster, Figure 5.13 Paper Trees, Figure 5.14 Bay Sculpture Figure 5.15 Farmscape, Figure 5.16 Farmscape Yarn,

-Hank Greeves, B-CC Club Figure 5.18 Three Rules of Recycling, Figure 5.19 Actions Figure 5.20 Before Cleanup, Figure 5.21 After Rock Creek Cleanup, Figure 5.22 Club Member Clean Up

-Tim Leitzkus Figure 5.23, Trees are important

-NASA Climate Kids Figure 5.24 Plant, Figure 5.25 A Terrarium

-April Sayre Figure 5.26 Thank You Earth Cover

-UN Figure 5.28 Downloadable Sustainable Development Goals Teaching UN Goals Figure 9.15 Thomas & Friends

-Jon Goldman Figure 6.16 I love you Daddy

-Domingue Pastor Figure 8.12 Dominique, Figure 8.13 Zoom Climate Change, Figure 8.14 Climate Justice

-Leah Namugerwa Figure 7.25 Leah and FridaysforFuture, Figure 8.10 Leah Grows Crops, Figure 8.11 School Strike

-Licpriya Kangujam Figure 8.7 Action, Figure 8.8 Global Plea, Figure 8.9 Greta and Licy

-Luna and Kirsten Darling Figure 8.15 Luna's Post, Figure 8.16 Cleaning up, Figure 8.17 Luna's Artwork, Figure 8.18 Self Portrait1, Figure 8.19 Self Portrait 2, Figure 8.20 Luna's Collage, Figure 8.21 Luna's Hair.

-Pet Picture Figure 9.2 Pets kellybdc, CC BY 2.0 Creative Commons

-Timiny Bergstrom Figure 9.6 Boating, Figure 9.7 Skiing, Figure 9.8 Frogs, Figure 9.9 An Igloo, Figure 9.10 A Salamander, Figure 10.10 Happiness

-Joyce Baker permission Figure 9.11 Oyster Recovery Zone

-Climate Dads Ben Block Figure 9.13 Electric School Bus

-UN Gordana Filipic, and Mattel Figure 9.15 Thomas & Friends

-Islam and Winkel, Figure 10.4 Effects of Inequality, Figure 10.5 Inequality and Climate Change Vicious Cycle

-Elder Climate Action Figure 11.1 Elders Act Now

-Alice Waters Edible Schoolyard Figure 11.3 The Table, Figure 11.4 The Garden, Figure 11.5 Classroom Lesson

-Scholastic, Ann Sandhorst, and EPA Figure 11.2 The Magic School Bus Clean

-Our Children's Trust Helen Britto Figure 10.11 Youth Plaintiff, Figure 10.12 Earth Guardians

-World's Largest Lesson Plan 11.6 World's Largest Lesson, Figure 11.7: The Solution, Figure 11.8 Nigeria's Largest Lesson, Figure 11.9 World's Largest Lesson Live

-*Istock* Photo by Madalin Olariu License 2073672819, Figure 12.5 Evolving Together

-*Children and Nature Network Laura Mylan* Figure 10.8 Green Schoolyard Infographic

-*Greta Thunberg* by Linda Astrom, media representative GSCC Network 8.9 Licy and Greta

-*Taylor and Francis* Figure 2.5 A Fire, Figure 2.7 Life Before and After, Figure 2.8 A Magical Place, Figure 2.12 Play Props, Figure 2.14 A Better Place/Planting, Figure 2.15 A Better Place/Trash

Index